Women's Bodies/Women's Lives
Health, Well-being and Body Image

Women's Issues Publishing Program

WOMEN'S BODIES/ WOMEN'S LIVES

HEALTH, WELL-BEING AND BODY IMAGE

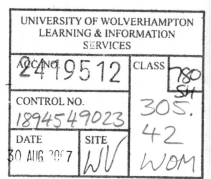

EDITED BY

Baukje Miedema,

Janet M. Stoppard & Vivienne Anderson

SUMACH

PRESS

WOMEN'S ISSUES PUBLISHING PROGRAM

SERIES EDITOR: BETH MCAULEY

CANADIAN CATALOGUING IN PUBLICATION DATA
Main entry under title:
Women's bodies/women's lives : health, well-being and body image

Includes bibliographical references.
ISBN 1-894549-02-3

1. Body image in women. 2. Self-perception in women.
3. Body, Human — Social aspects. 4. Women — Health and hygiene —
Sociological aspects. I. Miedema, Baukje. II. Stoppard,
Janet Mary, 1945- . III. Anderson, Vivienne.

HQ1206.W64 2000   305.42   C00-931773-2

The poems in Chapter Eight are reprinted with
the permission of Addena Sumter-Freitag.

Edited by Beth McAuley
Copyedited by Emily Schultz and Terra Page
Cover painting by Carolyn Livingstone,
reproduced courtesy of Jill Presser and John Duffy

Printed in Canada

Published by

SUMACH PRESS
1415 Bathurst Street, Suite 202
Toronto, ON Canada M5R 3H8
sumachpress@on.aibn.com
www.sumachpress.com

For Ajit, Aroon and Niels
— B.M.

For my sisters Judy, Anne and Bridget
— J.M.S.

For Richard
— V.A

CONTENTS

ACKNOWLEDGEMENTS

This collection is the end result of a great deal of work on the part of many. Its genesis was the 1997 conference of the Canadian Research Institute for the Advancement of Women (CRIAW). Many of the chapters in this collection were inspired by papers presented at this conference. We thank CRIAW for deciding to hold the 1997 conference in Fredericton. The collective work of women who were part of the conference organizing committee made this event possible and, without their help, this book could not have become a reality. The organizing committee included Anne Soucy who kept track of finances; Jina Rodas and Sherri Cameron, part-time staff who managed the conference office; Bev Woznow who used her knowledge of funding sources to good effect; Betty Lee who provided office and meeting space; Nusrat Arif whose advice on the conference theme and content was invaluable; Joan Hanley who provided assistance with "technical" matters; and Carmen Poulin who, along with Baukje Miedema, was the local representative from the CRIAW board. Janet Stoppard, Vivienne Anderson and Linda Eyre served as the program committee.

In the process of deciding which papers to include as part of this collection, we called on the expertise of several external reviewers. We would like to thank Gail Campbell, Barbara Cull-Wilby, Linda Eyre, Heather Sears, Patricia Hughes, Lorna Drew and Travis (Penny) Lane for their helpful feedback and insightful comments.

Last (but definitely not least) we would like to express our sincere gratitude to Sumach Press and to Beth McAuley, editor of the Women's Issues Publishing Program, for her support, encouragement, patience and tireless efforts in making this collection more accessible.

INTRODUCTION

Baukje (Bo) Miedema, Janet M. Stoppard and Vivienne Anderson

∽

THE TITLE OF THIS COLLECTION, *Women's Bodies/Women's Lives*, is intended to be a single phrase, reflecting our belief that women's bodies and women's lives are inseparable — each can be understood only within the context of the other. Yet, it is the case that throughout history, women have seldom had full control over their own bodies or their lives. According to Martha Ward, women's bodies/women's lives have often been owned by "others." She writes:

> The principle is that someone, somewhere, in most human groups, inevitably believes that he or she can, does, or should control the bodies of women. Ruling groups, gatekeepers, policy makers, the power elite, the patriarchy, tribal elders, religious authorities, relatives, kinfolk, cults, congresses, commissions, committees, whatever form they take, tend to worry about controlling women's bodies. Their concerns generally come to light in the areas of sexuality and reproduction.[1]

Not only are women controlled by others, they also are seen as "other."[2] Men's bodies are viewed as the norm and any deviation is defined as "unnatural" and often pathologized. Menopause, for instance, a normal physiological process experienced by all women who live long enough, is treated as an illness. Physician Jennifer Blake, in her editorial for the June 1998 issue of the *Canadian Family Physician*, stated that "menopause is quickly becoming one of the more intriguing areas for physicians to manage."[3] In medical discourse, menopause is discussed in terms of hormone "deficiency" and "symptoms." Thus, menopause has become a medical condition in need of medical management. This is just one example of how women's bodies become "other"; objects in need of control by *others*. And, as the historical record shows, such attitudes have contributed to oppressive living conditions for women.

This edited collection is the result of a long journey. This journey started in November 1995 during the biennial conference of the Canadian Research Institute for the Advancement of Women (CRIAW) in Prince George, BC. At the general meeting of CRIAW, held at this conference, the proposal was endorsed that the two members of the CRIAW board from Fredericton, NB, would organize and host the next CRIAW conference in November 1997. The conference theme, it was agreed, should focus on the lives of young women, perhaps addressing the body and body image. Following the 1995 conference, the CRIAW board members based in Fredericton initiated planning for the 1997 conference by establishing a volunteer committee to organize it. The core committee eventually consisted of twelve women, who stayed the course from planning to holding the conference. The first task of this committee was to develop the conference theme along the lines suggested by CRIAW. Although the body image theme was retained, the organizing committee felt that the theme should be broadened to include additional topics. The committee members decided this expanded theme should be one that could encompass a variety of aspects of the relationship between women's embodiment and women's lives under patriarchy. This overarching theme was expressed as *Our Bodies/Our Lives*, a phrase that seemed to reflect in a succinct way the integral connections between embodiment and social context in shaping women's lived experiences.

The conference was a rewarding, challenging and, at times, emotional experience, but above all, it resulted in a great deal of work for those involved with its organization. The final product was a highly successful conference, held November 7–9, 1997, in Fredericton, attended by more than 150 people (mostly women). Many excellent papers, artworks, performances and videos were presented. Following the conference, we three members of the organizing committee decided to explore the possibilities for publishing a collection based on papers presented at the conference. This book grew almost "organically" out of the conference. As prospective editors, we felt that a collection on embodiment and women's lived experiences would make a useful contribution to the growing literature on women and the body. Some additional chapters were invited to add to the overall consistency of the collection's theme.

The topics addressed in this collection, then, have links that can be traced to a set of historical and cultural processes in which women's bodies and women's lives have been conceptualized, ritualized and devalued in patriarchal social contexts. In Canada in the late 1800s, for example, most women were denied access to birth control methods because of male-dominated religious ideologies. The prevailing notion was that sexual intercourse should be "productive." For instance, Sylvanus Stall, writing in 1897, expressed concern that many young married women apparently did not want to have large families. Stall was horrified by this and claimed that women married "for the purpose of practically leading a life of legalized prostitution." According to Stall, these "selfish" women only wanted "greater luxury" so they could "self-indulge."[4]

Currently, medical doctors in Canada who perform abortions are targeted and threatened with harm by "pro-life" groups, resulting in reduced access to abortion services for many women. At the same time, sexuality is glorified, while many women lack easy access to birth control methods. During adolescence, young women need the consent of parents in order to obtain birth control and poor women often cannot afford to pay for birth control. As a result, some women have unwanted pregnancies, which places a heavy strain on their physical, psychological and economic well-being. Meanwhile, women with better financial resources are able to obtain an abortion if they wish to do so. Although having an abortion is not without physical and psychological risks, when this procedure is not equally available to all women, the sexual activities of some become controlled by patriarchal structures, a situation that has an impact upon the well-being of less privileged women.

In the past century, women in Europe and North America, as well as in other parts of the world, have enjoyed more protection under the law, achieved increased social status and gained more political power than ever before. However, these gains are often tenuous under patriarchy. In Canada, for instance, the federal government (currently formed by the Liberal Party) promised in their election platform a universal daycare system. Four years into their second mandate, they still have not delivered on this promise despite the fact that for many working parents it is very difficult to find affordable, licensed daycare. Nonetheless, in the government budget announced in February 2000, tax cuts for wealthy individuals and corporations were implemented.

Despite some gains, then, many women still have little control over their lives and have little public power and little institutionalized support. Women live their lives in a social and cultural context that exerts considerable power over them in subtle and indirect, but very persuasive, ways. For example, the fashion trade employs female models who have a body shape that is far removed from that of the average woman, but in a media-driven process, an "ideal" is created that is unattainable (and untenable) for almost all women. This engenders in many women feelings of inadequacy, or worse, may motivate some to emulate the "ideal" shape at any cost. As Susan Bordo has pointed out, the promotion of this "ideal" as a standard for women to aspire to undoubtedly underlies the "epidemic" of eating disorders (and generally unhealthy body practices) in women, both young and old.[5] Furthermore, everyday language, media reports and advertising images are permeated with negative, degrading and oppressive messages about women. It was not that long ago, for instance, that John Crosbie, an elected member of the Canadian House of Commons (Parliament) described a woman member as a "slab of bacon," an incident that received wide media coverage. In advertisements, women are frequently portrayed as being sexually available at all times, sometimes even against their will. These are just a few of the issues illustrating the pervasiveness of the social control of women's bodies and how such influences affect women's lives.

Nonetheless, it is too simplistic to argue that women are merely passive victims of processes outside their control. Women themselves are active agents in supporting "woman-unfriendly" social structures and cultural practices and so are implicated in the maintenance of patriarchy. Many women embrace the narrowly defined cultural ideal of female body shape and appearance, and some make money from promoting programs that promise a slender body, even though the "success rate" of such weight-loss regimes is minimal. Others sell clothing, makeup and so on, all promising to make women look "better." Margaret Thatcher may have been Britain's first female prime minister, but in this role she did little to question, let alone dismantle, patriarchy. In fact, during her tenure, from 1979 until 1990, Britain's welfare state was largely dismantled and displaced by free-market capitalism. As first minister, Margaret Thatcher's actions were often complicit with, and supportive of, social structures that devalue women. Thatcherite policies had many negative social and economic consequences for women, particularly those caring for children and working outside the home. For instance, maternity rights for women workers were weakened, a previously universal maternity allowance was abolished, and availability of preschool and daycare services was severely curtailed.[6]

In addition to social and cultural conditions that affect women's lives, some female bodies are ravaged by physical conditions that render the body "unwilling." A woman who seeks help for her bodily complaints often confronts the institution of western medicine with its history of medicalization of women's bodies. In this medicalization process, normal physical processes of the female body, such as menstruation, childbirth and menopause, become problems requiring medical control. At the same time, when women seek medical help for their physical complaints, they may be treated differently than men with similar symptoms and women's problems more often than men's may be attributed to psychological rather than physical causes. Western medicine is also to a large degree premised on the notion that illness is a set of objective, observable criteria, even though research has indicated that illness and well-being are very closely tied to social issues such as poverty and education. As stated in a recent report prepared for the Maritime Centre of Excellence for Women's Health: "Poverty is recognized as one of the most reliable predictors of poor health."[7] In western medicine the body becomes objectified as a biological entity, while social and subjective criteria of well-being may be ignored as irrelevant. One consequence of this medical focus on the bodies of individual women is that aspects of women's lives such as poverty, lack of support with childcare or an abusive partner are not considered pertinent to the provision of healthcare.[8]

In this collection, the focus is on how the material and the social are interconnected in women's lives and how one affects the other. In the same way that women's bodies/women's lives cannot be separated, nor can the material and the social be separated. The overall perspective follows an approach that has been termed "material-discursive," a perspective which allows a woman's lived experiences to be understood as being rooted in, and arising from, a reality that includes how she lives, where she lives and the kind of body she lives in. However as Lucy Yardley points out, this reality is not composed of fixed, concrete entities that are distinct from people's experiences. The material world is constantly being shaped and reshaped by individuals' perceptions, intentions and activities.[9] A fuller understanding of connections between women's bodies and women's lives can only be achieved when both material and social dimensions of existence are considered together.

In much of the literature on women, the focus is on the social conditions of women's lives, but less attention is given to how the social and the material might be interconnected. For example, how do women earning a minimum wage (a material reality) fit into the social image of a well-groomed professional woman? The way women's experiences are grounded in their material reality is overlooked. Material reality includes the context of a woman's life. So, for example, a woman who is married and has three children and lives within a low- income household will have a very different view of the world because these realities of a limited income affect how she lives, how she organizes her life and limits what she can and cannot do. It also includes a woman's physical body and the experiences she has because she lives in a female body. For example, how do menarche, menopause, childbirth, physical assaults on the body, serious illness and physical disability affect the way a woman lives her life? How do these material and physical realities shape what she does and what barriers they put in place for her?

In addition to these omissions is the omission of the discursive conditions that also affect women's lives. A discursive condition is the phrase used to define the cultural and social perceptions of women, how society and culture construct the image of woman and the female body. Beauty pageants, for example, set up "ideals" about how women should look, act and function in society. How do such ideals play out in women's personal experiences? How would a heavy-set teenager or young woman view her body when compared with the ideal of a tall and slender beauty queen? How does the "white ideal" play out in the lives of women of colour?

How, then, do material and social realities affect women and their perceptions of their bodies?

It is important to take into account how the material realities — both the physical and personal (income, housing and so on) — and the social realities work together or interconnect to shape women's lives. These interconnections are complex and multifaceted. The essays in this collection attempt to bridge social and material realities by exploring their interconnections.

The theme of this collection is also part of recent work that questions commonly accepted distinctions between concepts, for example between body and mind. It is usually taken for granted that body and mind are separate things that exist apart from each other. A different way of thinking sees these two as closely interconnected. That is, the body can only be understood by considering how the mind functions and the activities of the mind influence how the body functions. The material-social divide is another example where the usual way of thinking treats the two as quite separate from each other, rather than being inseparable. In western societies, this kind of "dualistic" thinking also shapes ideas about health and well-being among both professionals and ordinary people. When approaches to understanding women's experiences are based in these dualistic ideas, one result is that male-biased assumptions are more difficult to challenge and so this way of thinking is another factor that helps to maintain women's subordination within patriarchal structures. Seeing the material and the social as separate things and not looking for ways in which they are interconnected is one example of how dualistic thinking is a barrier to understanding women's experiences. A further aim of this collection, therefore, is to present examples of work that bridge the gap between women's bodies and women's lives and so contribute to undermining dualistic modes of thought.

The collection is divided into two parts, each consisting of eight chapters. In the first part, "Altered Bodies," the focus is on women's experiences in the context of changes within the "material" or physical body. In some instances, these changes are the result of illness, chronic conditions of ill-health or the aging process. In other cases, alterations to the body are actively sought (for example, through cosmetic surgery). The overall theme of Part I can be described as a concern with the experiences of women who live within "abnormal" bodies. Women's accounts are from an "inside" standpoint, from within the material body, looking out towards the social world, or the world around them. From this standpoint, the mind-body duality is explored as women cope with change or dysfunction in their bodies.

The opening chapter by Vivienne Anderson provides an account of her day-to-day struggles as a woman living with severe chronic illness. In "A Will of Its Own: Experiencing the Body in Severe Chronic Illness," she describes the constraints that her illness impose on her social relations and documents how stereotypical attitudes of healthcare professionals often impede the gaining of an effective treatment. She argues that control of the body is a myth for the hidden minority of the chronically sick.

The experiences of women who are breast cancer survivors are analyzed in the chapter by Roanne Thomas-MacLean: "Altered Bodies/Altered Selves: Exploring Women's Accounts of Illness Experiences." She shows how this life-threatening disease not only alters the body, but also changes identity as these women come to terms with the loss of a body part that symbolizes female sexual attractiveness in a patriarchal society. She discusses what it means to be ill and female, and how these women adjust to living a life after cancer.

Based on her work with asthma sufferers and her experience of her own asthma, Barbara Cull-Wilby explores metaphors around breathing and awareness of breath to reveal how prevailing knowledge rests on assumptions that separate body and mind, spirit and emotion. In "Breath and Body Wisdom: Experiencing the Personal Power of Self," Cull-Wilby describes the goals of personal growth and inner peace that can be obtained by following the rituals of healing.

In their chapter, "Understanding Depression From the Standpoint of Women Who Have Been Depressed," Janet Stoppard, Yvette Scattolon and Deanna Gammell contrast notions of depression as a disorder that afflicts individual women with one grounded in the experiences of women who have been depressed. Drawing on interviews with women, they describe ways of understanding women's depression that take into account both the activities performed by women in their everyday lives and the broader social context in which women live. They conclude that the experience of being depressed can be explained in terms of women's efforts to live up to socially prescribed standards defining the "good woman."

Women's treatment for mental health problems is also the focus of "Asylum or Cure? Women's Experiences of Psychiatric Hospitalization" by Baukje Miedema and Janet Stoppard. Interviews with women who had been psychiatric inpatients revealed that many viewed their hospitalization as a welcome respite from burdensome family responsibilities and unsatisfactory relationships. Rather than hospitalization being an unwanted incarceration, many women were reluctant to leave an environment in which they were free from performing domestic chores and could escape abusive partners. At the same time, disadvantaging social and material conditions, such as lack of work and poverty, having been sexually abused as a child or being stigmatized because of psychiatric hospitalization, which shaped and limited these women's lives, were rarely considered in treatment planning.

In their chapter "'Old Bags' Under the Knife: Facial Cosmetic Surgery Among Women," Diane Cepanec and Barbara Payne present an analysis of women's accounts of their experiences, good and bad, with facial cosmetic surgery. One of the fastest-growing medical specialities in North America, cosmetic surgery can be expected to increase in frequency due to the appearance concerns of aging "baby-boomers." Drawing on their interviews with women who have had cosmetic surgery, Cepanec and Payne reveal how women's decisions to change their appearance are rooted in cultural concepts of "old" and "ugly." They also point out the need for more informed decision-making.

Chris Egan discusses the impact of environmental pollution on the lived experiences of Inuit women in "Polluted Bodies: Inuit Identity and the Arctic Food Chain." The high levels of pollutants in traditional Inuit food sources are having an impact on the lives of the Inuit people, raising health concerns. And as Egan's analysis indicates, these environmental changes pose a threat not only to Inuit culture but also to the everyday lives of Inuit women.

A change of pace is provided by the poems of Addena Sumter-Freitag. Entitled "Witness: Testament of a Journey," her poems explore in vivid, expressive language the experience of living in a Black body in a predominantly white society. They speak of the growing feeling of pride in that body and the endless struggle to maintain self-esteem, especially among young Black women. Sumter-Freitag's poems conclude Part I.

The second part of the collection, "Objectified Bodies," focuses on the view from the outside. In these chapters, the lens is reversed to consider "normal bodies" from a standpoint that explores the impact of the outside (social and cultural) world on women's embodied lives.

In "Revisioning the Body/Mind from an Eastern Perspective: Comments on Experience, Embodiment and Pedagogy," Roxana Ng describes how she draws on the healing traditions of Traditional Chinese Medicine (TCM) in her own life and in her teaching. The assumptions of TCM are contrasted with those of western medicine to show how the former provide more holistic ways of understanding embodied experience. She concludes that TCM and related approaches offer directions for revisioning health and ill-health that acknowledge the integral connections between women's bodies and women's lives.

The relationship between chronological age and women's satisfaction with their weight and appearance is investigated in several chapters. For example, a young woman's appearance concerns are likely to differ from those of a fifty-year-old woman. Kate Rossiter's "Shattering the Mirror: A Young Woman's Story of Weight Preoccupation" provides a first-person account of a young woman's experiences in resisting the culturally constructed ideal of female slenderness. After a difficult and painful self-examination, Rossiter has come to accept her bodily self, a reconciliation that she expresses as a desire to initiate a social movement aimed at helping women resist the cultural equation of thin with good.

Gail Marchessault's "One Mother and Daughter Approach to Resisting Weight Preoccupation" highlights generational differences through an exploration of mothers' and daughters' attitudes to body size and appearance. Focusing on one mother-daughter pair, Marchessault illustrates how age-related and relational influences shape women's experiences.

The chapter by Michelle Lafrance, Marilyn Zivian and Anita Myers, "Women, Weight and Appearance Satisfaction: An Ageless Pursuit of Thinness," traces shifts over the past century in the body shape, size and appearance considered ideal for women. They then describe some recent findings based on data collected from almost two hundred women between the ages of thirteen and seventy-nine, revealing that pursuit of thinness is unrelated to a woman's age. They explain this finding as reflecting present-day cultural preoccupations with a slender body ideal.

In her study "Contours of Everyday Life: Women's Reflections on Embodiment and Health Over Time," Pamela Wakewich examines how women's ideas about body, health and identity vary across the life course and maps the shifts in women's embodied sense of self that occur with aging. Her research suggests that women's body images are fluid and multifaceted, rather than unitary and static. Her findings point to the importance of studying body image over time in relation to the specific social context of women's lives.

The theme of embodied experiences in cultural context and how women's sense of self is shaped by cultural location is explored in "Negotiating Sexuality: Lesbians in the Canadian Military" by Lynne Gouliquer. This chapter focuses on the experiences of lesbian women in the Canadian military, a predominantly male institution in which lesbians must also deal with a hegemonic heterosexual culture. Gouliquer documents the struggles faced by lesbian women as members of the Canadian military and outlines the survival strategies they adopt in an inhospitable cultural context.

The final two chapters by Fabienne Darling-Wolf and Mia Consalvo analyze the impact of technology on women and the shifts in demarkation of bodily boundaries in contemporary western culture. Fabienne Darling-Wolf's "From Airbrushing to Liposuction: The Technological Reconstruction of the Female Body" focuses on the role of technology in maintaining and promoting the western beauty myth, whether through image re-construction ("airbrushing" in fashion magazines) or by re-moulding female body parts (use of "liposuction"). As she points out, these technologically enhanced standards of beauty also reinforce sexist and racist ideologies, with effects that are both physically and psychologically damaging for many women.

In "From Razor Girls to Bionic Women: Extraordinary Cyborg Women in Popular Culture," Mia Consalvo discusses the figure of the cyborg — a body that has been technologically altered — drawing on examples from popular culture to explore what it means to be one. According to Consalvo's analysis, the cyborg serves as a reminder of the reality of the physical body while also undermining taken-for-granted assumptions about gender and bodies.

It is our hope that this collection will contribute to increased recognition of the need to develop knowledge about women's lived experiences that is based in an understanding of the interconnections between women's bodies and women's lives. A perspective that can address the materiality of women's bodies, while also keeping the social and discursive conditions of women's lives in view seems to offer more possibilities for emancipatory knowledge than alternatives that emphasize one to the neglect of the other. The contributors to this collection have a shared interest in developing knowledge that takes women's concerns seriously. We hope that women will find something that both reflects and validates their lived experiences among the topics addressed by the contributors. *Women's Bodies/Women's Lives* will also be of interest to scholars and researchers in a variety of fields, including Women's Studies, health psychology, cultural studies and sociology, while also offering a resource to practitioners whose work focuses on "problems" affecting women's bodies/women's lives. Included here would be social workers, transition house workers, counsellors and therapists, and primary healthcare providers such as nurses and physicians. This collection is directed, therefore, not only to those engaged in development of knowledge for understanding connections between women's embodiment and lived experiences, it is also intended for service providers who draw on this knowledge in their work with women. We hope the collection offers alternative and potentially transformative visions of women's bodies/women's lives and contributes to the dismantling of social and cultural influences that construct "woman" as "other."

Notes

1. Martha Ward, *A World Full of Women* (Boston: Allyn and Bacon, 1996), 13.

2. Jane Ussher, ed., *Body Talk: The Material and Discursive Regulation of Sexuality, Madness and Reproduction* (London, UK: Routledge, 1997), 5.

3. Jennifer Blake, "Hormone Replacement," *Canadian Family Physician* (June 1998), 1205–1206.

4. Angus McLaren, "Birth Control and Abortion in Canada 1870-1920," in S.E.D. Shortt, ed., *Medicine in Canadian Society: Historical Perspectives* (Montreal: McGill-Queen's University Press, 1981), 286–287.

5. Susan Bordo, *Unbearable Weight: Feminism, Western Culture and the Body* (Berkeley: University of California Press, 1993).

6. Sheila Rowbotham, *A Century of Women: A History of Women in Britain and the United States in the Twentieth Century* (Toronto: Penguin, 1997), 498.

7. Ronald Colman, "Women's Health in Atlantic Canada: A Statistical Report," (Halifax: Maritime Centre of Excellence for Women's Health, 2000), 15.

8. Deborah Findlay and Leslie Miller, "Through Medical Eyes: The Medicalization of Women's Bodies and Women's Lives," in B. Singh Bolaria and Harley Dickinson, eds., *Health, Illness, and Health Care in Canada*, 2nd ed. (Toronto: Harcourt Brace Canada, 1994), 276–306. Dr. Ian R. McWhinney, in his book *Family Medicine — An Introduction to Family Medicine for Medical Students*, acknowledges the impact of social conditions on peoples well-being. He states: "Factors such as social isolation and stressful life events are associated with higher mortality from all causes, not only from certain psychosomatic diseases" (New York: Oxford University Press, 1989), 48.

9. Lucy Yardley, ed., *Material Discourse of Health and Illness* (London, UK: Routledge, 1997), 9.

PART I

ALTERED
BODIES

�ग

Chapter One

A WILL OF ITS OWN
Experiencing the Body in
Severe Chronic Illness

Vivienne Anderson

☙

THE CHRONICALLY SICK are a neglected subset of the disabled. They are often overlooked, in part because the stereotypical public image of the person with a disability is of a young, healthy, athletic, paraplegic male, such as the celebrated wheelchair athlete Rick Hansen. The truth is very different. The inclusion of those with a severe chronic illness in the category of the disabled is controversial unless their disease causes some physical impairment. Yet the United Nations' definition of the disabled clearly includes those who because of some physical condition are unable to function in the same way as "the normate,"[1] the useful term coined by Thomson to use in opposition to "the disabled."[2] The severe fatigue that accompanies many chronic illnesses precludes a normal life and clearly leads to the inclusion of the chronically sick in the category of the disabled.

Many of these illnesses are far more common in women than in men and often strike in early middle age when the woman has a family to raise or a career to lose. I am concerned here not with the more familiar illness that strikes, develops, is treated and is subsequently cured, but with the persistent disease state, the illness that has its ups and downs but never goes away. These are the endlessly sick, those whom Cheri Register calls the "interminably ill."[3] This substantial group is largely silent; the sick are too preoccupied with surviving their illness to write of it and consequently social planners and even feminist theorists tend to overlook the realities of their lives.

We women with severe chronic illnesses lead lives of isolated suffering and I suspect that few of those whom I call friends know or understand the true circumstances of my life. The stiff-upper-lip syndrome, made worse in my case by my British background, causes one to "pass" for healthy whenever possible, contributing to the lack of knowledge of the lives of the chronically sick. In recounting my story I do not seek sympathy, rather I seek to place this life in the context of feminist thought about our bodies and our lives and show how the lack of information has led some to exclude this group from the current thought in this area.

In the spring of 1980, I became aware that something in my body had changed. I had permanent indigestion, the joints of my hands and feet ached, my fingers would change colour whenever I was cold, which was nearly all the time, my muscles were weak so that I found it hard to open swing doors or turn off taps, and I would wake up in the morning feeling as tired as if I had run a marathon during the night. On top of this I still had the sporadic attacks of severe abdominal pain that I had experienced for several years without finding any answer from my doctor, other than they were "all in my head" or due to "nerves," even though, when I tried to see if there was a consistent pattern, it was clear that the attacks of pain did not coincide with the ups and downs of daily living. I had given up mentioning them to my doctor. When I went to him with this list of new complaints, he examined me, told me I was looking particularly healthy and sent me on my way.

The symptoms worsened and I returned to my doctor. This time he listened to me more carefully and eventually decided to send me to a specialist in internal medicine. He appeared to take me seriously until he asked whether I was experiencing any stress in my life. I wanted to get to the bottom of the problem, so I told the truth. Shortly before I became ill I had been indecently assaulted then stalked by a powerful man in the office where I worked. When I complained to the police and to his supervisor, he denied everything and threatened to sue me for slander. So I answered that yes, I was under stress. The specialist smiled, said "Ah ha!" and proceeded to dismiss my complaints.

They did not go away, in fact they worsened and for two years I struggled as I returned to university and began a master's degree, until I reached a stage where my hands were practically useless and I could walk only with difficulty. I saw several other doctors, each time with negative results until the fall of 1982 when I was sent to see a rheumatologist. At last I was taken seriously. Various tests and X-rays were performed and finally I was told to sit down and prepare myself for some bad news. It appeared that I had a relatively rare chronic autoimmune disease called scleroderma.

Scleroderma means "hard skin," and the vast majority of persons with the disease develop just that, but it is possible not to have that symptom, as in my case, but to have the other symptoms — arthritis, muscle weakness and inflammation and subsequent scarring and malfunction of various internal organs; hence the disease's other name, Progressive Systemic Sclerosis. The prognosis was serious. It was possible to live a normal lifespan, but if the disease attacked and damaged certain internal organs, particularly heart, lungs or kidneys, the risk of an early death was considerable.

I came out of the doctor's office in an almost jubilant mood, inappropriate for the bad news I had been given. Instead I rejoiced that someone out there knew what was wrong with me, that there actually was a disease which matched my symptoms. It was a validation that rang true deep inside me. For two years I had been seeing patriarchal physicians who had denied what was to me an undeniable truth. Now someone had given me permission to be as sick as I felt, and I rejoiced. I had no intention of wallowing in illness, but this temporary euphoria helped me adjust to the situation.

The only symptom that did not seem to fit the scleroderma was the abdominal pain. Three years later, after more denials from a different set of doctors who thought they knew what was wrong, I had an operation and the doctors then would not believe me when the pain recurred. I finally learned that I had pseudo-obstruction of the bowel, a rare complication of scleroderma. Once more I rejoiced inappropriately, even though the revelation meant the pain had no cure.

With hindsight I can understand why I felt as I did. What I cannot understand is why I met with so much denial on my odyssey. I do not think that I give off an aura of mental instability, yet the doctors I met were so ready to attribute my symptoms to stress. Eighteen years later, having met many more specialists, nearly all of them male, I have come to believe that their behaviour is deeply rooted in a widely held view of women as weak and mentally unstable whose vivid imaginations lead them astray. Scleroderma is a disease in which women predominate by a ratio quoted variously from seven to one, to ten to one. Those few men with scleroderma I have met were without exception diagnosed quickly and efficiently. The women tell horror stories, many of them far worse than mine.

After the period of jubilation there was an opposite reaction, one I can only describe as a period of mourning. Hitherto I had been a relatively healthy person with a body that obeyed my commands. Now my body seemed to have a will of its own and I mourned my loss of function. Although I did not go through the five stages of mourning strictly laid out by Elisabeth Kubler-Ross,[4] it was nevertheless a prolonged process of readaptation with many stages, during which I gradually came to terms with my status as an invalid.

Once my diagnosis was established and it was acknowledged that I was suffering from a serious illness I found that physicians were by and large helpful. Even though their bedside manners vary, I have had a great deal of assistance from them over the years. In one aspect, however, they have had without exception a complete blind eye: the treatment or rather non-treatment of those symptoms that have a profound effect on daily living but are not medically significant. This is particularly true of fatigue.

Many of the symptoms from which I suffer are disagreeable to say the least, such as having dry foodstuffs and large food particles stick in the back of my throat because I have difficulty swallowing them. I suffer from pain severe enough that narcotics are prescribed for its treatment. Yet if you were to ask me which one of all my symptoms I would most want to get rid of I have no hesitation in naming not pain, but fatigue.

Extreme fatigue is totally debilitating, there are days when the sum total of my achievements is to get up, get washed and dressed and lie on the sofa until it is time to go to bed. It is impossible for me to work full time for a living. After dropping out of my PhD program and giving up my ambition of an academic career, I eventually developed a part-time job as an arts critic for the local daily newspaper, writing an average of eight to ten reviews or short feature articles a month. It is an ideal occupation, the feature articles usually have several days to prepare before deadline and if I am unwell or exhausted on the day of a performance there are other people only too willing to step in at the last moment. Above all, it helps my self-esteem. Extreme fatigue is demoralizing. Ours is a society which judges people by what they do. When you are introduced the first question is always "What do you do?" If the answer is "Nothing," you feel very small. I am fortunate to have a husband who is very understanding and who shoulders far more than his fair share of household duties without complaint. But even though he does not make me feel bad for spending a lot of time resting, I find it difficult not to be hard on myself and to feel with one half of my mind that I must be lazy, even though the other half is telling me from experience that unless I rest that day I will be very sick indeed the next.

Fatigue cannot be quantified and there is no medical cure available, hence the lack of interest on the part of physicians. They show a similar lack of interest in other symptoms which, although they are life-disrupting, are not seen as a medical threat. Two years ago I developed severe swelling in my legs. Once my doctor had satisfied herself that it was not caused by heart or kidney problems she lost interest. Meantime I was having more and more difficulty walking. When I went back to her in desperation, she sent me to a specialist who tested my liver, found no problem and dismissed me. By this time I was finding it almost impossible to bend my legs, I could not get in or out of the car, or sit without having my legs extended in front of me. In total frustration I went back to my doctor and wept. Finally she sent me to another specialist who immediately diagnosed a blood clot in an abdominal blood vessel, caused by the disease. As a result they began treatment of the swelling and my practical problems were partway to being solved.

Among the most difficult things to accept in chronic illness are external bodily changes. Before becoming sick I was of average build and was reasonably happy with the way I looked. After a few years the disease attacked my thyroid, which became extremely underactive. Not only did this add to my level of fatigue, but I began a steady weight gain. This was not helped by the fact that I had to take medications which caused retention of fluid. As my body changed so did my self-esteem. I became embarrassed by how I looked, fearful that other people would think me greedy and self-indulgent. I ceased to weigh myself since the results were so unsatisfactory. Dieting to lose weight was difficult given the medical restrictions on what I could eat, and it seemed to have no effect, anyway.

When my walking worsened and I had to take to a wheelchair outside the house, I found myself internalizing the embarrassment I saw on other people's faces. In a wheelchair one is simultaneously both an object of curious stares and invisible. In a restaurant with my husband I ordered my food and a coffee. The waiter promptly turned to my husband and asked, "Does she take cream in her coffee?" This was a typical response. However, I did not allow this or the stares to put me off using the wheelchair, since it made it possible for me to travel much further than I could walk.

Eventually my legs improved, so that I no longer needed the wheelchair, but used a cane instead, mainly for balance. This again required an adjustment in body image. I was no longer subject to stares (except when parking in a spot for the disabled), but in my mind only the elderly used canes, and I was young.

Another hurdle was learning to ask for help when necessary. I was brought up in England in a culture where one does not speak to strangers, still less embarrass them by asking for their assistance, and I found this hard to overcome, especially when as happened occasionally, I met with a rebuff. One time in particular sticks in my mind. My joints were very painful and I asked a student for a seat on the bus, explaining that I had arthritis. He replied, "Yeah, lady, and I've got bubonic plague," and went on sitting. For days afterwards I studied long hours in the library, although I was totally exhausted, so that I could take the bus home after rush hour and would not have to ask anyone for a seat.

I had a difficult journey to the university at that time, two buses and quite a long walk. I found my snail's pace walk frustrating, until I learned not to look for buses, or if I could not help seeing one, not to look at its number, unless I was actually standing at the bus stop, so that I would not have to face the frustration of just missing the bus because I could not hurry. Similarly, I trained myself not to look at the Walk/Don't Walk sign until I had reached the edge of the sidewalk: a trick that I still use eighteen years later. It was a very minor victory of willpower, but one which made me much calmer of mind.

One sentiment that had no such easy cure was the potent feeling of vulnerability to physical or sexual attack, which enveloped me as soon as I began to have walking difficulties. This preceded the development of external signs of physical problems, when to the average observer I simply looked like a woman taking a leisurely stroll. I became intensely aware that I could not walk with a confident stride, still less run away or fight back; even my vocal chords were affected by the disease so that I could not call loudly for help. When I became dependent on the wheelchair and subsequently the cane, this feeling of vulnerability increased, probably worsened by my recent experience of attack and stalking and by my knowledge of the dismal statistics of attacks on the physically disabled. I gained a measure of relief from attending a course on self-defence for the physically disad-vantaged, but to this day I do not feel secure when I am alone outside my home.

One problem that contributed to my feelings of isolation was the increasing dietary restrictions that I faced. The disease caused serious damage to the gastrointestinal tract and I ate less and less until finally I was put on a system of complete intravenous feeding for twelve hours at night and no oral intake except for occasional clear liquids. The carefully balanced flow of dextrose, lipids, vitamins and minerals was a space-age solution that completely replaced food. The fluids were life-sustaining, so according to my physicians, my eating problems were at an end.

But to say this is to ignore the whole social side of eating. Preparing food for those you love, sharing it with them, inviting friends to share the companionship of a meal, going out to eat at friends' homes or celebrating special occasions by eating in a restaurant are all important aspects of food consumption in which I could not participate. To say that my problems were at an end simply demonstrates that the medical model completely overlooks the social and emotional context in which we live. Our bodies do not operate separately from our lives.

I tried not to let others become embarrassed by my lack of participation in the rituals of mealtimes, but inevitably I became isolated from all but my closest friends. Because of the high levels of sugar in my bloodstream, I felt no hunger, but I had an acute longing for texture and crunch, which could only be assuaged by taking a mouthful of food and spitting it out. This became an accepted practice at home, and I became adept at carrying it out with the utmost discretion, but it was not socially acceptable, except in the homes of a few very close friends.

After eight and a half years on the intravenous feeding system a new drug was developed that enabled me to start eating again, albeit on a very restricted diet. The problem of social isolation is still there, though somewhat attenuated. Before I can eat anything I need a full list of ingredients, many of which I am unable to tolerate, so that spontaneous eating is still impossible. Only my closest friends have the courage to cook for me, and as a result, my husband and I are rarely nvited out for meals.

Although I have some friends who have remained faithful throughout my years of ill-health, the very fact of illness has alienated some people who are unable or unwilling to face the threat to their own continued well-being that it implies. My condition has been more stable recently, but there was a period of nine years during which I spent as much time in hospital as I did out, subject to frequent life-threatening infections. For some of our friends this continued stress was too much. Where others rallied round and became closer, for some it was as if they feared that my condition was contagious. On the other hand I gained friends through my stays in hospital. There is a subculture of the chronically sick. That someone is facing the same threat and difficulties as you are is a powerful basis for friendship that overrides differences in social background and lifestyle. Some of these hospital friendships have endured as long as fifteen years, throughout many ups and downs in our respective conditions, and I have lost others only to the early death of an individual. These friendships have brought a richness of the human spirit to my life that, in spite of the unfortunate circumstances of our meeting, I would not have missed.

My relationship with my husband has inevitably been changed by the disease. Although I seek out as many means as possible of being of help to him, the balance of our marriage has been changed so that most of the time I am dependent on my husband, including needing his help to put on and take off the thick medical stockings I must wear each day. Because of my fatigue, the responsibilities for cooking and house-work fall on his shoulders as well as all the tasks of house maintenance. For medical reasons I am unable to drive, so he must be the chauffeur. I spend so much time in hospital or sick at home that he has taken over the household finances and many other such jobs. In summary, he is the giver and I am the taker, which is not a healthy situation. My depleted energy levels and continuous battle with pain mean that I cannot take part in many of the activities of daily living, and the more intimate aspects of our lives are also affected.

Pain, though not quite as demoralizing as fatigue, is nevertheless a continuing struggle. I am fortunate enough to have a doctor who is not afraid to use powerful drugs in order to bring a measure of relief, citing recent research that shows that patients do not become addicted to narcotics when they take them not to induce pleasure, but to combat severe pain. When in pain I find that I have a short fuse, quick to feel anger or frustration. As the pain worsens I become more and more withdrawn until the pain reaches its maximum intensity, at which stage I am overcome with total inertia. The pain may be so all-encompassing that I am completely unable to take any action, including action that leads to pain alleviation. The world consists of me and my body, locked in silent combat. Other than pharmaceutical relief, the only trick that works is to engross my mind in some activity to such an extent that it blocks out the pain or reduces it to a tolerable level. This technique does not work for the most severe levels of pain, but it is effective for moderate or minor pain.

The ultimate experience of the body is death, and to be subject to a life-threatening disease makes one keenly aware of this reality. It is not something which hangs over one on a daily basis, although I am aware that the disease has begun to attack some vital organs. Yet as a result of an incident that occurred five years ago I do not feel threatened.

When I was taking the intravenous feedings I was subject to severe infections because of the open access to my central veins, coupled with a depleted white-cell count arising from the illness. On one particular occasion the infection struck with unaccustomed ferocity and my temperature rose to 41.8 degrees C (107.2 F), a temperature that it is often fatal in adults. At this point my blood pressure began to fall and I was wheeled out of the hospital room and into the CAT-scan department, as the medical personnel searched for an abscess. As my pressure fell further and further the nurses no longer spoke to me and told me later that they thought I was unconscious. Whatever the appearances may have been the reality was very different. Inside I was totally lucid. I knew where I was, I knew my husband was waiting outside and I overheard the nurses taking my blood pressure and saying that my doctor was at the desk, weeping. At that moment I knew with absolute clarity that all I had to do was to relax and let go and I would be at peace. But I knew with equal clarity that I did not want to die then, and I fought against the feeling that was so attractive. With every fibre of my being I hauled myself back into the world of pain and fever. I recovered from the infection after a long time, but from that day onward I have never been afraid of death. It was not a near-death experience like others I have read of, in the sense that I saw no piercing lights and did not see deceased loved ones as others have done, but although I have no religious beliefs I felt an overwhelming peace.

Fatigue may well be the hardest thing to bear; after fatigue comes uncertainty. With scleroderma the progress of the disease is sporadic. From day to day it is totally unpredictable. Unlike a disease which is the same each day or one in which there is a slow but steady decline, in my case I never know when I wake up how things are going to be. Will it be one of those rare days on which I have unaccustomed energy and can do whatever I want, even though I will pay for it the next day? Or will it more likely be a day of fatigue and pain, or a day I end up in the hospital for the umpteenth time?

Similarly, whenever a new symptom appears, as happens fairly regularly with this progressive condition, I never know whether all it will amount to is just some minor inconvenience or whether it will turn out to be a major problem entailing long and painful hospital treatments. Anxiety is inevitable whenever a new development crops up. There is a feeling of "here we go again," which is difficult to dismiss.

This unpredictability is hard to live with. I find myself reluctant to make plans in case I jinx them. I'm not superstitious but I hesitate to say I will do something on such and such a date in case I am sick by then. Although this sounds a minor inconvenience it is in fact a major disturbance of life. We don't realize how much we trust the body until it lets us down. I have found this measure of uncertainty very hard to accept, it is much more of a barrier in fact than walking with a cane or using a wheelchair. It also affects those around me. My husband states that he finds it very hard that there seems always to be some new complication or problem and that he cannot trust me not to be sick whenever we make plans to do something.

This uncertainty illustrates the lack of control I experience over my body. It is a tenet of some feminists that women should gain control of their bodies and lives. Although the theory deals with women liberating themselves from patriarchy and is nothing to do with health or illness, nevertheless there is an unspoken assumption that bodies and lives are controllable. It is what Susan Wendell refers to as "the myth of control."[5] For those with disabilities in general and with chronic illnesses in particular this control of one's body is elusive. Furthermore it should be borne in mind that aging is a disabling condition. Sooner or later we will all become disabled and lose our ability to control our bodies, and with this comes the inability to control our lives. Feminist theories need to take account of these facts and integrate the realities of the lives of the chronically sick so that they are not excluded, as has happened too frequently in the past.

With a severely malfunctioning body it is difficult not to think in terms of the mind/body split, with the mind representing the interior healthy self, and the body, all that is sick. This is especially true of the experience of severe pain. There is no question that it is the body that is at the root of the problem. Celebrating the body as some feminists would have us do is an alien concept to the chronically sick. It is difficult not to develop an adversarial attitude towards the body.

Yet some reconciliation of mind and body is possible. When I wrote a living will for my doctor, I asked her to do everything in her power to prolong my life, provided she was not just prolonging suffering. I wrote that in spite of my illness my near-death experience had taught me that I passionately wanted to live and that my life contained many good things in spite of my illness. I can still love and be loved; I can appreciate beauty of nature, music, art and literature; I can see the human qualities in my family and friends. I can still learn new things, the possibilities of life that remain are endless.

At first glance these things for which I wish to live are all things of the mind or spirit, yet that is misleading, for they are all mediated through the body. To give a few obvious examples, I use my eyes and ears to appreciate the beauty of art and music, and what is love without the physical gestures of tenderness with which to express it? In this way alone the chronically sick are able to celebrate the body, or rather to celebrate what they can do with it.

The theme of this book is women's bodies/women's lives. Women who have a severe chronic illness are intensely aware of their bodies and live their lives according to the vagaries of their disease. Although there are many negative aspects to this awareness, there are also positive ones such as the sheer physical joy one experiences on an unexpectedly good day. Socially the chronically sick woman must interact with others by means of the different body she possesses (note that I say "different," not "deficient"). The increasing visibility of disabled women cannot but help as long as it is remembered that those who represent this constituency must also speak and act for the hidden women whose lack of energy or severe pain must preclude their becoming spokespersons.

By and large the severely chronically sick have been an invisible minority. Unlike those whose disability level is the same every day and whose disability does not include severe fatigue, these women mostly cannot work and their extracurricular activities must be severely curtailed. Yet numerically when one considers conditions such as lupus, multiple sclerosis and cystic fibrosis, not to mention the many lesser-known conditions such as scleroderma, one is talking about a substantial number of women. This group of hitherto silent women live lives of quiet suffering. They need to be remembered in social planning and in feminist theory. These are women whose appreciation of the body's strengths and weaknesses are unusually acute, whose lives are intricately entwined with their bodies and who have much to teach to others on this topic.

I have lived with scleroderma for nearly twenty years. It is difficult for me to imagine how my life would have been had I not fallen ill. I might have had children. A professional career would have been intellectually satisfying and financially secure. Yet there are ways in which the illness has been a positive experience. I do not believe that "suffering is noble." But there is a certain grim satisfaction to be derived from meeting a difficult challenge well. I have had to learn to deal with pain, frustration and uncertainty, and to acquire patience. These are ways in which I think I am now a stronger person because of what has happened to me. I would not have chosen this path, but I had no choice. As doors have closed, so others have opened. As my near-death experience taught me, my life is still incomparably rich. When people ask me "How are you?" they don't really want to know how I feel. If they did, then, like Susan Wendell, I would answer, "Sick, but happy."

Notes

1. United Nations, *United Nations Decade of Disabled Persons, 1983–1992* (New York: United Nations, 1983).

2. Rosemarie Garland Thomson, *Extraordinary Bodies: Figuring Physical Disability in American Culture and Literature* (New York: Columbia University Press, 1997).

3. Cheri Register, *Living with Chronic Illness: Days of Patience and Passion* (New York: Macmillan, 1987).

4. Elisabeth, Kubler-Ross, *On Death and Dying* (New York: Macmillan, 1969).

5. Susan Wendell, *The Rejected Body: Feminist Philosophical Reflections on Disability* (New York: Routledge, 1996).

CHAPTER TWO

ALTERED BODIES/ALTERED SELVES
EXPLORING WOMEN'S ACCOUNTS
OF ILLNESS EXPERIENCES

Roanne Thomas-MacLean

ɔ

It is no small thing to have your body rearranged, first by disease and then by surgical and chemical interventions intended to cure that disease ... One step further and someone so ill would not return. I want that journey to be recognized.

— Arthur Frank, *At the Will of the Body*

THOSE WHO HAVE EXPERIENCED illness direct our attention to the importance of exploring their experiences. This type of knowledge — the experiential — is missing from much of the social science literature on illness.[1] More specifically, within feminist research, women's reflections on illness have been overlooked.[2] Yet it is essential for women to share their experiences of what it means to be ill. Currently, there are few forums that allow for personal explorations of illness, especially for women. Establishing such a forum is vital for three significant reasons. First, the leading causes of death in North America — cancer and heart disease — are those which may often involve lengthy illnesses. Second, serious illnesses are not necessarily terminal; for example, there are currently 1.6 million women in the United States who have had breast cancer — and are still alive. Third, such exploration allows for reflection and has the potential to reveal the meaning of an illness to the individual.[3] Thus, important questions for feminist research are revealed: What does it mean to be ill and female?

How do women experience illness? What is the social context in which they experience illness?

These are not simple questions. Both structural (macrological) and individual (micrological) approaches must inform the responses. For example, Arthur Kleinman, a psychiatrist and anthropologist, writes that society reacts to people who are ill by blaming the victim. Consequently, environmental links to breast cancer do not receive much attention, while women with breast cancer may be blamed for their illness through individual emphases upon low fat diets, for example.[4] There is, then, a symbiotic relationship between illness as a social phenomenon and illness as individual experience.[5]

This chapter explores individual women's experiences of breast cancer. In these accounts, the experiential takes precedence over structural realities and historical contexts. While these are important, it is equally as important to explore illness from individual perspectives.[6]

CONTEXTUALIZING ILLNESS

Before turning to the individual accounts of illness experiences, it is important to examine the social context in which illness occurs. The medical establishment and the media have played a large role in how illness is perceived in our society and how it is treated. The dominant model for treating illness is the cause/cure paradigm. Medicine emphasizes the discovery of the source of illness and its subsequent treatment. Deconstructing the ideology of "cause/cure" lets us see the limitations of allopathic (traditional) medical approaches to healing. Allopathic medicine and its practitioners have undoubtedly saved and prolonged millions of lives but have been somewhat limited in their ability to address all components of illness experiences.

While there have been recent movements away from the dominant paradigm of cause/cure, including an increase in qualitative research and a shift towards a more holistic definition of health and illness, North American society remains caught in a cause/cure discourse.[7] This is best illustrated through an examination of the workings of the medical system. People visit a doctor when they are experiencing symptoms of illness. Measures are taken to mitigate the physical response of the body to illness. Until recently, the social context of illness was ignored and only the moment of physical trauma was considered, along with a brief *medical* history. As medical sciences are becoming more aware of the significance of a holistic approach to the individual, it is also necessary to examine the issue of *ideology* in order to situate women's experience of illness.[8]

In addition, North American culture is extremely focused on life, and as Larry Dossey points out, this culture generally ignores issues such as illness, dying and death.[9] Dossey writes compellingly about society's dread of going to hospital and attending funerals.[10] Consequently, an illness like cancer, which is associated with a distinct possibility of death, is stigmatized.[11] Illness then becomes separated from the process of living. Dossey also writes of another separation — that of body and mind. This dualistic notion of being and knowing is a prominent theoretical underpinning of modern medicine and Dossey suggests that despite a widespread questioning of the ways in which medicine works, the dualism he describes is still a foundation of most physicians' practices.[12]

Allopathic approaches based within conceptualizations of body and mind as separate entities contribute to concepts of health and disease that function "prescriptively" (in order to fix or remedy illness) not "descriptively."[13] This means that modern medicine may divert attention from cultural meanings of illness as well as understanding individuals' experiences with illness (description) in order to cure (prescription). However, as Mary Rawlinson asserts, medical facts are not simply objective facts — they possess social, cultural and historical attributes. Different illnesses have held different meanings over time. For example, in the late 1800s, childbirth became an event directed largely by male medical practitioners and was treated as an illness, both to the benefit and detriment of women and their children. While childbirth is by many no longer defined as an illness, needless procedures are still performed on women each year.[14] In terms of treatments for breast cancer, Sharon Batt shows that radical mastectomies were being routinely performed in North America long after European physicians had found lumpectomies to be less invasive and equally effective.[15]

However, as medical professionals face the fact that the leading causes of death are now cancer and heart disease, medical science can no longer function so prescriptively. Medicine does not have complete cures for all illnesses. Medicine must now function more preventatively than it previously did. The emphasis still remains on the physical; "exercise" and "eat well" are two prominent messages we receive on a daily basis through the media. Little attention is paid to the social context of illness. Kleinman asserts that "one unintended outcome of the modern transformation of the medical care system is that it does just about everything to drive the practitioner's attention away from the experience of illness."[16] As a result, illness is largely treated as an isolated physical deviation that must be cured. In this research, I attempt to uncover the meaning of illness for five women who have lived with cancer, thereby moving beyond allopathic conceptualizations of illness to a more holistic, experientially based study.

Deconstruction of dominant medical frames of reference is an essential component in the development of knowledge of women's experiences with illness. Kleinman writes that understanding the construction of the meaning of illness can provide knowledge about caring professions and even a better understanding of life itself.[17] This understanding means exploring the implications of changing bodies/changing selves as they are shaped by illness experiences.

THE ALTERED BODY AND ALTERED SELF

Illness often involves a transformation of one's physical self. A person's "lifeworld," her social, cultural, historical and psychological context, is altered in a way that compels her to examine what she takes for granted, whether it is in terms of physical appearance or activity. This has much to do with our conception of the body as "object" or "something" that we must control rather than be. Sally Gadow describes this conception of "the object body" as experiencing "disrupted immediacy."[18] The body is seen as deficient and something to be controlled. It results in "the experience of *feeling encumbered by oneself*."[19] Gadow asserts that such conceptions also result in negative views of illness as there is only one way in which the body is experienced — as object. This conception is reflected in participants' accounts as they speak of their altered bodies. Joan Bottorff describes such experiences as "disease," thereby elaborating the fundamental qualities of disease.[20] What does it mean to be ill at ease? How does illness lead women to altered ways of knowing? How does it shape their being both in their bodies and in the world at large?

Five women participated in my study and their interviews took place in 1993 and 1994.[21] Of the women who participated, four had experienced breast cancer and one had non-Hodgkins lymphoma. The women ranged in age from 40 to 60 years. I spoke to Phyllis at the age of 51, ten years after her breast cancer diagnosis. Carol, who was 47 at the time of our interview, was diagnosed with breast cancer in 1992. Eileen and Jill are both midlife women who also experienced breast cancer and were treated with mastectomies. Jill's diagnosis and treatment occurred four years prior to our interview, while Eileen's cancer was diagnosed the same year of our interview. Unlike the other women, Eszter experienced non-Hodgkins lymphoma. Her treatment consisted of both surgery and chemotherapy. These women's narratives "enable us to grasp ... the complex inner language of hurt, desperation, and moral pain (and also triumph) of living an illness."[22] Exploring women's accounts of illness becomes a significant part of understanding the experiences of women in general. What does it mean to live in an altered body, to experience an altered self, to be ill and female?

The women's narratives allow us to hear the voice of the ill person authentically rather than through the "language of medicine."[23] This chapter represents one way of addressing the silence ill women may have suffered, thereby maintaining feminists' recognition that the personal is political. In *Medical Alert: New Work Organizations in Health Care*, the intersection of the political and the personal is demonstrated in one woman's account of surgery:

> My stomach is totally disfigured because they gave me a vertical even though I asked for the other incision. Because I'm a big girl they said I didn't have to worry because I'm not the type to wear a bikini. Like you have to have a certain body in their eyes to qualify.[24]

"Altered bodies" and "altered selves" cannot be generalized to others. Although research participants share some experiences, they also describe dissimilar experiences. For example, all of the participants were shocked by the revelation that they had cancer, but this shock was described in different ways. Eszter's body dramatically called her to attention when she became lame as a result of a tumour on her spine; Phyllis noticed a thickening of her breast tissue; and Jill saw a change in her breast. Unlike the other participants, Eileen states that, on some level, she believes she knew she had cancer before she received the results of a mammogram. What, then, does it mean to know that one's body and one's self are being altered by illness?

WOMEN'S VOICES: EXPERIENCING THE ALTERED SELF

Although I separate "bodies" and "selves" in this section, I recognize that they are both interconnected, and in reality, are not separable. This separation allows for ease in reading and understanding, for "the body is both our medium for having a world and the vehicle of our being in the world."[25] Arthur Frank writes, "Being ill is just another way of living, but by the time we have lived through illness we are living differently."[26] For example, Eszter shows how cancer may have shaken some of the faith she had in herself and in her experiences: in her being. When talking of the possibility of a recurrence, she says: "I do think about it. I don't dwell on it. I try not to — I always question myself now — is this a fear or just a normal question? I try to convince myself it is just a normal question."

She goes on to show that she has learned from cancer as well:

> I'm keenly aware that my priorities have changed and sometimes when I really get bogged down with the everyday details of work, or just existence, I say to myself, "Well, haven't you learned a lesson? Shouldn't you just be a little more aware of your priorities?" I certainly make decisions a lot quicker.

She continues by illustrating how she has converted these ideas to practice. Eszter accepts any opportunities to travel or to see her grandchildren. She also began taking lessons in yoga as it was something she put off for a long time. She says she has become "fearless." Is it the recognition of one's mortality that becomes an opportunity to learn about oneself?

Phyllis describes learning experiences that are similar to Eszter's. She no longer sleeps late and tries to live to the fullest. Similarly, Eileen says she "appreciates everything more" and that she looks at things differently. She says:

> You start to realize your mortality and think "I've taken all of this for granted." I shouldn't. I should appreciate more the good things ... A beautiful sunny day ... you really see how nice a day it is. I think it would be like looking at everything through a magnifying glass.

When asked if having cancer has changed her, Carol says she is not sure. She says she would like to be able to say she has changed and appreciates life more, but is not sure she can. She then says she has more confidence and realizes the value of friends. She calls these changes "little things."

Along with positive experiences, participants also describe negative ones. Jill, for example, describes how she received the impression from some people that they felt as if cancer was contagious. She does not describe their actions explicitly, yet to understand we have only to consider how we treat someone who has a cold that we do not want to catch. We keep our distance, nervously watching for any sign that the afflicted person is going to come closer, touch us, breathe on us, sneeze or cough on us. Surely, most people are aware that cancer cannot be caught like a cold. What is it about cancer that would prompt people to distance themselves from those who experience it? Is it the nature of the illness or the ideologies of health and illness that are associated with it? What causes discomfort amongst those who are in contact with people who have cancer? These questions have interesting implications if they are applied to members of the medical profession. Do doctors overcome such feelings of discomfort? Perhaps the seven minute appointment (on average) is a subtle form of distancing.

Alfred Schutz's concept of "fundamental anxiety" is a useful starting point for the consideration of such issues. Fundamental anxiety is described as follows: "I know I shall die and I fear to die." Further:

> It is the primordial anticipation from which all others originate. From the fundamental anxiety spring the many interrelated systems of hopes and fears, of wants and satisfactions, of chances and risks which incite man [sic] within the natural attitude to attempt the mastery of the world, to overcome obstacles, to draft projects, and to realize them.[27]

To grant death a central place may call into question all activities of daily life. Dossey writes that "for us, the most grievous problem is the fact of death," unless, as he advocates, death is an accepted aspect of living.[28] The effects of this problem are linked in a most interesting manner by Dossey: "Our society is aflame with resentment at ... the perceived inhumaneness of modern medicine ... It is anger that is overtly directed at the 'system', but at a system which is really ourselves."[29] He also states that this anger is a result of a loss of connectedness to the world and our recognition that living longer does not mean an improved quality of life. Neglecting death robs us of holistic experiences of life in all of its complexity.

In contrast to the negative experiences of some participants, Eszter describes a heightened awareness of, and connection to, the natural world around her — one that is quite intuitive. This awareness is similar to that described by David Rehorick in his phenomenological account of when he became more aware of his relation to the earth during an earthquake experience.[30] Eszter describes a connection with nature through the relationship she had with a tree. She walked to this tree in order to rehabilitate herself. It provided support for her when she was dizzy. She talks of appreciating the texture of the bark, the beauty of the leaves. She also describes another occasion of heightened awareness when her life passed before her eyes. She says it was the night when she faced the possibility of death. It is this recognition of death that Carol cites as a "lesson" she learned from her experience of cancer:

> The most prominent feeling is that you really never know from one day to the next, what it is that life has in store for you. And what I don't want to forget is that particular lesson which will make me more appreciative of the everyday things ... I think it's a blessing. You can get so caught up in things that, when it comes down to it, are not really important.

Jill describes this as "living accordingly." In contrast to this idea of living with a heightened awareness of one's mortality, perhaps living more spiritually, is the concrete and sometimes disagreeable reality of living with a changed body.

EXPERIENCING THE ALTERED BODY

Often illness involves a transformation of one's physical self. Although I primarily write about changes women experience in relation to their bodies and illness in this section, I do not believe that we can legitimately separate body from mind or being from knowing. Sally Gadow also contributes to this understanding of illness through her phenomenological approach to "body" and "self." Her orientation provides directions towards a rich concept of the physical body, one that is not solely concerned with the physical, but also with the self that interacts with the body. Gadow's unification of body and self is not an allopathic one — she does not equate the two; rather, it is a re-unification of body and self.[31] Similarly, S. Kay Toombs writes: "As embodied persons, we experience illness primarily as a disruption of lived body rather than as a dysfunction of biological body."[32] Meaning is central to the experience of illness. In order to understand what illness is, there must be an exploration that goes beyond the manifestation of disease, looking at, for example, its impact on everyday living and the body. Women who are ill may have to adjust their activities in order to live with illness. These adjustments illustrate society's conception of the body as "object." We can see how we objectify our bodies if we think for a moment about the language we use to describe them: we might speak of "recharging our batteries" or we might look for a quick fix. Illness alters this object body.

After her operation, Eszter experienced limitations. She states that it would take her twenty minutes to reach the couch from the bathroom, while previously, it was a journey completed in a matter of seconds:

> I was immobile and it took a long time to go from place to place. It was hard to live with — very hard to live with, especially for somebody who is very quick and athletic. But I never thought of it as a permanent condition.

Eszter also differentiates between this disabled body and what she refers to as her "able body." This is particularly evident when she discusses how she had to remain very still in order to have her lymph system dyed:

I mentally put myself into a situation where I would be guaranteed to be totally relaxed, like in a nice little bay in the sea where I'm just floating in the water or I mentally made myself recall, step by step, climbing a beautiful mountainside and I think through this I never lost sight of my able body — even while I would be lying down and miserable.

This illustrates certain points made by Toombs. She asserts that a person who is ill recognizes that she is her body. In this way, illness is also a threat to self.[33] This idea that illness affects self is not represented in dominant medical paradigms. Perhaps this connection (body and self) accounts for the strong feelings associated with the loss of a portion of Phyllis's body as a result of a mastectomy, for it is not just body that is lost, but also self. She explains it as: "Sadness. It's a type of mourning. You are mourning because you've lost part of your body and you always have to go through a mourning stage."

Toombs's idea is illustrated clearly when one replaces the word "body" with "self," as in "you've lost a part of your self." Phyllis's statement then becomes much more powerful and evokes further understanding. In a sense, these people experience the sensation of "leaving normal." Also present in the women's experiences is the notion "possibilizing," which "provides a way to detach oneself from the actual by seeking possibilities within the limits of the actual."[34] It can be a means of stabilizing the self, or of recognizing future limitations like the possibility of permanent disability. This is a recognition Eszter struggled with:

It did occur to me that this could become a continuous condition and I didn't really cherish that thought. It's not nice to be — well, I wasn't totally at the mercy of others, but almost. It's not a good feeling to realize that somebody else needs to be around you all the time to do the normal functions — to go to the bathroom and all of that. That's tough.

Carol experienced similar frustrations as it took a few months after her operation for her to get a full range of movement in her arms. She wanted to "be back as normal" — as "normal" as she could be.

"Normal" is a quality to which one must return. What does this say about "normal" and "abnormal" ways of being? Eileen says that after receiving her breast prosthesis and recovering from a disability associated with a temporary paralysis in her arm, she is "really back to normal." It is interesting to note what constitutes the condition of being "normal" for Eileen:

> I got my prosthesis. And that's working out really well. I felt fine before, but now I'm really back to normal and I can wear all the same clothes. I don't have to think about what I wear because it's all exactly the same. I don't think anybody would ever, ever know. I feel comfortable.

As healthy people, we recognize our shortcomings and adjust our goals accordingly, creating an "equilibrium," but "illness rudely upsets that equilibrium."[35] Normal equilibrium means not having to think about what to wear. It means returning to a state that previously existed. For Eszter, it meant returning to work, being productive, interacting with others. "Normal" means feeling comfortable; it also means not having to rely on other people to complete everyday tasks. This is significant for women: many women are accustomed to caring for others but illness may mean being cared for.

Can being normal also be considered having permission to take qualities like independence for granted once again? Although all of the women express concern that this should not happen, some express relief at not having to think about everyday tasks. For example, Eileen needed help to get dressed before her arm healed and was relieved when she did not have to give a great deal of thought as to what she would wear and how she would dress herself. Others discuss this enforced reliance of self upon others. Eszter describes it in the way she had to lean on someone to walk, and Carol expresses similar feelings. In a sense, Carol speaks of a way in which the body becomes enslaved:

> I remember the thing that bothered me the most. The first week I was out of the hospital, my sister had to clean out the bath tub. I couldn't do it. I hated that she had to do that for me. I really, really did. And she didn't mind one bit, but it seemed to me like the worst, awful thing for her to have to do for me.

What is so significant about this experience? Is it noteworthy because it made Carol "visibly vulnerable"? Barbara Cull-Wilby describes this trait as being "conscious of imperfection; it is an awareness of one's other-ness."[36] For women — already defined as "other" — illness may further contribute to feelings of isolation and difference. People who are ill may experience this otherness, this separation, in many ways.

Jill and Eszter underwent chemotherapy and as a result, experienced baldness. This experience results in a drastically altered appearance as hair is lost not only from the scalp, but from the eyebrows and lashes as well. Perhaps it is not so much a change in appearance that is difficult, but the association of baldness with illness, with passivity. Jill, for example, used scarves to hide her baldness while undergoing chemotherapy:

> I remember exactly when I started to lose my hair ... Something really turned me off wigs ... So I just decided I would wear scarves ... I had a bit of fun there — co-ordinating and matching them up.

There is some fear or anxiety associated with appearing ill. Yet there is a felt contradiction — participants espouse the idea that appearance is not important, particularly not when one is faced with an illness that may be terminal; but as Jill shows, looking good was important to her — she wanted her scarves to match her clothes. Perhaps appearance also enables blame to be passed on to the person with cancer. As a result of discourse surrounding the disease, cancer may be viewed by others as a result of poor lifestyle choices. Eszter, who did not cover her bald head, says she was surprised at the number of people who revealed to her that they had experienced cancer. She says of others that they "hid their disease so successfully." When surviving cancer becomes part of the dominant ideology, someone who is at a point during which they may or may not survive, is easily stigmatized. Perceptions that mind and medicine can heal cancer may contribute to a blaming of those who are visibly ill.

Connected to this idea is the notion of a cancer-personality as described by Susan Sontag in *Illness as Metaphor*.[37] Those with cancer may be thought to be repressed or too passive. Jill states, "I think a lot of people believe it's a disease that is preventable. You get it because of something you've done." And as Eszter shows, people perceive that cancer is something they must hide. There is fascinating interplay — those who are ill know that there are others who do not want to know.

Perhaps, for women, this arises from a fear that they will not be believed or that their illness will not be accepted as legitimate. Women may fear being labelled hysterical or may be told that "it's all in their heads." Nonetheless, despite the often negative context in which illness occurs, the women are able to describe a process of developing self-acceptance and new knowledge of their bodies/selves — an empowering process.

RECLAIMING SELF: A PROCESS OF REFLECTION

In all of the women's accounts, there is a perceptible movement towards acceptance of an altered body. Jill approaches her acceptance with a sense of wit and irony:

> I once forgot to wear my prosthesis ... I had an appointment and I walked downtown. When I got to the dentist's office and sat down, I realized I didn't have my prosthesis. My first reaction was "I've lost it!" ... I had visions of this announcement coming over the radio: "Lost on Regent Street somewhere, one left breast." I've laughed about that with friends.

At one point, Eszter was bald and had to use a walker. She recalls that she noticed people turning to look at her while on vacation at a lake in Canada. Yet she had a different experience while in Jamaica. A man told her he admired the courage it took for her not to cover up and said it was good to know people, like Eszter, survive cancer. She regarded his comments as positive.

It certainly takes courage to go without a wig or a hat, to acknowledge one's illness publicly, particularly when one considers what the media deem attractive in North American society. Despite her courage, Eszter did notice people's gazes, and Phyllis also says: "You do notice that they look. They sort of look at your breast, but then that's a very normal thing. That never bothered me at all."

Phyllis understands the gaze as normal. Eszter also experienced it and accepts it. However, rather than having the manifestations of her illness and cure being tacitly accepted as an everyday occurrence, a part of the nature of being human, she is made out to be a hero. What does this say about our conceptions of cancer, illness and body image? Are they solely elements of life that must be survived?

Unlike Jill and Eszter, Eileen did not notice people looking at her differently:

> I don't feel any different. I didn't know how people would react. You wonder whether people will look at you funny, think about you funny or whatever. People don't treat me any differently than they did before ...

While she was not stared at, Eileen wondered if such action would occur. To her, there was the possibility that she would be viewed differently. This recognition is as significant as the gaze itself. Knowing that we are voyeurs must influence the experience of illness as surely as the actual experience of becoming an object to be viewed.

Although Eileen does not perceive a change in the way people look at her, she still wears a breast prosthesis. Are both experiences indicative of an expectance of the gaze? For those like Jill, Eileen, Carol and Phyllis, the experience of cancer involved permanent change to the body as well. All of them experienced a mastectomy — the loss of a breast. Kleinman explores the meaning of such a loss through the accounts of one of his patients who had a foot amputated: "she grieved for the loss of a body part, physical function, body- and self-image, and way of life."[38] In contrast, Jill did not seem to mourn the loss of a breast: "My first reaction ... was 'Get rid of it. Cut the whole thing off if you have to, but get rid of it.'" Eileen had similar feelings; her reaction when learning she had breast cancer was: "I just want to be well. If it means losing a breast, it's not the end of the world, well, it's not the end of my life."

While Carol would undoubtedly identify with Eileen's statement, she, like Phyllis, describes a type of mourning. Her account links this idea of mourning to the concept of the gaze, only in this instance, the gaze originates from herself:

> For the most part, I'm not bothered by the change in my appearance and that surprises me because I wouldn't have thought so ahead of time ... Every once in a while, I have what I call a "reality check." I will actually look at myself and there's a sadness.

This action of "actually looking" is different from one's everyday look at oneself. It involves reflection. In that sense, it may also be different from the gazes imposed by others. What does it mean to truly look at oneself, to gaze at a reflection, to reflect? Perhaps reflections (from mirror or mind) enhance the process of knowing. Reflection does not only involve the act of seeing, but is also connected to the act of being thoughtful. Eileen states that with some reflection, she would have realized why she was tired all of the time while she was experiencing temporary paralysis in her arm. She visited the doctor asking what she could *do* about her tiredness. Such action shows how we perceive that we must always do — take action — rather than simply *be* in the world. Her doctor told her that she was tired because she had to think about everyday details of living so much, rather than following a routine. She says:

> If I had sat down and thought about it, of course I would have figured it out myself instead of having someone point it out. I felt better. It wasn't because the cancer had started up again. It was a perfectly natural reaction. My body was saying it's a little harder to do all of these things, so it's a little more tiring.

We are not encouraged to trust our bodies, to listen to them when they speak to us through "symptoms" such as tiredness. We rely instead on experts, on those who are outside of our experiences, to tell us what we are capable of knowing. Women in particular have been discouraged from listening to their bodies. In this information age where we are inundated with news about the world around us, we tend to neglect our immediate news that perhaps most directly affects us. In the effort to be faster and better, the process of self-reflection is viewed as being somewhat frivolous or a luxury. Who has time to think? Today, one in three feel they are stressed with no time to relax.[39] Participants both in Cull-Wilby's study on asthma and in this one, note the desire to escape to a desert island.[40] What are the characteristics of such a place? What types of activities would it permit?

Such a space allows for reflection free from interference — reflections on the altered body, altered self. It may be considered one destination of the journey to meaning; for me, as a researcher, it offers the metaphor of an inward place, somewhere to retreat, to explore the implications of research. It becomes a place in which assumptions about the workings of the world may be bracketed, in which implications for praxis — putting knowledge to work to create social change — may be considered. What can we do to understand what it is like to experience the body altered by illness? This final question directs attention to creating ideas for turning knowledge into practice.

∞

Modern medicine is part of a vast complex of values, ideas, beliefs, practices and institutional relations. Yet as Dorothy Smith asserts, we are a part of any ruling apparatus.[41] As such, we have the power to effect some sort of change in the ways in which we interact with the medical system and the ways in which we learn about the lived experience of being ill. Smith captures both the problematic and the potential that explorations of illness experiences may provide for women:

> Women have developed alternatives for women, which have been radical both in providing for a woman a place to begin from her knowledge of her own body and also in representing a radical departure from the professional forms of social relations in which knowledge is appropriated and controlled by "experts."[42]

This quote is a very empowering one and directs attention to the importance of practice or praxis. When applied to the query, "What does it mean to be ill and female?" praxis can mean many different things.

One way of effecting social change is to ensure that research remains accessible to those who give it voice. This may mean allowing research participants the option of using their own names in a research project or paper if they wish. Not one of my participants refused this option.[43] This represents a significant desire to own their stories. This wish needs to be addressed whenever possible and may contribute to the recognition of the true experts on illness — those with first-hand experience.

Praxis may also mean a rejection of dominant medical models of illness based solely upon dualistic notions of body and mind. Again, the sharing of illness experiences becomes an integral part of creating social change. Women need forums to express both personal and social aspects of illness. As a result, praxis may also mean questioning the ways in which knowledge is disseminated. This may mean recognizing the privilege of literacy in disseminating research findings as well as being open to new methods of dissemination (like art, for example).[44]

Finally, praxis may mean engaging in new forms of teaching and learning. One cannot overlook the vast potential that collaboration offers to developing understandings of illness. Collaborative research could integrate the perspectives of several disciplines and involve participants in research processes. If we continue to ignore the voices of those who are ill, we run the risk of developing systems of knowledge as sterile as operating rooms. While sterile conditions are important in a medical setting, the development of new knowledge about illness experiences should reflect the remarkable diversity of what it means to be human, and what it means to be a woman experiencing illness.

Notes

I am indebted to David Rehorick and his unfailing pedagogical support throughout my academic career. His comments and suggestions were vital to the process of completing my master's thesis, "'Cancer is ...?' An Exploration of Adults' Accounts of Living with Cancer" (University of New Brunswick, 1994), which forms the basis for this chapter.

1. For example, while much has been published in the area of cancer research, the focus has primarily been upon issues such as epidemiology, causes of cancer and prescriptions for coping with illness. It is a focus based on the discourse of cause/cure/cope. While this type of literature provides useful information, it neglects experiential aspects of illness. Recently, there have been some indications that research based on the everyday experience of illness is becoming more prominent.

2. V. Walters, "Women's Perceptions Regarding Health and Illness," in B.S. Bolaria and H.D. Dickinson, eds., *Health, Illness, and Health Care in Canada* (Toronto: Harcourt Brace, 1994).

3. B.S. Turner, *Medical Power and Social Knowledge* (London: Sage Publications, 1995).

4. Arthur Kleinman, *The Illness Narratives: Suffering, Healing and the Human Condition* (New York: Basic Books, 1988).

5. See Dorothy E. Smith, *The Everyday World as Problematic* (Toronto: University of Toronto Press, 1987) for an explanation of this type of theoretical framework.

6. One cannot deny the significance of historical circumstances and events and their role in shaping current ideologies of health and illness. Tracing the historical development of modern medicine and the consequences of its development for women today is beyond the scope of this chapter. However, Barbara Ehrenreich and Deirdre English provide a comprehensive "herstory" of modern medicine in *For Her Own Good* (New York: Anchor Books, 1978). More recent feminist research describes the roles that women themselves have played in facilitating the rise of the experts. See, for example, Leslie J. Miller and Deborah A. Findlay, "Through Medical Eyes: The Medicalization of Women's Bodies and Women's Lives," in Bolaria and Dickinson, eds., *Health, Illness, and Health Care in Canada*.

7. F. Saillant, "Discourse, Knowledge and Experience of Cancer: A Life Story," *Culture, Medicine and Psychiatry* 14 (1990), 81–104.

8. Holistic explorations of health and illness encompass all aspects of self, including physical, social and spiritual dimensions of experience.

9. Larry Dossey, *Beyond Illness: Discovering the Experience of Health* (Boston: Shambala, 1985).

10. Ibid.

11. J.N. Clarke, *Health, Illness, and Medicine in Canada* (Toronto: McClelland and Stewart Inc., 1990); Arthur Frank, *At the Will of the Body: Reflections on Illness* (Boston: Houghton Mifflin, 1991).

12. Dossey, *Beyond Illness*.

13. Mary C. Rawlinson, "The Facticity of Illness and the Appropriation of Health," in W.L. McBride and C.O. Schrag, eds., *Phenomenology in a Pluralistic Context* (Albany: State University of New York Press, 1983), 156.

14. Feminists have debated the merits and shortcomings of procedures such as episiotomies for years. See Suzanne Arms, *Immaculate Deception* (Toronto: Bantam Books, 1977). Other debates include those surrounding medical procedures involved with reproductive technologies. See Gina Corea et al., *Man-Made Women* (Bloomington: Indiana University Press, 1987). Interestingly, the retired director for health sciences for the Rockefeller Foundation suggests that only 20 to 25 percent of medicine is based on objective evidence that intervention would do a patient more good than harm. Lynn Payer, *Medicine and Culture* (New York: Henry Holt, 1996), xx.

15. Sharon Batt, *Patient No More: The Politics of Breast Cancer* (Charlottetown, PEI: Gynergy Books, 1994), 59–61.

16. Kleinman, *The Illness Narratives*, xiv.

17. Ibid.

18. Sally Gadow, "Body and Self: A Dialectic," in V. Kestenbaum, ed., *Phenomenological Perspectives* (Knoxville: University of Tennessee Press, 1982), 86.

19. Ibid., 90.

20. Joan Bottorff, "The Lived Experience of Being Comforted by a Nurse," *Phenomenology and Pedagogy* 9 (1991), 238.

21. A snowball technique was used to contact the research participants. Potential participants were referred to me by colleagues and by other people I interviewed. Each participant was given the choice of having a pseudonym assigned or having their real name used in my thesis. They were presented with this choice because I question, as does Janice Morse in "Subjects, Respondents, Informants, and Participants?," *Qualitative Health Research* 1, no. 4 (1991), 404: "Is not their information, used as a basis for interpretation, worthy to be linked with their name should they so desire?" Further, she asserts, pseudonyms may be "a signing away the right to have their knowledge, their ideas, and their insights recognized." None of the participants chose to use a pseudonym for the initial research. As some time had elapsed between the initial research and the writing of this chapter, I re-contacted Eszter, Eileen, Carol and Phyllis who confirmed that their real names could be connected to this publication. I was unable to reach "Jill" for similar confirmation and consequently assigned her a pseudonym. In addition, my original work refers to interviews completed with one male participant. Although his words are not a part of this research context, his understanding of cancer was significant in formulating my thesis.

22. Kleinman, *The Illness Narratives*, 28–29.

23. C. Mathieson, "Women With Cancer and the Meaning of Body Talk," *Canadian Woman Studies* 14 (1994), 54.

24. Pat Armstrong, et al., *Medical Alert: New Work Organizations in Health Care* (Toronto: Garamond Press Ltd., 1997), 94.

25. Merleau-Ponty in D. Rehorick, "Shaking the Foundations of Lifeworld: A Phenomenological Account of an Earthquake Experience," *Human Studies* 9 (1986), 381.

26. Frank, *At the Will of the Body*, 3.

27. Alfred Schutz cited in the "Introduction" of M. Natanson, ed., *Alfred Schutz: Collected Papers* (The Hague: Martinus Nijhoff, 1962), xliv.

28. Dossey, *Beyond Illness*, 20, 25.

29. Ibid., 27.

30. David Rehorick, "Shaking the Foundations of Lifeworld," 379–391.

31. Gadow, "Body and Self."

32. S.K. Toombs, *The Meaning of Illness* (Dordrecht, The Netherlands: Kluwer Academic Publishers, 1993), 201.

33. Ibid., 214.

34. Rehorick, "Shaking the Foundations of Lifeworld," 385.

35. Rawlinson, "The Facticity of Illness and the Appropriation of Health," 158.

36. Barbara Lynn Cull-Wilby, "Living with Asthma: A Phenomenological Search for Meaning" (PhD diss., University of Rochester, New York, 1993), 154. See also Chapter 3 in this book.

37. Susan Sontag, *Illness as Metaphor* (Toronto: McGraw-Hill Ryerson, 1978).

38. Kleinman, *The Illness Narratives*, 39.

39. T. Harpur, *The Uncommon Touch: An Investigation of Spiritual Healing* (Toronto: McClelland and Stewart Inc., 1994).

40. Cull-Wilby, "Living with Asthma."

41. Smith, *The Everyday World as Problematic.*

42. Ibid., 53–54.

43. See note 21 above.

44. Marianne Paget, *A Complex Sorrow* (Philadelphia: Temple University Press, 1993), provides an excellent example of a sociologist who explored an alternative means of disseminating the results of research. Before her death, Paget produced a play based on her research into physicians' management of their mistakes.

CHAPTER THREE

BREATH AND BODY WISDOM
EXPERIENCING THE PERSONAL POWER OF SELF

Barbara Lynn Cull-Wilby

⨕

WE WILL ENGAGE SIX TO SEVEN hundred million breaths in a lifetime.[1] Breathing is one of the few automatic processes of our bodies that we can bring under conscious control. Awareness of breath brings us to recognize its significance: breath both influences and is influenced by *every* experience in our moment-to-moment functioning.[2] It is used in every single word and movement; it is necessary for "all energy-producing chemical reactions in the body."[3] Breathing connects us to life, to spirit, to Self. It connects us with our environment. Breath is incredibly significant. It is remarkable that we breathe so much and are so dependent on breath yet often are not even aware that we are breathing.

Breath is simultaneously both a *literal* and a *metaphorical* function.[4] As a *literal* function, breath is focused primarily on the physical understanding: the pulmonary exchange of oxygen and carbon dioxide, for example. If breathing becomes difficult, the emphasis is on re-establishing the optimum functioning of the respiratory tract. Pharmaceuticals have been the main choice of treatment for breathing difficulties. Breath as a *metaphorical* function reveals one's life as it is experienced physically, but also spiritually, emotionally, mentally and culturally. If the breathing becomes difficult, the emphasis is on understanding the life experiences that are contributing to the breathlessness. Practising an awareness of breath, which could perhaps include the use of pharmaceuticals, might be used to help the condition.

Breath is both inhalation and exhalation. Inhalation means to inspire, literally breathing in oxygen and divine inspiration with each breath. Receiving, opening, accepting, allowing — these are all literal descriptions of the physical act of breathing in. They are also, at the same time and as equally important, descriptions of the metaphorical, the symbolic nuances of breathing in. How open are you to receive in your life? Are you open to accept loving gestures? Money? Friendship? Criticism? These questions may reveal obvious responses. Yet it is interesting to pay attention to the subtle ways we accept the experiences of our day. This receptiveness can be "tested" in any situation. Try it now. How open are you at this moment — can you stop reading and deeply notice the environment that you are in? Are you comfortable? Did you consciously choose your environment? Why? Why not? Is your breathing long or short? Are you open to thinking of your breath as divine inspiration? Do you resist that idea? Are you open to exploring the awareness that breath facilitates — the awareness that you can be who you desire to be now and always?

Exhalation means to exhale, literally and metaphorically expiring with each breath — dying, letting go, giving, releasing. How open are you to letting things go? What are you holding on to that no longer fits with your life? Whom are you holding on to? By breathing deeply in various situations, by consciously breathing in as well as out, you can direct and redirect the possibilities, as if to open the possibilities. Simply bringing your awareness to your breath — when breathing in know that you are breathing in, when breathing out know that you are breathing out — brings you to a point of focus that can facilitate a calming of your thoughts, your emotions and your body.

By doing so, we are more sharply aware of ourselves and our environment, which includes others. Being mindful of our breath can allow us to acknowledge that we might be resisting someone or something. Resistance is often accompanied by a shallow breath or a holding of breath. Therefore, there is reduced amount of oxygen and life energy being used to facilitate the vigour of bodily functions, to formulate thoughts and to recognize and understand emotions.

I have a dear friend who is quick to anger. Choosing to breathe deeply and consciously when she feels her anger rising offers her different possibilities to her predictable behaviour of blind rage. *Each* cell of her body benefits physically from an influx of oxygen, so does the clarity of her mind, emotions and spirit. She takes in more life (more air, more awareness of her environment, her feelings and mental formations) when she breathes deeply. Fear and anger constrict her respiratory and circulatory systems; she is not able to think or function with clarity. Through the calm, clearly felt field of energy that comes as a result of her focused breathing, she is better able to see the fear behind the anger and thus better able to understand and let go. It takes practice and a willingness to be open to try something new. Learning to respond to fear with blind rage is a familiar, inherited and well-practised pattern that has been subtly nurtured and reinforced in her life experiences, even with as innocent a comment as "Oh, she's always had a temper." Seeing herself holding her breath in anger allows my friend the possibility of reflecting rather than blindly ranting: perhaps she might ask, What is this anger about? What is it that causes me to hold my breath? Am I afraid to breathe fully, to speak fully, to act fully in this situation, with this person? Breathing with awareness not only nurtures the healthy functioning of her physical body but facilitates an understanding of her life and her choice of response. Her breath is significant, both metaphorically and literally, for a more centred life.

Using the breath to focus on our life energy and bring awareness to our actions and emotions is, on the surface, a foreign idea to our western way of thinking. Yet the origins of the diverse cultures that make up our western civilization, indeed even our language, are grounded in ancient roots and traditions based on an appreciation of breath. Cultural meanings of breath offer the individual possibilities to explore and experience breath as a life-giving force. For example, Chinese teachings depict the understanding of breath beyond a mere exchange of oxygen and carbon dioxide. The Chi (breath) is energy connected to all that is. This energy not only encompasses the body, it flows through it; it is it. The inhalation and exhalation of breath forms a part of this energy flow yet breath is also the metaphor for the vitalizing energy of life. It is, in the Chinese philosophy, the very essence of life:

> Therefore, the able, the wise and the scholars treasure life when it is not yet endangered . . . The way (TAO) is breath. The ruler of the body is this essence. This essence is the root of life. By loving the essence and treasuring the breath, you are likely to prolong life.[5]

Prana is the Hindu word for life principle. "Prana is not oxygen, but rather is that which gives *life* to the oxygen, the actual life force within the oxygen."[6] "To breathe deeply is to live fully,"[7] for breath contains prana according to Hindu belief.

The breath-of-life is a concept central to North American First Nations culture. It is understanding beyond what can be described in words:

> This concept of the breath-of-life is discovered everywhere in the unique spiritual world of Indians: in the ceremonial stem of the sacred pipe, in the heart line of animals imprinted on pottery, in the rite of inhaling the first light of day and the conferring of blessings by exhaling. All these symbolic images and gestures are associated with the wind and with the breathing of the universe — the invisible motion of the power that invests everything in existence.[8]

In Hawaiian culture, breath is a basic integral aspect of the language. For example, *ha* means breath, the breath of life, inspiration. Alo*ha* is the greeting for hello, goodbye. It means to go with, or to be with, the breath of life.[9] "*Ruh* in Hebrew and Arabic means both 'breath' and 'spirit.' The Dakota and the Sioux called it *niya*, the Aztec *ehecatl*."[10] Psychology is the study of *psyche*, a word commonly referred to in our language. The original meaning of *psyche* "is breath, life, spirit, soul, mind" derived from the Greek work *psukhe*. Spirit is derived from the Latin word *spirare*, to breathe. Similarly, in Hebrew, "soul, life, person" literally refers to "that which breathes."[11] Christian teachings record the connection between breath and spirit. God, having formed humans from dust, breathed into the nostrils the breath of life, and a living soul was created.[12]

Reminders that make us aware of breathing fully *can* be found everywhere, certainly in nature, with wind, for example. Reminders also exist in common breath-related expressions, such as "So hot you can't breathe." "Catch my breath." "You took my breath away." "Breathe new life into something old." Stop now. Close your eyes and in a symbolic way let go. Concentrate and with gentleness bring your awareness to your breath. Pause a moment and listen. Just listen. No judgement. Simply allow yourself, your thoughts, your emotions and your body to be still.

Reflecting on My Personal Knowledge

I do not remember the first time I became aware of my breath and its significance for my life; perhaps with my birth. Many of my past experiences offered me the opportunity to see, feel and learn to value the breath — tobogganing, falling, scuba diving, wheezing, pneumonia, asthma, loving, arguing, labouring, birthing, nursing, mothering. At the age of twenty-three (I am now forty-four), approximately one year after I was married, I was diagnosed with asthma. I was shocked with this verdict. Even though I had grown up with a wheeze, I had always seen it as a friendly wheeze. I had been taught in my nursing education to view asthma as an aberration. I was prescribed several pharmaceutical prescriptions. The dizziness, heart palpitations and bad taste of the medicine were difficult to accept, yet I dutifully took them as directed. I also began experimenting with my breathing as I walked up the hill to the university, monitoring my daily functioning and noting gradual improvement. I eventually stopped the medication and continued to experiment with other means to alleviate the breathlessness.

Although my primary focus at that time was on the physical act of breathing, I was, to a degree, aware that my new marital status had an influence on my breathing space. I relate this story because the meaning that I associated with asthma changed as I lived a life that was in contrast to what the physician and the textbooks told me asthma was, and what I felt and experienced as asthma. Essentially there was a blending of knowledge. I knew medically what asthma was. I knew the air became trapped in the alveoli, my air sacs. I knew in order to get a full breath in, I needed to exhale fully. I knew my body and mind functioned better when I concentrated on my breathing. It was this blending of knowledge that allowed me to experiment with the breathlessness as I walked to and from school. This blending essentially was an internal knowing, an awareness, perhaps even an empowerment that suggested I did not have to rely on the official view of treating asthma with medication if it did not feel right with me or feel good and easy with my body.

Years later, I discovered that my efforts to take control of this condition were not unlike those of others in similar situations. In the spring and autumn of 1986, I conducted preliminary interviews with four individuals with asthma as part of the course work for my doctorate. Analysis of the data generated from the interviews revealed that although individuals were using standard treatments, that is, medication, they were also alleviating breathlessness by using strategies based on personal knowledge. For example, a forty-year-old woman described how she achieved drastic improvement by listening daily, for one year, to an audio-tape that she had designed and taped to assist her in imagining a healthy respiratory tract.

Through my research I began to ask many questions of what I knew, and how I came to know. Again and again I recognized that as a society and as individuals we value and perpetuate dependence on external knowledge and regulation. I saw how we subtly encouraged the concealment and the disregarding of personal knowledge and subjective knowing. We all have personal knowledge as well as knowledge derived from objective and subjective points of view; they are different but not separate. Personal knowledge is often silent and invisible.[13] We bring personal knowledge, whether consciously or unconsciously, to every situation. It serves as a bridge for interpretation between objective and subjective knowing.[14] It became more and more obvious to me that we unconsciously encouraged, taught and even financially reimbursed illness and disease. In my pursuit to understand the personal meaning individuals brought to their illness experiences, I interviewed nine people for my PhD research on the experience of living with asthma. Five of the nine were women: Sophia, Joy, Olivia, Leah and Jane (pseudonyms). Deep contemplation on the breathlessness of asthma in their lives brought me back to an exploration of breath. I struggled with and resisted what I saw emerging from my data analysis because it did not fit with the way I had come to know illness, disease, breath, even life. My foundations were shaken. Others also resisted what I was saying and how I was saying it. It didn't fit with the expected way of being yet there was also growing recognition that as a global society our views of the world were changing.

My research revealed that there was an alternative movement towards understanding the journey of knowing breath as life, breath as soul, breath as Self. Funded by the Canadian Nurses Respiratory Society of the Lung Association, I portrayed this movement in a video featuring the stories of five women: *Living Each Breath. Asthma: A*

Dis-Covery of Self.[15] Over the past decade I have come to understand this movement as a healing process. It has not only influenced by research but also my work, my life. As a consequence, I made a change to my nursing practice. Honouring my body wisdom, I resigned from a tenured university position in the Faculty of Nursing. The energy demands of mothering three children spoke to a home-based business. My nursing practice now is defined by writing, public speaking and counselling, all focusing on breathing awareness in the experience of discovering Self.

Through the way I live and through my research, I intend to evolve and transform our understanding of life from the current disease-orientated health and illness to an understanding of life as integrated with equanimity, spiritual and personal meanings. I want to increase our awareness of what we take for granted and of the language we choose to describe how we live. I would like to see us increase our personal possibilities, acknowledge the inseparability of our lifeworlds, acknowledge the interrelatedness of our worlds and pursue an enjoyment of Self. This means there must be a desire to see the whole, not just symptoms of struggle or disease, for example, but also the *life* of the woman[16] as it is lived and all the elements that make up the totality of her Being: from the spiritual to the physical to the emotional to the environmental. *Everything* contributes to who and what we are and how we know what we know and how and what we pass on to future generations. Self, capitalized, is defined as "trusting, open, centered in a calm, clearly felt field of energy. The Self stands for *an ever-deepening experience* of Being and for a *wholeness* in relation to that experience that is open and expansive."[17] It is in the Self that there is an allowing, a recognition of our Essence, our essential nature. When we live with an awareness of this calm and clearly felt energy, we are living in an awareness of a personal experience of one's God, however God is or is not understood. My work is about honouring who we are as individuals. And so, it is about honouring Self and Other equally.

We gain insight into ourselves through allowing ourselves to listen and reflect on the experiences of others. My experience may relate to your experience and vice versa. We truly are not separate from one another. Even if we disagree, each perspective helps to create and picture the whole of reality that we, as individuals, understand.

Whether we like to admit it or not, we have created the world in which we live, perhaps with voice or action or silence. Every perspective has value and contributes to understanding the experience of what it means to be a woman. As we allow ourselves the gift of paying attention to our breath, we are more able to tap our inner and outer landscapes, our resources and our body wisdom.

LEARNING OUR BODY WISDOM

> If statistics are anything to live by (and surely they're as reliable as game shows), Leslie will be dead in five to ten years. *How* is still being decided by her cells. Will it be her stomach, where the ulcer has already made its presence known? Her heart or lungs, whose complaints she hears but manages to ignore? Right now, her cells are deciding her future.[18]

Because the body is our means of experiencing the world,[19] the search for meaning is inextricably connected to and is one with embodiment. Conscious embodiment is a "complex event and a task accomplished at every moment."[20] How aware of your moments are you? How aware of your embodiment are you?

Sally Gadow presents four progressive dialectic levels of relation between the body and the self.[21] I outline Gadow's body and self dialectic to help you engage in a dialectic with the experiences of your own body. Her writings inspired me to further explore the value of learning and trusting body wisdom. I perceive that it is through the process of mutual learning, of each learning the language of the other (whether the other is her body, a husband, a partner, a mother, an environment, an audience, a family, a religion, or a piece of art) that personal power is uncovered and consciously experienced. The dialectic is an honest exchange grounded in an open curiosity, a willingness to deeply listen, and a mutual respect allowing the other's validity.

In Gadow's first level, *Primary immediacy: the lived body*, the body and self form a unity of lived body separate and distinguishable from the world. In *Disrupted immediacy: the object body*, the second level, the body is opposed to self and is considered to be a source of impediment. The immediacy of being in the world, of breathing thoughtlessly is shattered as the self experiences the restrictions imposed by the body:

> The self either controls the body, through discipline, habituation and training, or is controlled by it through illness, awkwardness, disability. In either case, the relation is one of implicit struggle: I *will* master this musical instrument; I *will not* give in to this pain. Body and self are inevitably at odds with one another.[22]

Two directions are possible in an attempt to restore unity between self and object body. In one, *Renewed dichotomy*, the body and self continue to play out the master and slave scenario. "The self attempts to master the body conclusively by scientifically comprehending it, that is, relegating it to the abstract world of pure objectiveness and categories."[23] The second possible direction is a new unity, which Gadow identifies as the third level of the dialectical progression: *Cultivated immediacy: Harmony of lived body and object body.* Here the body and self are not opposed. The body becomes the means to fulfill the aims of the Self. Still missing, however, is the full recognition of the body as a respected and trusted member of the dialectic. Hence, the Self relies on learned ways to master, often masking the messages from the body. "Determination from the body is experienced as negative (limit, constraint) and, furthermore, as secondary to the determination imposed by the self."[24] The final possible level of the dialectic is *Aesthetic immediacy: completion of the dialectic in aging and illness.* It is in this final level that the idea of honouring Self and Other equally was triggered and hence the idea of honoring and understanding the messages from our bodies.

Coupled with what I saw emerging from my research data, Gadow's dialectic levels of relation between the body and the self revealed to me a possibility of teaching ourselves to listen to our bodies so that we may discover how we are responding to, and in a sense receiving, the experiences of our lives. Gadow posits that it is through aging and illness that we can choose to recognize the body as an equal in the dialectic of experience. This aesthetic immediacy, as she calls it, reflects the awareness of beautiful presence. It places both the body and the Self in a continual dance of each learning the language of the other. Gadow describes this "new relation between self and subject body" as intrasubjectivity. The self recognizes the body as another manifestation of selfness. She uses the analogy of a child within a family and recognizes that ideally "the child's reality *as a subject*, is of equal value with every other person in the family."[25]

I like this example of a child's reality being of equal value in a family because it is a concrete metaphor for symbolizing the potentially infinite expressions of the body. I have three children. Esther is seven, my youngest. Simon and Sarah, both in their teens, have evolved their art of being present in their reality through being heard — sometimes through vocal expression, sometimes through bodily gestures and sometimes through their chosen absence or presence. Esther's voice is not always heard, not always equally valued. To announce her desires, she may choose tears or change the tone of her voice to a pitch that gets attention. The body, through respiration, executes its "contact with the world," announcing its "mood and desires."[26] The personal meanings of our experiences are coloured with the interpretations we have learned from our own particular lives, each one filled with infinite, unique, individualized experiences. There are always many levels of interpretation possible in any given situation. We are all acting on personal meaning; acting on our level of awareness of embodiment. Esther has not yet learned to mask the messages from her body to suit the expectations of others. For example, she readily feels her own beautiful presence and is able to release easily her frustration with tears. Although not yet conscious, she trusts and therefore effortlessly acts with the messages her body gives.

We need to be aware of the messages our bodies give to us. It is an "out and in experience." We can "both move the body proper and are moved by it."[27] Touching something or someone and being touched by something or someone dramatically increases awareness if we can allow both to happen simultaneously; touching makes embodiment keenly and acutely felt.[28] Breath is both out and in. When I consciously embody my wheeze, I feel the restricted bronchi and am aware that I restrict the bronchi. As I fully embody the restriction, it releases. This process of allowing myself to join with the restriction is calming for it requires quiet poignant focusing. Often I gain insight into my own personal meaning of what the restriction is about. To live with an awareness of a possible dialectic is to uncover personal meaning in the search, the quest of finding what works and what doesn't work to release the restrictions I experience. Discovering embodiment is a quest; embodiment is a unique relation to the world; a unique way of being-in-the-world.

Without this embodiment, this body wisdom, I would not always *act* on messages my body gives. Indeed, it may seem and is often considered naive or trivial to heed our bodies as if they were communicating honestly and with authority. The women in my research project talked about how they learned to listen to their bodies — to embody their experience in breathlessness. They imagined themselves on a desert island where they could create their own space. On a desert island, the function of breathing switches its focus from the breathlessness of the restriction ("something happening to me") to the breath that is associated with the method to remain calm ("something I am doing"). It is not necessary to meet anyone else's expectations — only their own. On a desert island there is time to focus and centre. For these women, it is a way of coming into their being, to reorient themselves to the world, to Self. They can slow down, relax and focus inward. This image helped the women alleviate breathlessness, a technique used after all else had failed. This imagery and practice helped them learn to regulate their breathing in other situations. Joy, sitting at the legislator's table, consciously but discretely took "deep breaths in and out with pursed lips." Olivia has learned: "Sometimes you can wheeze yourself off by being quiet and just slowing your breathing down. It's like going into a meditation."

LISTENING TO THE LANGUAGE OF THE BODY

> Illness has always been of enormous benefit to me. It might even be said that I have learned little from anything that did not in some way make me sick.[29]

I compare the process of learning to value and respect communication with my body to learning to communicate in French with my friend, Jacinthe. It is a slow process and I improve with practice. If I do not practise, I do not improve, which is fine. Yet, as I learn to communicate in this new language, new possibilities and new experiences unfold; and so it is with the experience of listening to one's body. Emma, a young single mother who came to visit me, learned how to listen and trust her body's language. She told me that in the past during an asthma attack she never knew what her body was going to do. "I was afraid of it. I didn't feel I had any power over it but now I do. I always thought of my body as my enemy and now we're friends." Through listening and experimenting with understanding what relieved her breathlessness and what did not, Emma was able to value, listen and work with the communication from her body. She moved from seeing her body as an enemy to seeing it as a trusted, beautiful presence. This movement is what I define as the healing process. It is a process that allows oneself to embrace the fear and to practise living from a place of trust: trusting one's breath, one's way of knowing, one's values, even one's mistakes. It sounds so simple. And it is. Yet when we are in a state of being blinded with pain and fear, it can be very difficult to allow ourselves to be open to and nurture this healing movement.

Our bodies talk, not only through voice and thoughts and language but also through an infinite array of expressions: mobility, posture, breathing depth, sight, smell, touch, to name a few. Attending to these bodily messages acknowledges the inseparability of body, mind, emotions and spirit. At what level do we choose to heed the body wisdom? Interpreting "asthma attack," for example, based on the word's origins might imply that an asthma attack is battle with air, with breath, or a battle with a person's soul or spirit.[30] Often we do not take the time to explore the deeper meaning of the messages our bodies give. How do we experience these personal meanings? Jane was diagnosed with asthma and allergies at three years of age, shortly after her parents divorced. The synchronicity of these experiences is obvious. Jane, almost twenty at the time of the research interviews, had learned to maintain the asthma in her life through exercise and techniques she had learned from her mother, a nurse. She has learned to live the asthma experience. She learns to balance external control (for example, prescriptions, her mother's attention, the do's and don'ts of others) with her own internal sense of what feels right for her. Asthma is her "birthmark" as she says. It is part of her. To maintain it, she listens to her breath, she pays attention to the experiences of her life and when the asthma bothers her, she deals with it. The meaning Jane gives the asthma is wedded to the experiences of her life and to the depth of her openness and desire to understand it.

As we fully respect and attend to whatever sensations or messages our bodies reveal, we tap wisdom beyond rational knowing. We cross boundaries that have limited our understanding of ourselves and our lives. A salient example would be when I experience the beginnings of nasal congestion. I find this is an opportunity for me to recognize that my life has become overly congested. I have too many things on the go. If I slow my pace and allow myself to connect with that inner calm of Self, often the congestion will ease and not develop into a cold. A more subtle example is the feeling, that tug of sensation to contact someone. Often when I consciously value this message and act on it, my phone call comes at a most appropriate time; both for the person I call and for myself. "The body is a metaphor. Listen to it," Sheila Pennington, a Toronto psychotherapist advises.[31] What do arthritic fingers say about our ability to handle finely the experiences of our lives? Or an irritated digestive tract say about digesting life or about the relationships in our life? The messages of our bodies are wedded to context, to our experiences, our lifeworlds, and although there are common elements they are always unique to the individual. Joy, a forty-one-year old woman, experienced difficulties breathing when she was working in a factory with a specific glue. She took direct actions based on her awareness: "So I made a little stink at work and they did move us, move the area we were working in and put in some floor fans around us. I did continue to work with the glue. I started at that time using a prescription inhaler ... I think it was theroderm. I continued to be a smoker also." Joy experienced difficulties breathing when she smoked. She was aware of this but continued to smoke until, as she says, "I just reached a point where I couldn't inhale a cigarette."

There is a personal responsibility and with that a sense of freedom that comes when choosing to respect body's language and wisdom. And yet, the idea of being responsible for my being-in-the-world often has negative connotations. This responsibility with roots in a wholistic paradigm is different from blaming, which has roots in a separation paradigm. For example Leah, thirty-eight, says, "I would like to think that asthma is straight physiologic." This physical cause-and-effect statement of reassurance stems from our ingrained dualism that allows blaming. Joy's statement, too, reflects the ingrained separation of body, mind, emotions and spirit: "I get the feeling sometimes that others feel that you bring on the asthma yourself. Though I find it hard to think of myself as having a disease, I want to know that I don't bring it on myself." Although we want control, we do not want and have not reinforced, taking responsibility for our own lives, our own experiences. Choosing to listen to and act with the body's language reflects taking responsibility and allows for the opportunity of learning and personal growth. Valuing the body wisdom means respecting where you are at this time in your life. Sophia, who is sixty-two, has learned from her many breathless struggles: "I've learned," she says. "A day at a time, I guess."

RITUALS THAT SHAPE OUR LIVES

> Whatever I have encountered in my past now sticks to me as memories or as (near) forgotten experiences that somehow leave their traces on my being - the way I carry myself (hopeful or confident, defeated or worn-out), the gestures I have adopted and made my own (from my mother, father, teacher, friend), the words I speak and the language that ties me to my past (family, school, ethnicity), and so forth.[32]

All consciousness is consciousness of something. Each thought is a thought about something. Each thought is felt and experienced in our bodies. Our inherited knowledge is embedded in our way of knowing and in our way of being; it shapes our consciousness and our lives. We embody it. How has my consciousness been shaped? How has your consciousness been shaped? How do you know what you know? Listening to your body, paying attention to the experiences of your life enhances your personal power. How do you respond in situations, in relationships? How does your body respond? How aware of your bodily messages are you? Do you allow yourSelf to experience fully? When experiencing fatigue, do you rest, exercise more or have a cup of coffee? When you experience a full bladder, do you go to the bathroom or feel compelled to wait? We have learned and cultivated many ways to mask and cover up our true Selves by using business deadlines, caffeine, sugar, alcohol, fear, anger, medication and silence.

"I am what I say." Language (including all the "phenomena of expression") directs us towards possibilities. What language do we choose to describe our lives, our bodies, our possibilities? "I *am* language," Sartre wrote.[33] Language serves to create our rituals: the daily patterns of existence that we consciously or unconsciously live, day in, day out. *I am asthmatic. Asthma attacks.* This illness-specific vocabulary becomes internalized and directs, and perhaps limits, a woman's possibilities. *I can't breathe. I can't sleep. I have headaches. I take my medicine.* This language of disease is recited by rote in society, in the family, at work and in social gatherings. And so disease becomes a way of life. "It is a part of life," says Leah, referring to her asthma.

In his work with jazz players' unconventionality of language, Leonard recognized how their language stemmed in part from their "inarticulateness or the incapacity of ordinary language to express extraordinary feelings."[34] I wonder, does this reflect a gulf between what we experience internally and what is experienced externally? Are the internal feelings, intuitions, desires, wishes of women not expressed adequately in our ordinary language, in our external expected way of functioning? Jazz players come to grips with emotions so strong "that they are unable to cope with them in ordinary adjectives." Joy experiences emotions so strong she becomes breathless, has to leave the school board meeting and arrives home speechless. Verbalizing feelings led the jazz player to "the edges of language."[35] Keeping her feelings to herself leads Joy to prescribed valium. Somehow Joy has learned in her life not to breathe fully, and not to express herself fully. Allowing the time to reflect on the whole of life helps us to see patterns in our struggling.

Can I allow myself to become aware of my past — a past that "sticks to me as memories or as (near) forgotten experiences that somehow leave their traces on my being"? Can I consciously become aware of the inherited knowledge that influences and directs the rituals of my life? Can I then choose whether or not to maintain them? Attention, awareness of rituals facilitates the uncovering of personal knowledge and by renewing rituals (perhaps changing them, perhaps not) a personal way of Being is created and practised. It takes *courage* to look at the rituals of our lives and to allow ourselves to reflect on the experiences of the rituals and determine if they fit with our *desire* of how we want to be-in-the-world. Does our being-in-the-world reflect our *wishes* or are we living our *lives* with the expectations of others?

To reconnect with breathing as a ritual is to experience the miracle of each breath. It is to reconnect breath with life, with Self. Again: "Self is trusting, open, centered in a calm, clearly felt field of energy. The Self stands for an ever-deepening experience of Being and for a wholeness in relation to that experience that is open and expansive."[36]

TRUSTING OUR BODY WISDOM

Are we more aware of ourSelves when we breathe consciously? Do we take in more life when we breathe deeply? Are we restricting life when our breathing is shallow? Helen Luke in her book *The Way of Woman* reacquaints us with this miracle of breath:

> I am reminded of a beautiful sentence from an Indian Tantra which is thought to be as much as five thousand years old. It says, 'When in worldly activity, keep attentive between the two breaths (the in breath and the out breath), and so practicing, in a few days be born anew.'

> To the extent, then that we achieve this discrimination, this attention, our lives are freed from a sense of rush and begin to resemble the pattern of a dance instead of a wild plunging about, each movement dear and whole in itself yet related to all the others in the totality of the great pattern. This is the symbolic life. As Irene de Castillejo has said, in her book *Knowing Woman*, this end may seem very remote but all that matters is that we move toward it. Somehow in each tiny effort the whole is already there if we could but recognize it.[37]

Simply attending to the breath facilitates a learning and a trusting of the body wisdom. To experience personal power is to own our unique life journeys. To be a Woman of Power is simply to allow mySelf to be who I am. This means to speak what I know in a sharing, trusting, humble way. This, of course, takes courage because it is so simple, honest and authentic. Without masks to protect oneself there is vulnerability and we have not allowed ourselves to learn how to be vulnerable courageously. We have not taught ourselves to be honest without judgement.

My perspective of experiencing personal power through trusting body wisdom and breathing is based on the following assumptions. The "heart symbol" at the beginning of each assumption is a reminder to pause and breathe from a place of inner stillness. Although the heart symbol reflects, perhaps, more of a woman's craft than her science, I consciously chose it to provoke awareness of the often fast-paced, taken-for-granted lives we live and to invite awareness of the value of reading and living from a heart felt place of trust, openness, calm and clarity — something that breath can bring into focus.

- ♥ We, as women, are interested in taking responsibility for our lives. This means that we increasingly are letting go of blaming others or of blaming situations. Instead we are choosing to see deeply each experience of our lives with a sense of recognizing that every situation and relationship somehow contributes to the overall richness of Being who we are.

- ♥ We, as women, are interested in growing and "maturing" not only physically but also spiritually, mentally, emotionally and intu- itionally.

- ♥ We are interested in the power of understanding, the power of compassion, the power of peace; this contrasts, balances and transforms the power of dominance or control over someone or something.

- ♥ The values on which we have structured the various systems of our society (legal, economic, health, environmental) are out of balance. We have overemphasized the values associated with a more masculine perspective — production, manipulation, control, rationalization, analysis and competition. We need to emphasize with equanimity the values associated with a more feminine perspective — creativity, nurturance, intuition, synthe- sis, co-operation and mutual support.

- ♥ As women, either consciously or unconsciously in response to the multiple and varied experiences of our lives, we have taught ourselves not to breathe fully. Yet to breathe fully is to live fully.

♥ "Crisis" is always an opportunity to clarify, to renew and to recreate in such a way that more truly reflects the values on which we mindfully choose to live our lives.

♥ We, as women, are the experts in our unique, individual, and yet collective, lives. We already have everything we need to succeed. Our greatest contribution to this world and to our children, grandchildren, grand-nieces and nephews is to Be fully who we are, now.

♥ We, as women, have a desire to be authentic. This means, we have a desire to develop consistency in our lives among our thoughts, words, actions and felt energy (how we feel, what we feel). We recognize that this takes daily awareness, commitment, practice, compassion, gentleness and more practice. And practice means effortless effort.

♥ We have a desire to be the Self we want to be.

I perceive healing to be an ever-evolving process of clarifying Self. As we clarify our Selves we move to a deepening acceptance and an awareness of our Essence. Healing comes from this Essence, from within a person. It focuses on balance and harmony. The healing process is a journey, a life-long dance of experiencing and discovering Self. Essentially it is a journey of awareness; a journey of empowerment; coming to a place of trusting "I am who I am." Healing focuses on taking responsibility for our own health, our own lives. This involves becoming aware increasingly of the multiple influences on our lives and making conscious choices of which thoughts, words, emotions, actions and felt energy we desire to nurture. As we practise honouring ourSelves, this naturally embraces a deepening respect and trust of each other. In turn, our local, national and global communities will benefit. Imagine such a possibility.

Notes

1. L. Watson, *Heaven's Breath. A Natural History of the Wind* (London: Hodder and-Stoughton, 1984).

2. F.J.J. Buytendijk, "Regulation of Respiration," in *Prolegomena to an Anthropological Philosophy* (Pittsburgh: Duquesne University Press, 1974).

3. E.N. Marieb, *Human Anatomy and Physiology* (California: Benjamin/Cummings Publishing Co. Inc., 1989), 709.

4. Barbara L. Cull-Wilby, "Living with Asthma: A Phenomenological Search for Meaning" (PhD diss., University of Rochester, New York, 1993). My research was supported in part by the Leonard and Kathleen O'Brien Humanitarian Trust, the Canadian Nurses' Respiratory Society of the Lung Association, the University of New Brunswick, the University of Rochester, the New Brunswick Nurses' Association and the National Health Research Development Program of Health and Welfare Canada (NHRDP); and Barbara L. Cull-Wilby and Jacinthe I. Pepin, "A Theory of Healing as an Ever Evolving Process of Experiencing Self (and Other)," unpublished manuscript in author's possession.

5. Jane Huang, trans., *The Primordial Breath: An Ancient Chinese Way of Prolonging Life Through Breath Control*, vol.1 (California: Original Books, 1987), 32.

6. Sondra Ray, *Celebration of Breath (ReBirthing, Book II) or How to Survive Anything and Heal Your Body*, rev. ed. (Berkeley, CA: Celestial Arts, 1986), 114.

7. Kenneth K. Cohen, *Imagine That! A Child's Guide to Yoga* (Santa Barbara, CA: Santa Barbara Books, 1983), 9.

8. J. Highwater, *Ritual of the Wind: North American Indian Ceremonies, Music and Dances* (New York: Viking, 1977), 16.

9. Laura Kealoha Yardley, *The Heart of Huna* (Honolulu, Hawaii: Advanced Neuro Dynamics, Inc., 1991).

10. Watson, *Heaven's Breath*, 327.

11. Ernest Klein, *A Comprehensive Etymological Dictionary of the English Language* (Amsterdam: Elsevier Scientific Publishing Company, 1971), 599.

12. Frank Thompson, ed., *The New Chain-Reference Bible*, 4th ed. (Indiana: BB Kirkbride Bible, 1964).

13. Jean Watson, *Nursing: Human Science and Human Care: A Theory of Nursing* (New Jersey: Prentice-Hall, Inc., 1985).

14. Michael Polanyi, *Personal Knowledge: Towards a Post-Critical Philosophy* (Chicago: University of Chicago Press, 1962).

15. Barbara L. Cull-Wilby, exec. dir., Daphne Curtis, prod./dir., and Ilkay Silk, dir., *Living Each Breath. Asthma: A Dis-Covery of Self,* videotape (New Brunswick: Software Excellence, 1994). This research has informed many other projects: "Trusting Body Wisdom" and "Letting Go: Reclaiming Personal Power," papers presented at the 1993 and 1995 Nurturing Ourselves: Women's Health Issues Annual Conferences; "Notice Your Breath," paper presented at the Rotary Club of Fredericton, 1995; "Complemenatry Healing Approaches," a university course offered to senior baccauleaureate students, 1995; "Joining With What Is: A Healing Process," paper presented at the Women's Celebration of Healing, Wholeness and Empowerment

Conference, 1998; "Living in the Light," paper presented at the 1999 Annual Meeting of the United Church Women of the Woolastook Presbytery. My researsh has been shared with an international audience through newsletters: "Applying Research: Integrating Knowing and Doing," *Cooperative Connection, Newsletter of Nurse Healers-Professional Associates, Inc.* 17 (1996), 14, 17. My healing workshops offered to diverse groups have provided further "life testing" of the broad nature and practical use of my research. I have worked with the Breast Cancer Support Network, Osteoporosis Support Group, Palliative Care Practitioners, Mental Health Staff, Department of Social Work as well as women's church groups and elementary school teachers.

16. I use the feminine gender here and throughout the chapter because of the focus of this book and also because of my desire to contribute consciously to balancing our predominantly masculine view of the world. Albeit, the work is intended for all people, all ages, without prejudice.

17. David Michael Levin, "Logos and Psyche: A Hermeneutics of Breathing," *Research in Phenomenology* 14 (1984), 124. Emphasis added.

18. Bronwen Wallace, *People You'd Trust Your Life To* (Toronto: McClelland and Stewart, 1990), 115.

19. Maurice Merleau-Ponty, *Phenomenology of Perception*, trans. by C. Smith (New York: The Humanities Press, 1962).

20. R.M. Zaner, *The Context of Self* (Ohio: Ohio University Press, 1981), 57.

21. Sally Gadow, "Body and Self: A Dialectic," in Victor Kestenbaum, ed., *The Humanity of the Ill: Phenomenological Perspectives* (Knoxville: The University of Tennessee Press, 1982), 86–100.

22. Ibid., 89.

23. Ibid., 90.

24. Ibid., 93.

25. Ibid., 95.

26. Buytendijk, "Regulation of Respiration," 288, 289.

27. Ibid., 283.

28. Elizabeth Behnke, "Matching," *Somatics* (Spring/Summer 1988), 24–32.

29. Alice Walker, *In Search of Our Mother's Gardens: Womanist Prose* (San Diego: Harcourt Brace Jovanovich, 1983), 370.

30. Klein, *A Comprehensive Etymological Dictionary*, 37, 56.

31. A. Frampton, "Thinking Well," *Saturday Night* (February 1988), 26.

32. Max van Manen, *Researching Lived Experience: Human Science for an Action Sensitive Pedagogy* (London, ON: Althouse Press, 1990), 104.

33. Jean-Paul Sartre, *Being and Nothingness* (New York: Philosophical Library, 1956), 485–486.

34. N. Leonard, *Jazz, Myth and Religion* (New York: Oxford, 1987), 89.

35. Ibid., 89–90.

36. Levin, "Logos and Psyche: A Hermeneutics of Breathing," 124.

37. Helen M. Luke, *The Way of Woman: Awakening the Perennial Feminine* (New York: Image Books, 1995).

CHAPTER FOUR

UNDERSTANDING DEPRESSION FROM THE STANDPOINT OF WOMEN WHO HAVE BEEN DEPRESSED

*Janet M. Stoppard, Yvette Scattolon
and Deanna J. Gammell*

IN THIS CHAPTER, we explore a way of understanding depression in women that is rather different from more familiar medically informed or "mainstream" conceptions in which depression is viewed as an illness or disorder that affects individuals. Our approach also has a different starting point than more usual concerns with treatment of women who are depressed. Treatment of women for depression is not the focus of this chapter. In fact, one implication of our work is that contemporary approaches to treating women for depression miss the mark because they fail to consider women's experiences. This is the primary reason why our work has focused on talking to women about being depressed, rather than beginning with theories of depression proposed by medical and other "experts."

We begin by describing how we became interested in women and depression. We then outline reasons for our disenchantment with prevailing or "mainstream" approaches to explaining depression and why we find them counterproductive for addressing the problem of depression in women's lives. Following this, we describe our research and the alternative approach to understanding women's depression that is emerging from our work. Our approach, which focuses on what women say about being depressed, reflects our feminist conviction that this is an important place to begin the process of understanding women's depressive experiences.

BACKGROUND TO OUR INTEREST IN WOMEN'S DEPRESSION

All three of us are psychologists with training in clinical psychology and our interest in women and depression stems from this background. Janet Stoppard trained as a clinical psychologist in Britain in the mid-1960s where she worked for several years before emigrating to Canada. In 1976 she earned a PhD in clinical psychology. Currently, Janet is a professor in psychology at a university in the Maritimes, where among other activities, she teaches graduate courses in clinical psychology. Janet's interest in women's depression crystallized during her graduate training and when she did post-doctoral work in clinical psychology.[1] In the year after completing her PhD, her clinical work was focused on treatment of depressed patients. She soon noticed that most of the depressed people she saw were women and because she had specialized in gender and mental health issues for her PhD research, she became intrigued by the overrepresentation of women among depressed patients. Much of Janet's work since then has been on women's mental health, particularly depression in women.[2]

Yvette and Deanna, both in their mid-twenties, were graduate students in clinical psychology with Janet as their supervisor when the research we describe in this chapter took place. The study by Yvette was carried out for her PhD thesis and concerned depressive experiences among women living in rural communities in central New Brunswick.[3] Deanna talked to women who had been diagnosed with, and treated for, depression by health professionals (e.g., physicians, psychiatrists). Most of the women in Deanna's study had been treated with antidepressant drugs.[4]

All three of us are feminist psychologists whose work focuses on the mental health of girls and women. We also share an interest in qualitative research methods and the contributions they can make to understanding depression in women. An important reason for using qualitative methods is that they enable women's voices to be more "audible" and also allow women's experiences *as women* to become part of the knowledge about depression. In the next section we furthur discuss our reasons for using qualitative methods rather than the quantitative methods usually employed in mainstream research on depression.

MAINSTREAM RESEARCH: PROBLEMS AND LIMITATIONS

A key requirement of mainstream research is "objectivity," something which researchers assume is achieved by adopting the role of a detached, impartial observer and using "objective" measures. In research on depression, typically this means using questionnaires to assess people's (or "subjects'") symptoms or applying diagnostic criteria to determine which diagnosis best fits a person's (or "patient's") symptoms. The diagnostic criteria currently used in most research on depression are those for depressive disorder contained in the *Diagnostic and Statistical Manual of Mental Disorders* (DSM) published by the American Psychiatric Association.[5] An important reason for use of objective measures such as questionnaires and diagnostic criteria is that they are a source of information that can be counted and then analyzed using statistical procedures. Quantitative and statistical methods currently hold a dominant place in the fields in which depression is studied. One consequence of this situation is that qualitative information, including what people have to say about their experiences and everyday lives, generally is considered unimportant, or even irrelevant, for understanding problems like depression. When research draws on qualitative information, it is often dismissed by mainstream researchers as lacking in "rigour" and as less "scientific" than research employing quantitative data and statistical analyses.

Quantitative methods have been useful in providing certain kinds of information. For instance, large-scale quantitative studies have shown that rates of depression in the population generally are higher among women than men.[6] This kind of research has also been helpful in identifying which groups in society face an increased risk of depression. Among women, for example, depression appears to be more prevalent among those who are younger, those caring for children at home, those living on low incomes, and those who are divorced or separated.[7] Studies employing mainstream research methods, however, are limited because they don't tell us much about why depression is more common in women than men or why women in some social categories are more vulnerable than others to becoming depressed. In part, this is because little attention is paid to the substantial information produced by feminist activists and scholars about women's experiences and how women's everyday lives are shaped by patriarchal practices and beliefs. But it is also because of the assumptions on which mainstream approaches to research are based.

Mainstream research begins from the assumption that something called "depression" exists within individuals before researchers begin their work. The job of researchers is to discover knowledge about depression using scientific methods, primarily quantitative and statistical, to gather data. A key assumption in this research process is that use of objective procedures will generate facts leading to an understanding of the causes of depression and, eventually, its cure. Researchers who use these methods also assume that depression and its causes can be studied separately from the lived experiences of those who become depressed. Thus the knowledge produced is assumed to be unrelated to the larger social and cultural context in which researchers, as well as research participants (or "subjects"), live and work. The issue of how people's experiences are influenced by the social processes which make up the context of their everyday lives has not been the concern of mainstream research on depression.[8]

Instead of considering people's experiences, mainstream research is most likely to focus on the physical body, particularly biochemical mechanisms in the brain involving substances called neurotransmitters and their role in controlling mood and emotion. Investigation of brain mechanisms is based on the assumption that knowledge about the body's biology will ultimately prove most important for explaining depression. This is a form of biological reductionism.[9] One outcome of this biological approach has been development of "antidepressant" drugs, such as Prozac and Zoloft, currently the main medical treatment for depression.

As feminists have pointed out, the predominance of women among those treated for depression means that women are the major consumers of antidepressant drugs and so are most often exposed to these drugs' negative effects.[10] A complication for users of antidepressants is that their "side effects" include symptoms that are also associated with depression (e.g., anxiety, insomnia, fatigue and appetite disturbance). To date, however, little is known about the effects that antidepressants have on the female body. Relatively few studies on these drugs' effects have been done with women because of the risk of damage to the health of unborn children and breast-fed infants.[11] Yet many women who use antidepressants are in the age range where pregnancy and breast-feeding are common occurrences. Nevertheless, pharmaceutical companies are increasingly targeting women as the recipients of their products; for instance, antidepressants like Prozac are frequently advertised in magazines read primarily by women. In newspapers, it is also common to see articles about antidepressants which are aimed at women readers. The daily paper in the town where Janet lives recently carried articles with the following headlines: "Prozac said safe for expectant mothers" and "Antidepressants used in treating severe PMS." As illustrated by these examples, processes within the physical body have been the main focus of research on depression.

When the scientific method is applied in this way, the result is a form of "stripped-down" knowledge, which is almost totally disconnected from the background context in which people live and become depressed. This context includes the social conventions, customs and practices that are part of people's everyday lives. Language, particularly talking to others, plays a crucial role in the social processes that enable people to participate in daily life, to make sense of what is happening around them, as well as sharing their experiences with others. In research, too, words are used to talk and write about the things studied; language forms an important, but often taken for granted, part of the social context in which research takes place. Typically, language is viewed only as a medium for transmitting information. The particular words chosen and how they reflect the language used more generally are completely ignored.

This "decontextualized" research approach can be contrasted with another, rather different approach in which language and social context become the focus of research and an important part of the process of creating knowledge. An approach to research in which language is considered an integral part of the process of generating knowledge is one referred to as "social constructionist." Many feminist researchers consider a social constructionist approach more useful than mainstream methods because it allows women's everyday experiences as women to be studied in their own right rather than being relegated to the margins of scientific research. In a social constructionist approach to studying depression in women, what women say about their experiences becomes an important focus, rather than research being restricted to investigation of biochemical processes within the brain.

The following example illustrates how knowledge is socially constructed and the important role of language in this process. The term "premenstrual syndrome" or "PMS" is a familiar one to most women. It is also an established area of research and many scientific studies on PMS have been conducted in the last few decades. Many books on PMS have been published and articles on this topic appear frequently in magazines read by women. Prior to the early 1980s, however, hardly any information existed about this disorder, which by definition is unique to women, and it received little attention from either researchers, health professionals or women in general. Now PMS is a household term. As Amanda Rittenhouse's work has shown, interest in PMS as a problem affecting women began to emerge in the early 1980s through the combined influence of research on PMS and the dissemination of this information in the media.[12] Interest in PMS among researchers and the lay public was stimulated by two widely publicized cases in England in which women charged with manslaughter used PMS as a legal defence. Before the 1980s, however, few studies on PMS had been carried out and it was not until the late 1980s that PMS was formulated as a medical diagnosis for which women could seek treatment.[13]

Does this sequence of events imply that PMS is a newly discovered disorder affecting women? Does it imply that some fundamental change has taken place at the level of women's bodies so that many women now experience PMS? From a social constructionist perspective, this way of defining and understanding some aspects of women's menstruation-related experiences is interpreted instead as part of a broader shift in cultural meanings associated with the female body and is also linked to women's increased participation in the public world outside the home. In this changing cultural landscape characterized by growing publicity in the media about PMS, women are more likely to pay attention to their menstrual periods and to draw on the notion of PMS to explain experiences they associate with menstruation. Moreover, others in women's lives (e.g., husbands, boyfriends, co-workers) also have access to the PMS concept both as a label and an explanation for female behaviour. As a consequence of this train of events, PMS has been "socially constructed" as a problem that is widely presumed to afflict many women.[14]

When research on women's menstruation-related experiences is conducted from a feminist standpoint, women's experiences become the focus, rather than experts' concepts. The result is more woman-centred knowledge that not only validates women's menstrual experiences, but also suggests new directions for understanding what women and others call PMS. For instance, research from a social constructionist perspective in which close attention is given to women's talk about experiences they attribute to PMS, is beginning to reveal that such experiences can be understood as responses to the conditions of women's everyday lives, such as living with an abusive partner, caring for small children, or coping with poverty.[15]

The term "depression" is also culturally and historically specific. Both the diagnostic terminology and the groups in society identified as particularly likely to suffer from depression have changed over time. For instance, several centuries ago there was a condition known as "melancholy" that was thought to afflict men with literary or artistic talents.[16] Over time, the term melancholy gradually disappeared, replaced by "melancholia," a diagnosis used during the first half of the twentieth century. A condition called "involutional melancholia," for example, was believed to characterize those in middle age, particularly women. The present-day word "depression" came into wide usage following changes in diagnostic terminology introduced in the third edition of the DSM published in 1980. Attention was first drawn to the overrepresentation of women among those suffering from depression by American researchers Myrna Weissman and Gerald Klerman in a paper that appeared in 1977.[17] Since that time, a great deal of research, most of it using mainstream methods, has been carried out to explain why women are more vulnerable than men to this mental illness. Women's particular susceptibility to depression has now attained the status of a fact that is well-known to researchers, health professionals and the general public alike.

UNDERSTANDING DEPRESSION
FROM THE STANDPOINT OF WOMEN

Numerous theories have been proposed to explain women's apparent vulnerability to depression. Some of these explanations have focused on hormonal changes associated with menstruation, pregnancy, childbirth and menopause. Others address sources of stress in women's lives, particularly those connected with women's roles as wives and mothers, and the demands of their work in the home. Another type of explanation has highlighted women's psychology, particularly "feminine" personality traits, as a key to understanding women's vulnerability to depression.[18] Although frequently discussed in the media, a drawback of all these explanations is that they reflect experts' theories rather than being based in women's experiences. In short, they draw on mainstream research approaches, while language and the social context of women's lives are virtually ignored.

In our research, we believe it is important to find out what women have to say about their depressive experiences as a starting point for understanding women's depression. Our work is ongoing and here we describe findings from two series of interviews with women. Deanna interviewed women who had been treated for depression by a health professional, usually their family doctor or a psychiatrist, and in some cases also by a counsellor. The twelve women interviewed to date live in the same town as Deanna and Janet. We were particularly interested in what the women told us about why they became depressed, how they explained their depression, and their thoughts about their treatment — what helped and what didn't help. The interviews carried out by Yvette were with women living in small communities in the mainly rural area surrounding the university town where Yvette was a student. The fifteen women interviewed by Yvette identified themselves as depressed and none had sought treatment for their depression. These interviews focused on how the women understood and explained their depressive experiences and how they coped when feeling depressed. Most women were interviewed at home and the interviews usually lasted between one and two hours. Although focused on topics related to the women's experiences with depression, and so "semi-structured," the interviews took the form of an extended conversation.[19]

The women who had been treated for depression were seen initially by their family physician or another health professional who diagnosed them as depressed. At that point, they were usually encouraged to take an antidepressant drug and all but one woman had done so. All of the women stated that their depression was caused by a "chemical imbalance in the brain," the explanation given to them by a physician. As well, some women indicated that their depression was caused by hormonal changes. For instance, Jane, a forty-seven-year-old married woman who was on disability leave from her job when interviewed, said:

> It's the chemical imbalance plus everything else. Plus I went through menopause when I was forty and so I'm on hormone replacement therapy. I think it's a combination of everything ... my body had spoken.[20]

Gloria, a sixty-six-year-old homemaker with two grown children explained her depression in a similar way: "It's a chemical imbalance and, to me, it just happened. It may have something to do with my menopause."

Younger women also explained their depression in terms of physical causes but were less likely to mention processes specific to the female body. When Tracy, a nineteen-year-old student, was told by her doctor that her depressive feelings were due to premenstrual syndrome, she had dismissed the suggestion as "ridiculous." The younger women tended to explain their depression in terms of physical causes that were not gender-specific. Susan, who was twenty at the time of the interview, single and working part-time, said: "I'd love to say that it was something I couldn't avoid and it's hereditary, that I got it through my grandmother ... I know that most likely it has to do with me being someone who was susceptible to depression."

Some women also explained their depression as arising from particular events in their lives. In the following excerpt, Ann, a homemaker in her early fifties, describes the events that led to her first becoming depressed:

> [It was] an accumulation of stressful things. My husband was trans-
> ferred to [city] ... I stayed behind in [town] for quite a few months,
> before our house was sold ... and I came down here and got a job
> right away, unexpectedly ... and of course [that] involved working
> evenings. My kids weren't very happy that I was working, I'd never
> really worked out of the home. And then the final crunch was that
> very close friends of ours marriage broke up and I couldn't do any-
> thing for them, couldn't fix it.

Debbie, a homemaker in her early thirties with small children at home,
said, "I believe it [depression] was because of the sexual abuse I had
gone through ... When I started going through all that healing for my
sexual abuse, the depression started to lift."

Although some women, particularly those who were older, believed
the cause of their depression was entirely physical, others also considered events in their lives to have contributed to their depression.
Nonetheless, all but one of these women complied with their doctor's
treatment recommendation and had taken antidepressants. Tracy was
the only one not to have taken antidepressants, preferring to see a
counsellor instead. She gave the following reasons for not wanting to
take a drug in order to feel better:

> I think partly it's fear of the drugs themselves. Like I'm not really
> sure what, in terms of side effects and in terms of addiction. I guess
> the idea of needing whatever drug to feel okay is kind of a nasty
> idea.

In contrast, the older women were more likely to consider drugs the
most important part of their treatment. As Ann said, "I was afraid that
she [her physician] was going to say that I didn't need an antidepressant
drug ... I think I would fight tooth and nail if anybody refused to prescribe it for me." Sarah, aged fifty-two, married and working part-time,
also saw antidepressants as the key to her recovery from depression: "I
know I do need medication ... we've tried three, well, four different
drugs now and this is the one that seems to be working the best."

Younger women's feelings about drug treatment were more ambiva-
lent. Susan said the following about taking drugs:

It made me feel weak to have to take a chemical ... and then I got thinking about the medication. So what does this mean if I have to take this medication in order to be normal? Like it just felt so weird. I haven't told my doctors but I have stopped taking my medication.

Several of the women who had used antidepressants also told us that drugs alone were not enough. They had wanted to talk to someone about their feelings in addition to taking drugs. Sarah's experience was not atypical:

I felt I couldn't talk to my psychiatrist. You're in five minutes and okay, we'll try you on this pill. We'll try you on that pill and there was no counselling. And I'd come home and there was no counselling, like there was nowhere to go. And so Dr. [name of psychiatrist] said I'll put you in touch with a [counsellor] and he did, and that was the best thing that ever happened.

Debbie found counselling more helpful than drugs:

I think counselling probably was the best thing more so than the Paxil [an anti-depressant drug] ... I shouldn't say that. But I think I probably could have healed without the Paxil too, but the Paxil's like an aid ... giving you your ability to calm down.

These interview excerpts tell us something about how the women explained their depression and about their treatment experiences. They reveal how medical ideas shaped the women's understanding of their depressive experiences. "Medicalization" refers to a process through which depression comes to be understood as a medical condition caused by a disorder within the physical body. This "medicalization" theme was apparent in the willingness of most women to take antidepressants and in their use of biological explanations for depression such as chemicals in the brain, female hormones and genetic influences. Medicalization is also reflected in the language used by women to talk about their experiences, for example "menopause," "hormone replacement therapy," "medication," "pills" and "side effects." Thus, even though some of the women did link their depression to events in their lives, all attributed it to an "imbalance in the chemicals in the brain," an explanation given to them by physicians.

In marked contrast, the medicalization theme was almost totally absent in Yvette's interviews with women who had not sought professional help for their depression. These women had coped with, and in many cases overcome, their depression on their own without help from a physician or another health professional.[21] In many cases, these women were living on a low income and caring for young children at home. Generally, they explained their depression in terms of the conditions of their everyday lives. For instance, Lucy, who was thirty-nine, a single-parent with two children, and living on income assistance at the time of her interview, said the following about why she became depressed:

> I still think that my problem would have been that I had no money, I don't even care for help. I know what my problem is. But if I went to the doctor, he probably would have said, well, you're depressed or something. And I probably would have said, yeah, and said, what's the use, whatever, you know. I know I am depressed and I don't know how you can help there. Are you going to give me some money?

Linda, a thirty-three-year-old woman, with six children under the age of seventeen, who was living in a common-law relationship, also emphasized lack of money as the main reason she became depressed: "You're sitting on welfare, you're bound to get stressed out. You're alright for about two weeks and then everything comes crashing down. You're bound to be depressed and stressed out."

Other women talked about their depression in terms of their experiences as wives and mothers. Gina, in her early forties and married with three children, described her depression in the following way:

> Just keeping strong and trying to be happy for both of us [Gina and her husband] ... that was very stressful ... but always trying to cope because the children were young. During the day you had to cope because at the time I had no washer, no dryer, we lived very poor, and I had to do everything by hand and the children, have to look after them every minute. So you keep busy you know, changing diapers, and feeding and crying and put them to sleep ... I wasn't doing anything for myself.

Linda also linked her depression to the responsibility of looking after children:

> Because the kids are going to be the kids, they are at the age where they are going to make you depressed. And like I said, whether it's rich or poor, they are at the age where they are never going to be satisfied anyway, so of course, I'm the one that's gonna end up depressed or upset.

Some women connected their depressed feelings fairly directly to their ability to provide for their children. Sue, forty-eight and divorced with four grown children, said, "I would feel panic set in, I'm not providing the basics, right, and to this day that will upset me, that will depress me if I don't have food in my house. It scares the life right out of me." Linda also talked about having depressed feelings when she didn't have enough food for her children:

> With these children you try and tell them you got your food, take it easy on the food, and then when there's nothing left, of course they sit and cry and of course, we get depressed ... because it's not there. We don't have the money to get more. I just go in the room and cry. I'll go sit in the bathtub and read if I get too depressed or just stay in my room.

According to the women Yvette talked to, their depressed feelings arose in the course of everyday lives marked by chronic poverty and daily struggles to meet their children's needs. Although none had sought professional help, they used various strategies to cope with their depressed feelings. One way they coped was by "getting on with life," carrying on with their daily activities. Pat, age thirty-five, a single-parent with one child, who was unemployed and living on income assistance, described how she coped:

> I just said, somebody's got to look after the house, somebody has got to look after the lawn, and it was me who had to do it. I got through that by realizing that somebody had to do stuff around here, you knew it, stuff wasn't getting done.

The daily routine of looking after their children helped some women to get through times when they felt depressed. As Linda said:

No matter how depressed or stressed out you are, for me, I know I still have to get up every morning and I still have to get them their breakfast. I don't know if you'd say they were my anchor, for me it always comes down to the kids.

Several women had supportive friends and others found that contact with women living in similar situations was helpful in coping with their depression. Sue turned to a friend for support:

Thank god I had a friend two doors away. Before she went to work, and then when she came home, she'd run over and have a cup of tea or something. I give her all the credit for pulling me through that because I didn't go to a doctor.

Bridget, aged twenty-six, married with two children and working part-time, talked about the importance of spending time with a friend whose situation was similar to her own:

We need to just get out. Her and I just need to after the kids are in bed because you get too busy and you get caught up in things. You're already stressed out from having the daily routine ... you still need that time for yourself. I used to do a lot of [hobby], go out one night a week. I don't do that anymore, but yet once in awhile, once a month or once every two months, I call her and say, let's go out for a coffee, let's get out and you both need that. You still need that out away from it all for like an hour. That keeps my sanity, I think, even though it should be more often.

Women living in rural communities who had not sought professional help understood their depression as part of their everyday experiences, as something explicable in terms of poverty and burdensome family responsibilities. They coped by getting on with life as best they could, often with the support of friends. This is a rather different picture than the one presented by women who had received treatment for depression.

Apart from taking antidepressants, and in some cases seeing a counsellor, the responses of women who had been treated for depression focused on eliminating sources of stress in their lives. This involved reducing the scope of their activities, for instance, by switching from full-time to part-time employment or in some cases giving up paid work altogether. The women who were students when interviewed reduced stress by dropping courses and changing their educational goals. Susan was reconsidering her plan to attend law school: "I want to go to law school and that's another seven years and I just think, if I can't handle second year Arts, how in the hell am I supposed to be able to deal with this?"

Women who had received treatment were unlikely, however, to make changes in their lives at home. Describing how she coped with her depression, Sarah, who was married with two children, said: "They [family members] did not see a whole lot of change in me except that I couldn't work [outside the home]. You know, because I worked around here [at home]." This theme of continuing with responsibilities in the home was also present in interviews with women who had not sought treatment when depressed. For instance, Sue said the following about looking after her adult children: "I still make their supper, and I would still do their laundry, and I would still do whatever I feel is my duty to do for them." For many of the women we interviewed, fulfilling their responsibilities as wives, as mothers or as both, seemed to take priority over other activities in their lives; even when depressed they continued to prepare meals and do other domestic chores for family members. The pervasiveness of this theme in the women's interviews suggests a connection between their lives as women and their depressive experiences. In the final part of this chapter, we explore one way to understand women's experiences of being depressed that take their lives as women into account.

WOMEN'S BODIES, WOMEN'S LIVES
AND DEPRESSION

As we saw earlier, women who had received treatment for depression tended to adopt a medicalized way of understanding their experiences. They explained their depressed feelings as the result of a disturbance in internal bodily processes ("chemicals in the brain") or associated with hormonal changes in the menopausal body. Women who had not sought treatment were much less likely to draw on these kinds of explanations. Instead, they explained being depressed as an understandable consequence of the arduous and often stressful conditions of their everyday lives, especially lack of money. None of the women, however, identified their everyday lives *as women* as a source of their depressed feelings. Generally, women took the work they did in the home as wives and as mothers for granted, as something they carried out as a matter of course. The following interview excerpts provide a sense of what these women's lives were like both before and while they were depressed. In the first, Linda, thirty-three and living in a rural community with her common-law partner and several children, describes her daily routine:

> So I get up at 5:30, use the bathroom, make lunches [for the children to take to school], make breakfast ... supper time comes, they eat, leave the dishes in the sink and go and they listen to music, on the phone or in bed. I get stuck with the dishes, then cleaning up.

At the time of her interview, Linda had just started a full-time job, while her partner was unemployed. The next extract is from the interview with Jane, in her late forties and married with grown children. She worked full-time until her "breakdown," when she was treated for depression. Here she describes herself as she was before her "breakdown":

> I looked after my family, plus my husband's family. Whenever anybody got sick, they always called M [Jane refers to herself as "M"]. M would go. She could never say no ... I used to do fifty things at once. I look back and see, not that I want to get back to that person, but even if I could do five things at once I'd be happy.

These two women, like many of the others who talked to us, depict their everyday lives as being governed by the caring needs of family members. Their lives seem to be organized around the ideal of being a "good woman," something which is expressed through their activities as a housewife and mother. Failing to perform family caretaking activities in a manner that conforms to the standards of this ideal can be a source of guilt which is likely to exacerbate feelings of distress. As Jane said about doing less at home than she had before becoming depressed:

> You can't see anything at all that's good. Everything is bad ... and there's no way out, it seems like there's just no way, it's never going to get any better. And guilt is the big thing, you feel guilty because you're not doing this, you're not doing that.

For Sarah, the feeling that she could no longer carry on as usual with her work at home was a turning point which led to her decision to shift from full- to part-time employment:

> I still did my daily activities ... had supper ready, had dinner ready, had their lunches ready. Did the wash. None of that had ceased, you know. But I did it because ... well you do it. Then you went to bed. But I think this time I had to allow that because I was tired of ... putting on this mask and ... keeping going.

Being unable to match some ideal standard of how a woman should carry out her responsibilities in the home seems to have contributed to the depressed feelings of many of the women who talked to us.

One way to make sense of what these women told us is to consider how the image of the "good woman" represents an unarticulated backdrop to their accounts and also provides the impetus for their activities in the home. Being a good woman involves being a good wife, mother and housewife, ensuring that family members' caring needs are met. The activities that contribute to a woman's sense of herself as a "good woman" are based in the home — cooking, washing clothes, cleaning house and so on. At the same time, several of the women had jobs outside the home, others were students or defined themselves as "unemployed" although expecting to be employed sometime in the future. Regardless of these women's employment status, they continued to do work in the home, caring for others. They did not question the idea that they *should* take care of family members. As Sue said when talking about her grown-up children: "I would still do whatever I feel is my duty to do for them." In a similar vein, Sarah said, "I did it because ... well you do it" as her reason for doing work in the home.

The women's depressed feelings seemed to arise in circumstances where they saw themselves as failing to live up to the ideal of the "good woman." However, a woman's efforts to meet this ideal are always limited, on the one hand, by her own bodily resources (physical energy and ability to work under time pressures) and, on the other, by the external resources (e.g., financial, social services, employment opportunities) available to her. The nature and extent of such resources accessible to a particular woman will be determined by broader societal conditions (e.g., the economy of the region in which she lives, laws regulating employment, availability of childcare services) and also by her living arrangements (e.g., whether she is supported financially by a partner, the location of her home).

When a woman's activities take place in a family setting in which her relationships are reasonably congenial, she has adequate resources and her life is similar to that of other women with whom she identifies, she is likely to feel "good." For too many women, however, caring work in the home becomes routine and family members take it for granted. In addition, prevailing economic conditions mean that many women must earn a living in order to meet their own and their family's financial needs and so are locked into a "double day" of work outside as well as inside the home. One outcome of such conditions is that a woman will experience her everyday activities as burdensome chores. In striving to be a "good woman," she is more likely to feel overburdened and that her efforts are unappreciated by others. The reality for many women is that by attempting to live up to the good woman ideal they become physically exhausted (are chronically tired) and feel discouraged and hopeless about their situations.

The ideal of the good woman still persists strongly within society despite being criticized by feminists. It is maintained by images of women perpetuated in various media (TV, movies, magazines) and transmitted to girls and young women in the course of their upbringing and schooling. The good woman ideal is also reflected in beliefs about women and women's lives held by those in power (politicians, policy-makers, business leaders). Because these influences are so pervasive, it is difficult for individual women to make significant changes in how their everyday lives are organized. In any case, being a "mother" holds such a central place in most women's sense of themselves as women that few would contemplate abandoning their mothering responsibilities.[22]

Thus, when women's lives involve stressful responsibilities and they feel they are failing as "good women," the only avenue open to most is to continue to expend their energies in an attempt to attain the standards inherent in being a good woman. Failure to do so only increases a woman's chances of being considered a "bad woman" by herself and others, something that most women want to avoid. A woman's physical body, however, sets a finite limit on her efforts, so that her continued attempts to act as a "good woman" are more likely to exhaust her body while also undermining her sense of morale and self-esteem. In keeping with this interpretation, tiredness, fatigue and feelings of stress are commonly reported by women in surveys of their health problems, complaints which they typically attribute to their burdensome family responsibilities.[23] Such complaints are also part of what physicians and other health professionals may call depression. This leads us to conclude that women's depressive experiences do not result solely from disordered biochemistry within the body nor are they produced only by events that happen in women's lives. Instead, being depressed can be understood as experiences that are closely interwoven with the everyday activities that women do *because* they are women. These activities, central to many women's lives, also draw upon the physical resources provided by women's bodies. To understand experiences which currently are labelled as "symptoms of depression," knowledge about women's lives *as women* must be taken into account. Talking to women about being depressed is an important part of this endeavour.

Notes

1. Janet spent 1976–77 as a post-doctoral fellow in clinical psychology at the Health Sciences Centre Hospital, University of British Columbia, in Vancouver.

2. Janet acknowledges the support of the Social Sciences and Humanities Research Council of Canada for a grant awarded during 1997–2000 which enabled her to carry out the research on women and depression described in this chapter.

3. Yvette acknowledges the support of the Social Sciences and Humanities Research Council of Canada for the doctoral fellowship she was awarded during 1995–97 while she was completing the research for her thesis. She also acknowledges receipt of a grant from MindCare New Brunswick in 1996 and a Hyde Graduate Student Research Grant awarded in 1997 by the Psychology of Women Division of the American Psychological Association in support of her research.

4. This study was supported by Janet's research grant from the Social Sciences and Humanities Research Council of Canada (see note 2).

5. American Psychiatric Association, *Diagnostic and Statistical Manual of Mental Disorders: DSM-IV,* 4th ed. (Washington, DC: American Psychiatric Association, 1994).

6. Studies of this kind are carried out by epidemiologists. Epidemiology is concerned with the distribution and causes of disease in human populations. For a review of

epidemiological studies on rates of depression in women and men, including studies conducted in Canada, see Janet M. Stoppard, "Gender, Psychosocial Factors and Depression," in P. Cappeliez and R.J. Flynn, eds., *Depression and the Social Environment: Research and Intervention with Neglected Populations* (Montreal: McGill-Queen's University Press, 1993), 121–149.

7. For a detailed overview of findings on women and depression, see E. McGrath, G.P. Keita, B.R. Strickland, and N.F. Russo, *Women and Depression: Risk Factors and Treatment Issues* (Washington, DC: American Psychological Association, 1990).

8. This "decontextualized" approach to research is a feature of positivist methodology. For a discussion of limitations of mainstream research on depression, see Janet M. Stoppard, "Why New Perspectives Are Needed for Understanding Depression in Women," *Canadian Psychology* 40 (1999), 79–90.

9. Reductionism is the idea that one way of understanding the world is more important or fundamental and ultimately will be closer to the "truth" than another way. The assumption that knowing how the brain functions will provide a better foundation for understanding depression than knowledge based in understanding women's experiences is an example of biological reductionism.

10. For a discussion on the lack of research investigating the effects of antidepressant drugs on women's bodies, see J.A. Hamilton, "Sex and Gender as Critical Variables in Psychotropic Drug Research," in C.V. Willies, P.P. Rieker, M.M. Kramer, and B.S. Brown, eds., *Mental Health, Racism, and Sexism* (Pittsburgh: University of Pittsburgh Press, 1995), 297–349, and J.A. Hamilton and M.F. Jensvold, "Sex and Gender As Critical Variables in Feminist Psychopharmacology Research and Pharmacology," *Women and Therapy* 16 (1995), 9–30.

11. M.M. Weissman and M. Olfson, "Depression in Women: Implications for Health Care Research," *Science* 269 (1995), 799–801, identify the need for investigation of potential health risks for women when they use antidepressants while pregnant or breastfeeding.

12. C.A. Rittenhouse, "The Emergence of Premenstrual Syndrome as a Social Problem," *Social Problems* 38 (1991), 412–425.

13. A.E. Figert, *Women and the Ownership of PMS: The Structuring of a Psychiatric Disorder* (Hawthorne, NY: Aldine de Gruyter, 1996) documents the events that resulted in a "PMS" diagnosis being included in the DSM by the American Psychiatric Association. The current term for this diagnosis is "Premenstrual Dysphoric Disorder."

14. To say the PMS concept is socially constructed does not mean that experiences women (and their doctors) might call PMS are therefore imaginary or unreal.

15. These findings were described by C. Swann, "Reading the Bleeding Body: Discourses of Premenstrual Syndrome," in J.M. Ussher, ed., *Body Talk: The Material and Discursive Regulation of Sexuality, Madness and Reproduction* (London: Routledge, 1997), 176–198, based on talking to women who were attending a PMS clinic in London, England.

16. J. Radden, "Melancholy and Melancholia," in D.M. Levin, ed., *Pathologies of the Modern Self: Postmodern Studies on Narcissism, Schizophrenia, and Depression* (New

York: New York University Press, 1987), 231–250, traces historical shifts in the terms used to label experiences, which currently are called depression, and also analyses reasons for the current preponderance of women among the depressed.

17. M.M. Weissman and G. Klerman, "Sex Differences and the Epidemiology of Depression," *Archives of General Psychiatry* 34 (1977), 98–111.

18. For a discussion of theories proposed to explain women's vulnerability to depression, see Janet M. Stoppard, *Understanding Depression: Feminist Social Constructionist Approaches* (London: Routledge, 2000).

19. More detailed information on the methodology of these studies is reported in D.J. Gammell and Janet M. Stoppard, "Women's Experiences of Treatment of Depression: Medicalization or Empowerment?" *Canadian Psychology* 40 (1999), 112–128, and Y. Scattolon and Janet M. Stoppard, "'Getting On With Life': Women's Experiences and Ways of Coping with Depression," *Canadian Psychology* 40 (1999), 205–219.

20. In this extract and those that follow, identifying information (including names) has been omitted or altered. Extracts have been edited slightly for readability. Material in square brackets was added for clarification. Three dots (...) indicate where material has been omitted.

21. The women who talked to Yvette identified themselves as depressed. They also completed a questionnaire which is used widely by mental health professionals to assess "depressive symptoms." The questionnaire scores of all but one of the women fell in the depressed range. The majority of the women's scores were in the "clinically depressed" range.

22. This point is discussed by Sharon Hays, *The Cultural Contradictions of Motherhood* (New Haven: Yale University Press, 1996) and Martha McMahon, *Engendering Motherhood: Identity and Self-Transformation in Women's Lives* (New York: Guilford Press, 1995). Hays talked to mothers in California and McMahon talked to mothers in Ontario.

23. This finding was reported by J. Popay, "'My Health Is All Right, but I'm Just Tired All the Time': Women's Experience of Ill Health," in H. Roberts, ed., *Women's Health Matters* (London: Routledge, 1992), 99–120, with women in England, and by V. Walters, "Stress, Anxiety and Depression: Women's Accounts of Their Health Problems," *Social Science and Medicine* 36 (1993), 393–402, with women in central Canada.

CHAPTER FIVE

ASYLUM OR CURE?
WOMEN'S EXPERIENCES OF PSYCHIATRIC HOSPITALIZATION

Baukje (Bo) Miedema and Janet M. Stoppard

ॐ

IN CANADA, AS WELL AS other western countries, in-patient psychiatric treatment is one of the main forms of service available to women experiencing mental health problems. Over the years, there has been a shift from psychiatric hospitals to psychiatric units in general hospitals as the primary location for delivery of psychiatric treatment services. The majority of people who receive treatment for a psychiatric illness or mental health problem now do so through psychiatric units within general hospitals. Relatively few people are treated in psychiatric hospitals, and those admitted as in-patients tend to have much longer stays than people treated in general hospitals. The average length of time spent by patients in psychiatric hospitals is slightly less than a year (326 days), while the average stay in psychiatric units in general hospitals is just over a month (40 days). Between 1993 and 1994 (the most recent time for which information is available), the leading diagnosis among women admitted to psychiatric units was "affective psychosis" (23 percent) and the second most common diagnosis was "neurotic disorder" (13 percent). In comparison, among males hospitalized in 1993–94, the most common diagnosis was "schizophrenia" (33 percent).[1]

Contemporary psychiatric treatment has its roots in the confinement of "madmen." In past centuries, no clear distinctions were made between the "mad," the unemployed, the criminal and the poor. All such individuals were considered "deviants" and, according to seventeenth-century authorities, had to be confined.[2] During the nineteenth century, the "mad" were gradually isolated from the poor and the deviant, with the latter being subjected to new social control measures such as prison and the discipline of work in factories.

Feminists have argued that psychiatry and treatment of madness continue to operate as effective means of social control for the purpose of keeping women "in line." The day-to-day difficulties experienced by women in performing their socially prescribed gender roles may be interpreted by mental health professionals as symptoms of a mental disorder, rather than as understandable responses by women to experiences within a social context in which they lack personal, political and economic power.[3] In her classic book *Women and Madness*, feminist Phyllis Chesler proposed that one of the few resources available to women when they seek escape or relief from the burdens of their social roles as wives and mothers is to go "mad."[4] This may explain why Canadian statistics for in-patient psychiatric treatment indicate that women predominate among users of these services, a pattern similar to that observed in both the United States and Britain.[5]

Given critiques by feminists of women's treatment within the mental health system, it is of some importance to learn more about women's experiences as psychiatric patients. A key goal of our research, then, was to ask women who have been hospitalized for psychiatric treatment to describe their experiences in their own voices. To date, research on the experiences of psychiatric patients typically has been conducted from the perspective of mental health professionals and so usually reflects the medical model of psychiatry. Within a medical model approach, mental illnesses are conceptualized as diseases caused by biochemical disorders within the body and psychiatric treatment involves treating the underlying biochemical disorder (most often with drugs).

Our own interest in the topic of women's treatment by psychiatry has its roots in our backgrounds as mental health professionals. Baukje Miedema trained and worked as a psychiatric nurse in Holland before emigrating to Canada and Janet Stoppard is a clinical psychologist who has worked in Britain and Canada. Based on our experiences in the mental health field, we share the conviction that the medical model approach has distinct limitations as a way of understanding and explaining women's mental health problems. Our paths crossed at the University of New Brunswick where Baukje was doing graduate work in sociology and Janet is a professor in psychology. The project we describe here arose from our common interest as feminists in women's experiences of psychiatric hospitalization. We wanted to hear the voices of the women who had been hospitalized and to understand their experiences. From the women's accounts, we learned that for some hospital admission was experienced as an unwanted incarceration, for others hospitalization represented a welcome escape from an untenable situation. Although feminist theoretical approaches begin from the standpoint of women, they are not entirely able to explain women's experiences in relation to psychiatric hospitalization. The issues involved are more complex than some feminist analyses would imply. When discussion about women and psychiatric treatment is couched in terms of curing a diseased part of the body (or the mind) versus social control of women who rebel against existing gender conditions, an important source of information is excluded because the voices of women who have been psychiatrically hospitalized are ignored.[6] Our research focused on southern New Brunswick and involved interviews with twenty-seven women who had been psychiatrically hospitalized at least once. The women were recruited with the help of local self-help groups.[7]

Healthcare, including mental health, falls largely under provincial jurisdiction. In the past, provision of psychiatric services in New Brunswick was the exclusive domain of two psychiatric hospitals: one anglophone in Saint John and the other francophone in Campbellton. At present, only the psychiatric hospital in Campbellton remains, and the majority of those who receive psychiatric treatment do so through psychiatric units located within general hospitals. According to figures for 1993–94, New Brunswick had the third highest rate of psychiatric hospitalization (in general hospital psychiatric units) in Canada.[8] Delivery of mental health services is governed by the *New Brunswick Mental Health Act* of 1967 (amended in 1985). This Act describes procedures concerning involuntary admission of patients to psychiatric services.

The ages of the women who agreed to be interviewed ranged from twenty-one to sixty-one years. Fourteen were married, one was in a common-law relationship, seven were single and five were divorced or separated. More than half of the women had at least one child. A majority of the women (eighteen) were not in paid employment at the time of the interview, and only five had completed more than a high school education. None of the women were members of a visible minority group and most lived in small or medium-sized towns. In general, therefore, the women who participated in this research were both poor and poorly educated. The women's social characteristics are in keeping with a pattern often observed by researchers in the mental health field. For instance, sociologist Joan Busfield noted that there is a "consistent pattern of higher levels of mental illness among those of lower social status."[9] This association, however, overlooks the way in which psychiatric hospitalization might itself be a cause of poverty rather than the reverse. The downward drift on the social ladder creates a disproportionate number of poor people among psychiatric patients.

ADMISSION: VOLUNTARY OR INVOLUNTARY?

Legally there is a marked difference between voluntary and involuntary admission to psychiatric in-patient facilities. In general a person can be admitted against their will to a psychiatric unit when they pose a danger to others or are a danger to themselves. When admitted involuntarily, a person can be forced to accept treatment. The *New Brunswick Mental Health Act* outlines the procedures a physician must follow in order to admit someone to hospital as an involuntary patient. A person's initial involuntary admission can last up to seventy-two hours. After this time, if a patient is deemed to be unfit for discharge and unwilling to remain in hospital voluntarily, a psychiatrist has the option of applying to the Lieutenant-Governor's in Council Tribunal for an order to detain the person. A patient may also be detained pending application to the Tribunal. In either case, a first period of involuntary admission can last up to one month, a subsequent period can be up to three months, and thereafter up to six months. This process of involuntary detainment can go on indefinitely.

Of the twenty-seven women interviewed, seventeen had been admitted at least three times to a psychiatric unit and ten had been admitted once or twice. The women's accounts of their experiences of psychiatric hospitalization yielded several recurring themes with respect to their admission. When admitted to hospital, a common experience was lack of information about whether their status was voluntary or involuntary and many had not known the reason for their detention. Some also complained about the use of police cars to transport them to a hospital, something which made them feel like criminals. Once in hospital, the women complained about being overly controlled and restricted in their freedom of movement. In general, however, the women had been in agreement with their admission, citing the need for respite from problems with their family or spouse, or unsatisfactory living arrangements as reasons for their hospital admission.

In theory, each woman should have been informed about her legal status[10] at the time of her admission. The *New Brunswick Mental Health Act* (Amended) states that:

> [t]he attending psychiatrist shall inform a person detained in a psychiatric facility under an examination certificate of the reason for the detention and of his [sic] right to retain and instruct counsel when the person is initially detained in the psychiatric facility.[11]

In practise, however, some women could not recall having been told whether their admission was voluntary or involuntary. There might be various reasons for this — a woman might be agitated or severely depressed during admission, or her admission status might not have been discussed with her. The women were not always able to recall clearly the circumstances of their admission. Nevertheless, of the seven women who knew that their admission was involuntary, none was informed of the "reason for the detention" as required by the *Mental Health Act*.

In addition, involuntary hospitalization sometimes occurred for reasons apparently unrelated to a woman's mental health condition. Alice, who had been hospitalized twice before, was again seeking help but was unwilling to be admitted to a psychiatric unit some distance from her home. She wanted to go to her local hospital, but was told that she had to go to a hospital 100 kilometres away. She recalled:[12]

> Just the fact that I said I did not want to go ... put me on an involuntary list. I was in there [psychiatric unit] eighteen days and never taken off [the list]. I was so afraid they would keep me longer, and

that they would not let me out, that I hardly dared talk to anybody.[13]

Beth was taken from her home to the hospital by the police. At the hospital, she was admitted as an involuntary patient. According to Beth:

> The police came to the door and I was taken to [a psychiatric unit]. I felt absolutely terrible to be taken by the police. I only showed a temper. I never hit anybody or anything like that. So I could never understand why the police took me. The police never told me any reason, they took me by the arm and put me in the back of the car. They never said why, or who called them or anything.[14]

Beth did not know who had called the police and it is beside the point whether she needed psychiatric treatment. From her perspective, it was disturbing that she was taken from her house by the police without knowing why. She described herself as having "paranoid" tendencies, something which her hospitalization experiences seem quite likely to have exacerbated.

For many of the women, admission meant escape from the home environment, and generally they were very eager to be admitted to hospital. One woman said she was "very happy to be admitted" and another recalled that she "was very glad [to be admitted], I knew I was in an awful state." The story of Susan provides an example of why women sometimes want to be hospitalized. Susan lived alone and became lonely and frightened while housebound because of a physical health condition that made her lose control of her bladder. When her situation became unbearable, she took action:

> I took all the medication [along with me], went to out-patients [at the psychiatric unit] and sat there and I was angry and I was crying and I wanted something done. I said I cannot go on with this any more.[15]

This was not Susan's first psychiatric admission, she had been hospitalized several times before. Clearly, for her the psychiatric unit represented a much safer place than her home. Another woman, Connie, was receiving treatment as an out-patient, but felt that she was not "getting anywhere." She asked her family doctor to "send me somewhere. I don't care where or how long but I have to get better."[16]

Twelve women explicitly mentioned family or marital problems, ranging from having been molested as a child by a close relative to being battered by a spouse, as difficulties that led to their hospitalization. According to these women, however, when they were hospitalized, their family and marital problems were hardly addressed at all. It did not seem to be part of the treatment to explore these women's family relations and social living arrangements.

Whether women were admitted to hospital voluntarily or involuntarily, they experienced restrictions on their movements during hospitalization. Many were not allowed to leave the unit for the first couple of days and later on had to request permission to go for a walk or to go shopping. Julie said that she was "voluntary" but "I could not go off the ward. I gather that was for our own good because we might be suicidal and do something. But I did feel very kept in."[17]

TREATMENT AND DIAGNOSIS

Feminists have also been critical of the treatment women receive for psychological problems, particularly the assumption in mainstream approaches that the causes of mental health problems are rooted within the body's biochemistry, rather than the conditions of women's everyday lives under patriarchy. The logic of biological psychiatry leads to heavy reliance on psychotropic drugs, such as antidepressants (e.g., Prozac) and tranquillizers (e.g., Valium) to ameliorate the problems that bring women to the attention of mental health professionals. Further compounding women's difficulties in gaining help for their distress, as Miriam Greenspan points out, is that mental health services are based on the "father knows best" assumption which itself is part of patriarchal structures within society that cause women's "madness" in the first place.[18]

Because mainstream psychiatry is based on the medical model, with its emphasis on biological treatments, it should come as no surprise that all but two of the women interviewed had been prescribed drugs while in hospital and that most of these women felt that medication was the most important component of their treatment. In general, the women were accepting of their drug treatment. Debbie, for instance, said, "... nothing seems to help; it was a matter of getting the medication and over a period of time it seemed to work out. It was gradual."[19] At the same time, some women did complain about problems associated with taking medication. Julie, who had been hospitalized many times in her life, had fallen while in hospital and had broken her wrist. She attributed this to being given too much medication. "I think he [the psychiatrist] gave me too much. I didn't feel drowsy, but there was nothing to keep me standing up." Debbie also described having symptoms of "tardive akathisia," a side-effect of long-term medication use. One of these side-effects is the feeling of being compelled to engage in physical activity. After her discharge from hospital, Debbie was unable to stop pacing and consequently became exhausted. "I walked miles ... there was one day that I never stopped walking. I could not even sit down to eat." Eventually her husband contacted the doctor who then reduced the medication.

According to the women, they were told little about the potential side-effects of the drugs they were given.[20] Stephanie recalled having withdrawal symptoms when her medication was reduced. She had not been informed about this possibility and became very anxious. When she tried to discuss her symptoms with the hospital staff, she felt that her experiences were trivialized. She recalled:

> They just told me they were going to give me this for the panic attacks and the anxiety ... I had withdrawal symptoms and I felt rotten ... I could not understand why. A student nurse, who does not know the ropes, explained that the symptoms were withdrawal symptoms. It levelled itself out, but they could have explained. Don't get me wrong, if it was not for them I would not have been where I am now, but they could have explained a little bit more [about the drugs and their side-effects].[21]

Eight women received electro-convulsive (or shock) treatment (ECT).[22] Although most thought the treatment had been useful, they also expressed fear of the procedure and some felt that their memory had been affected. Julie, who had received her first ECT some twenty years earlier, recalled, "They saved me from dying. For a long time afterwards I felt they damaged my brain, but they ... made me ... they got me well." Another woman, Maggie, had been very fearful of having

ECT "because nothing was explained."[23] However, she felt that when the treatment "wore off" she was back at square one.

Thus according to their accounts, the women's treatment consisted primarily of medication or ECT or both. Possibly as a consequence of the type of treatment they received, many women described feeling bored while in hospital. As Julie said, "... there is very little to do in the [psychiatric unit], I learned to sit and do absolutely nothing for hours on end ... I found there is a lot of time in a psychiatric [unit] when there is nothing to do." At the same time, the women generally had complied with their treatment, although few recalled being consulted about it by hospital staff. For instance, Connie said, "I don't think that anybody asked me. I was willing to do whatever I had to do to get better." These women apparently were willing to go along with the treatment they received because they wanted to feel better so they could return home and resume their everyday lives. In a largely rural province such as New Brunswick, where few mental health services are available, treatment options are quite limited. Unless women have the financial means to pay for the services of a therapist, they have little choice but admission to a psychiatric unit for treatment of their mental health problems. At minimum, hospitalization offers women a brief period of respite from burdensome family responsibilities and stressful living conditions.

In addition to lack of consultation about their treatment, few women were informed about their diagnosis.[24] For some, not knowing their diagnosis had had serious implications in their lives. Brigid, for example, who had been hospitalized many times, recently had learned that her diagnosis was schizophrenia. She said that she felt much better having this knowledge: "I feel I am not crazy, it is an illness ..."[25] As a result, she has made a major change in her life. A single-parent of a nine-year-old boy, Brigid had found it hard to care for her child with the regular recurrence of her illness and she felt that her child had suffered emotionally. Based on the prognosis of her illness, she decided to give her child up for adoption to spare the child from further suffering. "If I would have known years ago, [the child] would not have been traumatized by my illness ..." Although Brigid's decision made sense to her, perhaps if more support had been available, she could have continued to raise her child instead of giving him up for adoption.

In other cases, women had been told their diagnosis, but this was not always perceived as being helpful. Lana remarked that she would get a different diagnosis every time: "I guess I got so after a while I didn't pay much attention to the diagnosis."[26] Michelle stated that her diagnosis was not discussed with her but with her husband. At that time it did not bother her, however, now that she is better, she says, "I feel that it should have been discussed with me and I should have been consulted and they should have talked to me about it."[27]

It was evident from what the women told us that they wanted to be better informed about their treatment and to understand what was happening to them. They wanted to learn what made them sick and they wanted to participate in their healing. Many of the women made it clear that they had tried hard to comply with what the hospital staff had wanted them to do because they were eager to get better and believed that full participation in treatment would aid their recovery. As Lana said, "I wanted to go to the bottom of what was troubling me. I bent over backwards to get help."

A few women, however, did express reservations about their treatment and had participated only because they felt forced to. Jennifer described herself as being a "rebel" on the psychiatric unit and said that when she would not participate, the staff gave her "a hard time." Jennifer had been in and out of several psychiatric units in several provinces. She always refused to take medication and according to her own recollection, was therefore considered a rebel by the staff.[28] Marie characterized the situation faced by psychiatric patients in the following way: "You have to work twice as hard to get half as far. Your input is never taken seriously. If you choose to disagree you're a raving lunatic who does not know what she is saying."[29]

When the women were first hospitalized, most had expected to receive drugs and many welcomed this form of treatment. However, they also had expected that a systematic effort, characterized by regular contact with a psychiatrist, would be made to help them to solve their problems. Lack of contact with a psychiatrist during their hospitalization was cited as a major problem by many women who had expected that the psychiatrist would be the main treatment provider, something that in most cases did not happen. Several of the women said that they saw the psychiatrist only every "two to three days for ten to fifteen minutes." Marie recalled that when she saw the psychiatrist during morning rounds, "it kind of consisted of good morning, how are you? How did you sleep last night? Eat your breakfast okay? See you tomorrow." Nancy explained how her psychiatrist dismissed her and downplayed the importance of talking to her about her problems. "He was treating me with drugs for a disease and he did not go along with the psychological garbage as he put it."[30] Obviously, this psychiatrist adhered to the medical model of psychiatric illness and did not believe that social influences played a role in causing mental health problems. Debbie complained that she saw her psychiatrist only about "four times" during her five-week hospital stay. "That was the problem, I would have liked to see him more often ... everyone else is the same way. They also would like to see him more often. I did not see him enough."

Not only did the women indicate that they lacked support from staff, particularly the psychiatrist, while in hospital, they also indicated that their own family members often were not very supportive. Loneliness was another condition some women faced. For instance, the only family member to visit Mavis while she was in hospital was her husband.[31] The women excused this neglect on the part of close relatives with such comments as "they are too busy," and "they don't have time to visit." For others, failure of family members to visit them in hospital was because relatives could not accept that someone in the family had a mental illness. According to Marie, her brother thinks "mental patients are loony" and he maintains that there is no "mental illness in the family."

The lack of family support was difficult for women to deal with. Also, when they were discharged, they were often unable to talk about their experiences because this meant revealing their psychiatric hospitalization to others, something that their families do not want to be reminded of. As indicated in these women's accounts, psychiatric illness is still a very stigmatized condition. Cheryl aptly described the dilemma faced by those who have received psychiatric treatment:

> I don't want to be labelled as a loony. If people would know, they would hold it against you. If two people apply for a job and all things are equal, and one has a history of mental illness and does not lie, it is not hard to tell who will get the job.[32]

In most cases, the women were not consulted by hospital staff about plans for their discharge and for many their discharge seemed to come "out of the blue." One woman was told that she was going to be discharged the next day. "They tell me that they think I am ready to go home and they will be discharging me." She did not feel that she had enough time to prepare herself, "If they could give [me] a few more days notice that would be nice." It is surprising that so little attention is paid to the discharge process because many women did not feel ready to leave hospital when told that they were being discharged. Kathy, who had been in and out of the psychiatric unit numerous times, said:

> I didn't want to go but I knew they were going to boot me out any-way. The day of discharge was really hard. I didn't think I was ready, but when the doctor thinks you're ready, you are ready. I could have stayed there the rest of my life. I had no worries, I didn't have to worry about meals, everything was planned.[33]

Kathy's story offers several insights. First, it is the psychiatrist who de-termines when a patient is ready to go home, not the patient, a situa-tion in which the doctor holds most of the power over a woman. Second, it seems ironic that someone who does not spend much time talking to patients and who does not appear to be very interested in women patients' lives or experiences, such as sexual or physical abuse, which have an impact on women's mental health, is the person who makes the decision that a woman is "cured" and ready to go home. Kathy's story also reveals why some women do not want to leave the psychiatric unit. Women with recurring mental health problems may have difficulty surviving outside the hospital environment. If they are on social assistance, for instance, they face a life of poverty often with little family or community support. In fact, for many women the psychiatric unit is a place where they feel safe and protected. As Connie said about being discharged, "I was putting up a brave front but I think underneath that security is the uncertainty of how will I cope. A plan gives you something to go by."

Yet nine women expressed more positive feelings about being discharged from hospital. Beth had been admitted as an involuntary patient, and was very eager to go home. She had been made to wait until a certain date before being discharged. Two weeks before her discharge date, she took a taxi to her home, a trip of 100 kilometres, because she was unable to handle being on the psychiatric unit any longer. As soon as she reached home, the police, who had been alerted by the hospital, arrived and she recounted that "they took me down to the detention centre overnight and brought me back to the [psychiatric unit]." She had to stay another week in the hospital before her final discharge. She said, "When you do something like that you are naughty." As Beth said, "Discharge day was one of the happiest days in my life."

AFTER-CARE

Given that people who have been hospitalized in a psychiatric unit or hospital are stigmatized, that they lack family and community support and are often living in poverty as well as being unemployed, it is hardly surprising that returning "home" posed a considerable challenge for many of the women interviewed. In some cases, women reported experiencing severe anxiety in the days following their discharge. One woman described her first few days at home as being "hell." She was very afraid because she did not know whom to contact. Connie recalled that "I was expected to run my house, enter the community on my own." She pointed out that "when you have a mental illness you are expected to be back in full swing, while if you have diabetes you don't have to do that." After-care typically consisted of seeing a psychiatrist two to four weeks after discharge, although eleven women did not receive even this level of after-care. Cheryl described the lack of after-care as "the worst part" of her psychiatric experience. Some women attributed their re-hospitalization to the lack of after-care services because there was nothing to "ease the transition" between the hospital setting and the outside world. Even those women who had received some form of after-care felt that the first few days following discharge were very difficult. The women who were most satisfied with their after-care arrangements were those referred to day-therapy programs offered by some psychiatric units. Such programs were important to these women because of the social contacts they provided.

All of the women who participated in a self-help group as part of their after-care felt that this involvement was very important because it filled the gap created by the lack of after-care services. These self-help groups, attended by both women and men, were usually established by voluntary organizations, most often a local branch of the Canadian Mental Health Association. Several women felt that without being able to go to meetings of the self-help group they would have become very lonely. These women felt that being in a self-help group had prevented them from being re-hospitalized. As Brigid said, "If you don't get help and are not followed in everyday life, you just end up in the ward."

∞

There are two underlying themes that these women have identified: the desire to seek "asylum" and feelings of powerlessness and being controlled. The accounts of many of the women reflected a view of hospitalization as offering a respite from the stresses and strains of everyday life, whether these involved social isolation, unemployment, unsatisfactory living conditions or an abusive spouse. The hospital provided a safe, protected place where their everyday responsibilities were taken care of by others. Many of the women had expressed reluctance to be discharged when the staff decided they were ready to leave hospital. In her work with socially disabled clients, Rachel Perkins has also described the psychiatric hospital as a place where women feel safe and protected, while at the same time relieved from expectations that they cope with day-to-day family responsibilities.[34] Perkins goes so far as to suggest that, for some women, a long-term stay in the psychiatric hospital may be preferable to returning home. She concludes that for some women the community is not always the best place to be.

Although a number of women wanted to be admitted to hospital, many were critical of the care they received and aware that the power to determine central elements of their hospitalization experiences was outside their control. They had little or no input into decisions about their treatment or, more fundamentally, whether services were received. Control over hospital admission, subsequent treatment and discharge rests with the psychiatrist. To a large degree, therefore, women are rendered powerless by the way psychiatric services are administered. Judi Chamberlin who was psychiatrically hospitalized twenty years ago, has recounted similar experiences. She writes, "Power, not illness or treatment, is what that system [mental health system] is all about."[35] Many of the women we spoke with would agree with her.

Furthermore, no attempt is made to incorporate the women's experiences into planning of service delivery. For instance, despite the common experience that the period immediately following discharge was a particularly difficult one for many of the women, only a few received any after-care services. For these women, the self-help group was perceived as a "life-saver," not only offering a source of support following discharge but also providing an alternative to hospitalization.

If mental health care is to improve, it is critical to attend to the experiences of women who have been psychiatric patients. The medical model, as practised by many psychiatrists has little to offer these women. A more inclusive treatment model that takes women's lives into consideration would, we believe, be much more beneficial to women. The women who spoke to us wanted respite from debilitating symptoms, but they also wanted problems in their everyday lives addressed. The difficulties experienced by these women that brought them into contact with the mental health system need to be understood from a perspective in which women's experiences are treated as having validity in their own right. To see these experiences as a "disease" or to ignore them altogether is to invalidate an important source of information about women's mental healthcare needs. If more effective strategies for improving mental health among women are to be developed, they must be grounded in women's experiences and incorporate women's participation more fully than is currently the case. Some feminists who work in the mental health system have been instrumental in developing approaches that better respond to the needs of women with mental health problems. In England, for instance, Sue Holland has developed a community-based program for women with mental health problems which combines individual psychotherapy with social action with the aim of improving the women's living conditions as well as their mental health.[36] Canadian feminist psychologist Eva Szekely has outlined strategies that professionals working in hospital settings can employ to help women patients to negotiate a service system that is often unresponsive to their needs.[37] These examples along with the women's voices presented in this chapter underscore the continuing need for improvements to the mental health system so that the services women receive can be healing rather than merely perpetuating the often oppressive conditions of their everyday lives.

Notes

Baukje Miedema would like to thank the Canadian Federation of University Women for the award of the Alice E. Wilson Scholarship held while conducting this research. She also acknowledges the funding received from the Nels Anderson Fund, Sociology Department, University of New Brunswick, in support of this research.

1. Jean Randhawa and Rod Riley, "Mental Health Statistics, 1982–83 to 1993–94," *Health Reports* 7 (1996), 55–61.

2. Michel Foucault, *Madness and Civilization* (New York: Vintage Books, 1965).

3. Phyllis Chesler, *Women and Madness* (New York: Doubleday, 1972); Susan Penfold and Gillian Walker, *Women and the Psychiatric Paradox* (Montreal: The Eden Press 1983).

4. Chesler, *Women and Madnes*; Carol Mowbray, Susan Lanir, and Marilyn Hulce, *Women and Mental Health* (New York: Harrington Park Press, 1985); Jane Ussher, *Women's Madness: Misogyny or Mental Illness* (London: Harvester Wheatsheaf, 1991).

5. Ussher, *Women's Madness: Misogyny or Mental Illness*; Nancy Felipe Russo, "Forging Priorities for Women's Mental Health," *American Psychologist* 45 (1990), 368–373.

6. Baukje Miedema and Janet M. Stoppard, "Asylum, Bedlam or Cure? Explaining Contradictions in Women's Experiences of Psychiatric Hospitalization," in Houston Stewart, Beth Percival, and Elizabeth Epperly, eds., *The More We Get Together* (Charlottetown, PEI: Gynergy Books, 1992).

7. Self-help groups provide support, information and social activities to their members. Many groups are organized by the Canadian Mental Health Association and its local branches. Others are organized based on American programs like the group known as Recovery.

8. Randhawa and Riley, "Mental Health Statistics, 1982–83 to 1993–94."

9. Joan Busfield, *Managing Madness* (London: Hutchinson, 1986).

10. Legal status refers to being a voluntary or involuntary patient as stated in the *New Brunswick Mental Health Act*. This is a different category than the category "criminally insane." The Canadian judicial system has the power to declare somebody criminally insane. A physician has the power to commit somebody involuntarily, for a certain period of time, to a psychiatric hospital.

11. *New Brunswick Mental Health Act* (Amended) (Fredericton, NB: Queen's Printer, 1985), Section 7.4.

12. In order to protect the identity of the women who participated in the research, fictitious names have been used to identify them. Interview with Alice, July 4, 1989, at interviewer's residence.

13. In the interviews the women did not always explain the reasons why certain things happened, or who had told them something. We are dealing with retrospective experiential accounts of events that may have occurred some time ago. The events, as told by the women, were not corroborated. The intent of the research was to document how women had experienced psychiatric hospitalization. For a more detailed discussion, see Baukje Miedema, "A Critique of 'Oversimplified Images: Comments on Control or Treatment?'" *Canadian Journal of Community Mental Health* 14 (1995), 133–136.

14. Interview with Beth, September 21, 1989, at a self-help group club house.

15. Interview with Susan, September 27, 1989, at a self-help group club house.

16. Interview with Connie, October 2, 1989, at her residence.

17. Interview with Julie, July 17, 1989, at her residence.

18. Miriam Greenspan, *A New Approach to Women and Therapy* (Blue Ridge Summit, PA: McGraw-Hill, 1993).

19. Interview with Debbie, September 6, 1989, in a hotel room.

20. During the interviews the type of drugs the women were taking was never discussed. In some cases the women knew the name of the drug and the reason it was prescribed. In other cases, however, women referred only to the "blue pill" and were not always clear why they had to take the drug, except that it would make them better.

21. Interview with Stephanie, September 5, 1989, at her residence.

22. Electro-convulsive therapy (ECT) is the treatment of mental disorder by inducing a brain seizure through the use of an electric current. Between 70 and 170 volts of electricity are applied to the brain via electrodes for a fraction of a second. ECT is used primarily as a treatment with patients who are severely depressed. This procedure was developed in the 1930s in Italy.

23. Interview with Maggie on September 22, 1989, at a self-help group club house.

24. Diagnosis in itself is not that important. During the interviews, the first author did not focus on the type of illness the interviewees may have been suffering from. First of all, it is a very personal issue and some interviewees may have been uncomfortable disclosing the nature of their mental illness. Some mental illnesses are more stigmatized than others. Being hospitalized for depression, for example, is less stigmatizing than suffering from schizophrenia. Second, the type of mental illness the interviewees suffered from was irrelevant to the research questions. The research examined hospitalization experiences of people hospitalized in a psychiatric unit of a general hospital or a psychiatric hospital. Psychiatrists are required to provide a diagnosis to Medicare in order to be reimbursed for his/her services. All mental health diagnoses are described in the American Psychiatric Association, *Diagnostic and Statistical Manual of Mental Disorders: DSM-IV*, 4th ed. (Washington, DC: American Psychiatric Association, 1994). If a condition is not described in the DSM, it simply does not exist.

25. Interview with Brigid, September 22, 1989, at a self-help group club house.

26. Interview with Lana, September 11, 1989, at her residence.

27. Interview with Michelle, September 5, 1989, at her residence.

28. Interview with Jennifer, September 27, 1989, at a self-help group club house.

29. Interview with Marie, September 26, 1989, at a self-help group club house.

30. Interview with Nancy, July 21, 1989, at her residence.

31. Interview with Mavis, September 1, 1989, at her residence.

32. Interview with Cheryl, September 1, 1989, at her residence.

33. Interview with Kathy, July 21, 1989, at her residence.

34. Rachel Perkins, "Working with Socially Disabled Clients," in Jane Ussher and Paula Nicolson, eds., *Gender Issues in Clinical Psychology* (London: Routledge, 1992), 171–193.

35. Judi Chamberlin, *On Our Own* (New York: Hawthorn Books, 1978), xiii.

36. Sue Holland, "From Social Abuse to Social Action: A Neighbourhood Psychotherapy and Social Action Project for Women," in Ussher and Nicolson, eds., *Gender Issues in Clinical Psychology*, 68–77.

37. Eva Szekely, "Can Feminist Therapy be Practiced in a Medical-Hospital Setting?" paper presented at Eating Disorders and Body Image Conference, The Toronto Hospital, Toronto, Ontario, February 6, 1993.

CHAPTER SIX

"OLD BAGS" UNDER THE KNIFE
FACIAL COSMETIC SURGERY AMONG WOMEN

Diane Cepanec and Barbara Payne

႟

COSMETIC SURGERY IS the fastest growing medical specialty in North America and over 80 percent of the current recipients of cosmetic surgery are women, even though men are increasingly undergoing this procedure.[1] In North America, cultural expectations influence and regulate behaviours related to physical appearance, resulting in cosmetic surgery being required for women in ways that it is not required for men.

To gain an understanding of why women decide to have this procedure, attention must be paid to the meaning of cosmetic surgery from the perspective of women themselves. With few exceptions, researchers have not listened to the personal accounts of women regarding their decisions to have the surgery.[2] To date, no research on Canadian women's experiences with cosmetic surgery has been reported. To fill this gap, we have undertaken interviews with ten women living in Manitoba and present an analysis of their personal accounts. Canadian women, like most women, are pressured to look young, sexy and maintain their beauty as they grow older.

Women from many cultures have a long tradition of undergoing painful and sometimes mutilating procedures for the sake of beauty. In China, countless women were crippled for life by the centuries-old custom of foot-binding. During the Victorian era, women achieved "hourglass" figures by wearing constraining corsets or by having their lower ribs surgically removed. While standards of female beauty have varied greatly from culture to culture and have shifted drastically over the years, the underlying assumption seems to be that beauty is worth spending time and money on, enduring pain and sometimes even sacrificing life itself. Standards of beauty are cultural creations that are "narrow, restrictive and set impossible expectations for most females all of the time, and by virtue of human aging, are impossible for all women at least some of the time."[3] The "universal" ideal of beauty mirrors Caucasian characteristics and neglects the diversity of women's bodies and appearance. Lip reduction in Black women, nose-reshaping surgery among Jewish women and eyelid surgery to westernize Asian women's eyes, all demonstrate that beauty is often defined in Caucasian, ethnocentric and racist terms. This standard of beauty is also influenced by age. As a woman ages, failure to replicate society's ideal becomes all the more apparent. Beauty and youth tend to be seen as synonymous in our society. In short, surgical alteration of the face and body is a procedure that women in many cultures undergo in order to improve and transform their bodies to meet the cultural requirements of youth and femininity.

At the close of the twentieth century, North American women are living in a cultural milieu that supports and encourages them to invest heavily in their appearance. The media abound with features on body image, cosmetic surgery and how to keep the body looking young, sexy and beautiful.[4] According to Marcene Goodman, "that women of all ages ... are willing to undergo painful, intrusive medical procedures in the name of self-enhancement is not surprising given the media drive to socialize women in that direction."[5] Women are bombarded with images that the majority can never attain, which perpetuates the consumption of products and services to construct and maintain a desirable appearance. This plethora of idealized body images in the media coincides with changes in the medical specialization of plastic surgery.

Plastic surgery has a long history; its oldest form is rhinoplasty, which was first recorded around 1000 B.C. in India, where women's noses — which had been mutilated by their jealous husbands — were reconstructed using flaps of skin from the forehead.[6] In addition, more than fifteen hundred years ago, the Chinese were surgically repairing noses and harelips.[7] Although technology for surgically altering the appearance of the human body has been available for centuries, it was not until the large number of casualties produced by both World Wars that plastic surgery emerged as a full-fledged medical specialty.[8]

The field of plastic surgery encompasses two categories of operations: reconstructive procedures and cosmetic procedures.[9] Reconstructive procedures "restore or improve physical function and minimize disfigurement from accidents, diseases, or birth defects."[10] Cosmetic procedures purport to offer elective aesthetic improvement through surgical alterations of facial and bodily features on otherwise healthy bodies.[11]

The emergence of cosmetic procedures in the mid-twentieth century altered the field of plastic surgery, which until then was confined to restoring or improving physical function and minimizing disfigurements from accidents, diseases or congenital deformities.[12] By the mid-twentieth century it had expanded to include the creation of new physical properties as well as dealing with phenomena that are part of the "natural" process of aging — wrinkles, jowls and sagging skin.[13] This new use of plastic surgery came to be known as cosmetic surgery. There are two basic types of cosmetic surgery: type-changing and restorative.[14] Type-changing cosmetic surgery attempts to improve parts of the face and body that are perceived to be an undesirable shape or size (such as nose-reshaping surgery). These procedures are type-changing because they create an appearance the person has not previously had. Restorative cosmetic surgery, such as facelifts or eyelid surgery, attempts to rejuvenate and minimize the effects of aging. Restorative procedures restore previous physical characteristics of the individual.

Cosmetic surgery, like all surgery, carries a number of health risks. However, unlike most surgical procedures, the risks of cosmetic surgery are weighed solely against the value of a more attractive appearance. While there may be no physical justification for cosmetic surgery, there is, according to some cosmetic surgeons, a psychological justification. Some physicians argue that cosmetic surgery improves the mental health of their clients and that the benefits are psychotherapeutic.[15] However, "in the name of the 'feel good' factor, the benefits of beauty procedures are played up, while the dangers are played on a low key."[16] To their financial advantage, cosmetic surgeons function in a society that promotes bodily improvement, defies age-related bodily changes and worships beauty that is youth-related.

The beauty in the fifty-year-old model or actress is valued precisely because she does not look her age; unaltered fifty- or sixty-year-old women are not held up as the styles for women to emulate as they age.[17] In Naomi Wolf's view, "women have facelifts in a society in which women without them appear to vanish from sight."[18] "Baby boomers" (women born between 1946 and 1966) are the current lucrative market for cosmetic surgeons and they are expected to continue to use this technology into later life.[19] In Canada, "baby boomers" are the largest cohort of the population and will continue to be so until the middle of the next century.[20] In short, the aging of the population has generated an increasing number of potential consumers for cosmetic surgery, the majority of whom are women.

There is a growing academic and popular interest in cosmetic surgery. Academic research has relied heavily on critiques of the pervasive cultural beauty system,[21] while research based on empirical data is sparse. As well, the relationship between aging and cosmetic surgery has been virtually unexplored. The most comprehensive study on cosmetic surgery is the work by Kathy Davis.[22] In *Reshaping the Female Body: The Dilemma of Cosmetic Surgery*, Davis reports on her study with women in the Netherlands. Davis spoke to women who had undergone cosmetic surgery purely for "looks"; she did not talk to women who had had reconstructive surgery. The focus of Davis's research was on women's decision-making to have cosmetic surgery and their satisfaction with the outcomes of the procedures. Her work drew heavily on women's accounts of breast cosmetic surgery. Davis identified three major themes from these experiences: identity, agency and morality. Contrary to feminist scholarship — which situates cosmetic surgery in women's involvement in the beauty system[23] — Davis contends that for her participants, cosmetic surgery is about identity. That is, cosmetic surgery could be an occasion for a woman to renegotiate her identity and become an embodied subject rather than "just a body." Davis argues that cosmetic surgery is about agency in that it is a possible action women can take to remedy their dissatisfaction with their appearance. She concludes that cosmetic surgery is about exercising power and control over conditions which are not of women's own making. The women Davis spoke to "treated cosmetic surgery as something which was morally problematic for them and had to be justified." Using the three themes of identity, agency and morality, Davis developed a framework that allowed her to explore cosmetic surgery as a dilemma — being critical of cosmetic surgery without uncritically undermining women who decide to have cosmetic surgery. This framework enabled her to listen and take women's reasons seriously without having to agree with what they said.[24]

Despite Davis's major contribution to the developing literature on cosmetic surgery, there are a number of disadvantages to her approach. Her claim that cosmetic surgery is first and foremost about agency (taking one's life into one's own hands) deflects attention from the socio-cultural context in which women's agency operates. More importantly, Davis's work is problematic for its noncommittal position on cosmetic surgery as well as her discussion of agency. According to Davis, cosmetic surgery is both "profoundly disempowering and a road to empowerment at the same time."[25] Despite her recognition of the potential negative impacts of the procedure, she remains uncritical of the beauty system. Her conclusions that cosmetic surgery is both disempowering and a road to empowerment can be used to endorse cosmetic surgery. As Davis herself admits, the systematic or structured patterns of women's involvement in the cultural beauty system have not been taken into account.[26] In addition, she does not address the importance of aging issues that plague women as they grow older.

This failure to incorporate structure and age into an investigation of women's use of cosmetic surgery supports the need for a wider socio-cultural exploration. In contrast to Davis's exploration of cosmetic surgery — primarily breast surgery — and neglect of aging issues, we focus exclusively on facial cosmetic surgery and take into consideration the age factor. This chapter examines how women make the decision to have facial cosmetic surgery and explores the relationship between aging and the socio-cultural context. Critical to this examination is the consideration of external forces such as cultural images and social relationships which can influence women's decisions.

The ages of the women we interviewed range from 23 to 73. The six younger women (ages 23 to 35) were single, and the four older women (ages 57–73) were married. All ten women were Caucasian. In class terms, all the women described themselves as being middle to upper-middle class. Three of the women were university students, two women worked in a professional occupation, one woman was employed full-time and attending university part-time, and the remaining four women were retired. Of the ten women, two had graduated from university, five had some university education and the remaining three had graduated from high school.

Of the ten interviewees, five had undergone one procedure each of type-changing cosmetic surgery (surgery designed to create a new appearance). Three women had nose-reshaping surgery, one woman had dermabrasion to remove acne scars and one women had her eye muscles tightened for cosmetic reasons. One woman had multiple type-changing cosmetic surgery, which included jaw, chin and lip surgery. The remaining four women had undergone multiple restorative facial cosmetic surgeries to restore their previous appearance, including two women who had facelifts and eyelid surgeries, one woman who had two facelifts and one woman who had eyelid surgery and neck liposuction. The women who had type-changing facial cosmetic surgery were younger than the women who had restorative facial cosmetic surgery (age range 23 to 35 versus 57 to 73 respectively). A summary of the participants' ages and procedure(s) is shown in Table 1.

The questions we asked these women examined the relationship between social, cultural, economic and individual factors, and their

TABLE 1

PARTICIPANTS BY AGE AND TYPE OF COSMETIC PROCEDURE

PARTICIPANTS*	AGE	TYPE OF COSMETIC PROCEDURE
Amy	23	Nose-reshaping surgery
Grace	25	Nose-reshaping surgery
Stephanie	27	Jaw, chin and bottom lip surgery
Victoria	29	Dermabrasion
Tamara	30	Muscles in eyes tightened
Sharon	35	Nose-reshaping surgery
Marlene	57	Facelift, eyelid surgery
Rachel	58	Mid-line facelift, eyelid surgery
Rose	66	Eyelid surgery, neck liposuction
Lillian	73	Two facelifts
*Pseudonyms		

decisions to have facial cosmetic surgery. Also included were questions that explored the relationship between aging and cosmetic surgery. Each interview began by asking participants "Could you please tell me a little about yourself to give me a sense of who you are?" Questions then followed on body image ("How satisfied are you with your physical appearance?"), reactions to aging ("How do you feel about aging?"), media influence ("How do you think the media portrays women?") and beauty routines ("What steps do you take to keep up your appearance?"). Participants were then asked to tell the story of their facial cosmetic surgery and a number of probes were used to explore how these women reached their decision to have facial cosmetic surgery. Examples of some of the probes were: "Can you tell me about the circumstances that led to your decision to have the surgery?" and "When did the thought of having cosmetic surgery first enter your consciousness?"

A number of key themes in their accounts reveal the nature of their involvement with facial cosmetic surgery. At the level of the individual, decision justification and normalization, self-identity, agency and choice played important roles. Their decisions were also influenced by a number of social forces such as the role of the medical profession, social relationships, and cultural images of beauty and aging. To protect their identities, the names of the women are changed; their age follows in brackets.

JUSTIFYING THE DECISION

All the women interviewed sought to normalize and defend their decisions to have facial cosmetic surgery. They justified their decisions in a number of different ways. Lillian (73) felt that cosmetic surgery falls into the same category as other forms of body improvement, such as losing weight, wearing makeup or colouring your hair. She felt more women would have cosmetic surgery if they had the financial resources and more information. Similarly, Amy (23) said in reference to her nose-reshaping surgery:

> I expected just really an increase in the angle. It seems so tedious, stupid, lame, but a nose can do so much for your face. It can and I know it can because I've always studied faces. And I wanted, by

increasing the angle between my upper lip and my nose, [to] accent the rest of my face and bring out the good features. Like makeup or anything else would. For me it was an extension of makeup. I guess the same principle of putting on makeup. And that's why I wanted to. I've always done shading along my nose and I thought I won't have to shade my nose any more.[27]

Cosmetic surgery was often viewed as one of many, and no different from, other body maintenance techniques and practices. This normalization of a potentially dangerous procedure is not surprising given that the vast range of services and products that are "produced, marketed and sold, point to the significance of appearance and bodily preservation" within Canadian society.[28]

One might deduce from such statements that women's decisions to undergo cosmetic surgery may be empowering to them because their surgery provides them with a more permanent solution than "makeup" for "personal" dissatisfaction they have about their features. However, an examination of their descriptions of the natural appearance of their features reflect the larger social/cultural negative evaluation of certain inherited ethnic features — as well as aging — in women.

While body maintenance was an important factor, heredity and genetic destiny were also used as a justification for a decision to have facial cosmetic surgery. Marlene (57) explained that she had her eyelids tucked because they were "literally hanging down to her eyelashes" and that this was a family trait. Using the same argument, Rachel (58) explained that she had the same deep lines under her eyes as her father. Inherited features were also invoked as justifications for nose-reshaping cosmetic surgery. As Amy (23) explained, "I'm of German descent and we come from a family with large noses and it grows as we get older." Similarly, Sharon (35) stated, "I always thought my nose was a lot longer because I'm Ukrainian and a lot of us have a typical long thin nose."

In addition to body maintenance and heredity as justifications for surgery, unique personal circumstances were also cited. For Grace (25), her decision to have nose-reshaping surgery coincided with reconstructive surgery following an accident. Rationalizing that since she was already having her nose corrected due to the accident and that she had always felt that her nose was too large, she would have it made smaller.

She was adamant in asserting that she would never have undergone nose-reshaping surgery just because she did not like her nose.

A common belief is that cosmetic surgery is a decision based on vanity. The women who participated in this study both rejected and feared this notion. Statements such as "I don't associate vanity with trying to look good" (Amy, 23) and "It's okay to look good sometimes and it's okay to feel good about the way you look and it doesn't mean that you're vain" (Victoria, 29) suggest that women's decisions to have cosmetic surgery are not reached based on vanity. At the same time, eight women expressed fears of people judging them as vain. Victoria explained, with reference to her dermabrasion for acne scars:

> The vain thing was a problem with me when I decided to do this. That was [the] whole justification or legitimacy from it being covered in Medicare was that they saw it as a psychologically upsetting, traumatic thing for a person to go through and that's why it was covered — and that was acceptable because I've always had a problem that somebody might think I'm vain.

Sharon (35) described how the fear of people judging her as vain is the basis for her withholding the fact that she elected to have facial cosmetic surgery. She stated:

> I would have a hard time telling people I don't know very well that I had nose surgery done because I didn't like the way my nose looked. I think that I'm lucky in the sense that I was able to just say it was part of my sinus surgery thrown in. And to tell you the truth, I haven't told a lot of people that I paid for it because I think I'd be embarrassed to tell them I did because they'd think I'm vain.

For eight participants, justifying their decision to undergo cosmetic surgery involved presenting themselves as not being vain — because they felt that unless their decision was "valid," the larger culture would conceive them as being vain. As Tamara (30) explained, "A lot of people would think it's due to vanity. I guess you can say so, but I wouldn't say vanity in that negative connotation. I would say vanity, in how does it make me feel? Do I feel like a stronger, more confident person?" The fact that many of the women in this study felt a tension between their desires to look good and feel good about their appearances and their fears of being judged as vain for these decisions, points to the primacy of appearance in their lives.

SELF-IDENTITY

The literature on cosmetic surgery suggests that identity is an important concept in women's decisions. Davis's research found that for a woman who felt trapped in a body that failed to match her sense of self, cosmetic surgery was a way to renegotiate her identity.[29] The theme of identity was also raised in Goodman's study of American women. Reporting on older women who had all undergone facial cosmetic surgery, she found "cosmetic surgery enabled them to stop the clock; to put their faces in synchrony with their inner feelings of youthfulness."[30]

The theme of self-identity was also supported in our analysis of the interviews. More specifically, self-identity was raised in relation to reconstructing one's identity. Marlene (57) said the main reason she underwent a facelift was to avoid looking like her mother. At the time of deciding to have cosmetic surgery, Marlene was undergoing intense psychotherapy to deal with child abuse issues from her past that surfaced in her later life. Her mother and her sister were in total denial of the abuse. She explained, "In order to gain my own identity, in order to, to just try to find out who I was after being so connected to them for so long, that's what I had to do." Her decision to have a facelift was based as much on wanting to be herself as on not wanting to look like her mother. For Marlene, cosmetic surgery was part of the process of reconstructing an identity different and separate from her mother.

Self-identity was also raised in relation to "ideal" versus "real" self-identity. Rachel (58) explained her decision to have eyelid surgery and a mid-line facelift as, "You just want to come out looking more like your image of what you think you look like. And I guess I only wanted to remove the bags under my eyes and get back to the way I looked before they started to appear." Lillian (73) explained that she wanted a younger-looking face to match her more youthful-appearing figure. When asked if she had other expectations of the surgery beyond the physical change, Tamara (30) responded:

> I knew that once I had this surgery I was going to be like everybody else. And once I'm on the same par as everybody else, it was sort of

like the real me could show through. That's what I think I wanted.
I wanted people to see the real me because I had this tendency to be
shy before and I knew that I wasn't shy.

For these three women, cosmetic surgery enabled them to reconcile the
discrepancy between their "real" and "ideal" self-identities.

Agency and Choice

As with Davis's findings, agency emerged as an important theme in our
analysis. Davis contends that women who have cosmetic surgery are
not victims of the cultural beauty system, but can be seen as competent
and knowledgeable subjects who act upon conditions which are not of
their own making. She argues that cosmetic surgery is a way for women
to be active agents and to take action over their dissatisfaction with
their appearance. In our study, agency surfaced in relation to the decision-making process and resolution. This is captured by Marlene (57):

> It's kind of like the surgery for me was a symbol, or the doing of it
> — not so much the effect, but the doing of it — the deciding to do
> it and the carrying out of my decision. And having the courage to
> discuss the financial situation with my husband, all those sorts of
> things, the doing of that was a very brave act for me.

Victoria (29) also expressed how carrying through her decision was
more important than the results of her cosmetic surgery. She explained:

> Just saying this is what is going to make me feel better, I'm going to
> admit that, and I'm just going to do it. And I'm just going to take
> charge of it and that's I think what gave me satisfaction as opposed
> to the percentage of improvement. That was a big part of it. Be-
> cause that helped me understand that I can do what ever I want ...
> It kind of broke that barrier [of] me sitting and wishing and won-
> dering to ... feeling better and taking charge.

Also expressed was how cosmetic surgery was a decision they reached
on their own and that making the decision to proceed, rather than the
cosmetic surgery per se, was the key factor that gave them confidence
in their decision-making abilities. In this sense, making the
decision was what made some of the women agents; however,
cosmetic surgery itself is not about agency. In fact, the conditions of

genuine choice were questionable for all the women, particularly given the influence of social forces such as the medical profession, social relationships and the pervasiveness of cultural images of beauty and aging.

THE ROLE OF THE MEDICAL PROFESSION

Some women make their own decisions, while some wait for others to make decisions for them. It was not uncommon for women in our study to be influenced to have cosmetic surgery on the recommendation of a male physician. Tamara (30) discussed how she always dreamed of getting her eyes fixed because they were not straight. But no one, not even her eye doctor, ever suggested it until she was in her early twenties. She said:

> It wasn't until I went to see another doctor, I think it was about my acne or something, and the doctor just came out and said, "Have you ever thought about getting your eyes fixed?" And I did. It was always on my mind. It was like, I think it was everyday, I thought about my eyes. I am sure of it. And when he said that to me … I couldn't believe it. It was like somebody actually sort of finally suggested it. And I said, "Yes I have, but I don't know how to go about doing it." And he got me hooked up with a guy who specializes in this particular type of surgery. And that's how the ball started rolling.

Similarly, Stephanie (27) hated her profile as she had no angle to her chin and also thought about getting it fixed. If she saw a picture of herself displaying her profile, she would immediately rip it up. The opportunity arose when she was seeing an oral surgeon about removing her wisdom teeth and he offered to fix her jaw. Stephanie elected to have jaw, chin and lip surgery, which required her mouth being wired shut, and an eight-week recovery. Rose (66), who had liposuction on her neck and eyelid surgery at the same time, related how the eyelid surgery was the physician's suggestion. She recalled, without comment on the inappropriateness of the remark, that the physician said to her, "'Do you want these bags removed or are you packed to go away somewhere?' And he said I'll just do them and I said okay … [But] I didn't go there for that." Rachel (58) recalled how after she had her lower eyelids done and a mid-line facelift, she was persuaded to do more. She recalls thinking:

> Oh god, I'll never do this again and for some reason or another I
> was going back for my follow-up and we started talking about my
> upper eyelids, and [he] and I came to the conclusion: Why half do
> it? You might as well do it. So I went ahead and did it again and I
> couldn't believe it.

Sharon (35) described her visit to an ear, nose and throat specialist, not
for cosmetic purposes, but for some sinus trouble she was having.
However, her first consideration of nose-reshaping surgery came at the
suggestion of the surgeon. As Sharon described:

> I never ever at any point said, "Oh, I'd like to get my nose
> changed." NEVER. And he's the one [who] said, "We can make
> some changes to your nose." I didn't think anything of it. He said
> to give it some thought and I asked him what it would cost and he
> said $700. So I left it at that.

Sharon later elected to have the nose-reshaping surgery at the same
time she was undergoing the sinus surgery. For these women, male
physicians had a strong influence on their decision to have facial
cosmetic surgery.

There is another reason that supports our contention that the conditions for making an independent choice were not met: the amount of
information available to these women to equip them to make an
informed decision. While the medical profession has been actively promoting cosmetic surgical procedures, the women's accounts suggest that
four of the women were hampered by the lack of information available
to them. Lillian (73) said, "Other than what the physicians tell me, I
don't have any other source of information." Three of the women
expressed dismay over the information provided by cosmetic surgeons
as they felt they were not adequately informed as to what to expect
from the surgery. When Tamara (30) was asked whether the results
were what she expected, she said:

> The first little while, no. I almost regretted the surgery for the first
> little while. Actually, that was one of the first things [I thought]
> when I woke up, 'cause you know the doctor assured me that this
> [wouldn't] be so bad and I think that [what] I said when I woke up

was, "You told me that this [wouldn't] be so bad."

Amy (23) described her anger at her physician for failing to inform her of the risks associated with her nose-reshaping surgery:

> I'm just saying when you pay $2,000 and put your trust in some-one who is supposed to be a specialist in the area ... I believe they have a duty to inform you of all the risks — and I wasn't informed my nose could come out larger than what I went in with. He said, at the worst — this is an exact quote — "At worst, your nose will be the same." I knew there was a risk of death with the anaesthetic ... And that is kind of ironic, I ... would have acknowledged the fact that yes, I know I could die, but [not that] my nose [was] going to come out worse. Because he didn't tell me that, that just didn't cross my mind.

Her surgery left her with a nose that is classified as a severe secondary deformity and in order to get it repaired she would have to see a specialist in the United States at a cost of approximately $20,000. Other potential risks of cosmetic surgery include infection, hemorrhaging and blood clots, all of which can cause severe impairment and, in rare cases, even death.[31] It is estimated that 10 percent of cosmetic surgeries entail some unexpected and negative outcomes.[32] The lengthy duration of recovery from the swelling and bruising left most women anxiety-ridden over what the actual results would look like. For four of the ten women interviewed, the anxiety was justified when results required additional cosmetic surgery.

Grace (25) was told by her cosmetic surgeon, "Three things could go wrong with the surgery but I have never experienced any of them. One, you could get an infection; two, you could end up being rushed into emergency; and three, you could need more surgery." All three of these potential risks happened to her. In addition, two other women who participated in this study also had infections and had to be rushed to hospital for emergency care.

For three of the women, aside from their surgeon, their only other source of information for cosmetic surgery was the media. By her own account, Rose (66) was introduced to the idea of having liposuction on her neck from watching a program about liposuction on TV. Two of the women interviewed were led to believe, by relying on media as a source of information, that cosmetic surgery was a "piece of cake." Women's magazines often glorify cosmetic surgery as a means to improve appearance and resist the ravages of time.[33] Among the before and after photographs, there is no trace of a "between" stage, showing bruised faces and bodies, rent with surgical stitches. Rachel (58) described her expectations and experience of cosmetic surgery:

> I felt that there was probably not much to it and I think that was an image I got from listening to other people ... on TV [who] said "Oh, I've had facial surgery" or, "I've had my eyes done and I was back out on the street in two days." And I thought there can't be much to this. NOT TRUE! It took six weeks before I felt that people wouldn't ask me what happened to me.

Likewise, Sharon (35) warned that, "If some of these women saw what they might look like or feel, a lot of them wouldn't get it done. I guarantee it." The lengthy periods of pain and the unintended deformities are absent from pages of photographs in magazines.[34] Reading women's magazines, a woman might learn of possible complications and risks of cosmetic surgery, but not their probability.[35] While some women in our study drew upon media as a source of information, social relationships were not often used since most women did not know anyone who had undergone cosmetic surgery. Rachel (58) said, "The one thing I feel was lacking with me was I didn't talk to anybody who had surgery." Nonetheless, social relationships appeared to have a bearing on these women's decisions to have facial cosmetic surgery.

SOCIAL RELATIONSHIPS

While all the women dismissed the influence of significant others on their decision to have cosmetic surgery, five women's decisions were related to social relationships, particularly family relationships. As mentioned above, Marlene (57) underwent a facelift in order to look different from her mother. Grace (25), who underwent nose-reshaping surgery, explained that she had a cousin who had a large nose. When she was a child, Grace's father often said to her that if her nose turned out like her cousin Kim's, they could get it fixed. Grace said, "He always put this bug in my head that my nose was going to be so hideous.

And so, when I got my surgery he said, 'You definitely don't look like Kim.'"

Lillian (73) explained that the importance she placed on her physical appearance was greatly influenced by her mother, who had invested a lot of time and energy to keep up her own appearance. This maternal modelling of appearance from her early adolescence was something Lillian felt she carried with her throughout her life. She explained her desire for a third facelift as, "Even at age seventy-three, a woman wants to look as good as possible." In her study, Marcene Goodman found that women who developed an appreciation of their merit as females through their appearance carried this value into middle age and late adulthood.[36] Tamara (30) described that both her parents are "very much centred on the way they look" and that she thought she was brought up that way too.

Amy (23) recounted how her peers greatly influenced her decision to have nose-reshaping surgery. She said, "Being under the influence of a lot of superficial people, I thought, well, what can I do to try and perfect the way I look?" She described her friends as "being very Cosmo-type people [and] ostentatious." Amy and her peers felt the pervasiveness of cultural images of beauty and aging.

CULTURAL IMAGES OF BEAUTY AND AGING

The younger women in this study, more readily than the older women, acknowledged the social pressures on women to conform to standards of physical attractiveness. Amy (23) explained:

> What I guess I really wanted to do, why I did the surgery, was you know, you just have to open a magazine and go walking through a mall and you see so much emphasis put on the way people look. And people are very superficial and pretentious. You see men going after the best looking, the smartest … you want to be the best you can be … But I think society really puts more importance on the way you look rather than living … And I think I got sucked into that.

Only two women discussed feeling societal pressures to conform to standards of physical attractiveness for economic reasons. Sharon (35) said, "I've done a lot of reading through some of the classes I've taken and they have always commented on how more attractive people tend to get the more successful jobs and all that kind of thing. And you know what? I wouldn't say that's not true." Even if a woman consciously resigns herself to the fact that she cannot match up to societal standards of beauty, or even if she rejects them outright, the dominant culture still judges her by these cultural images of beauty. The cultural messages of how women should look and act are endlessly disseminated in mass media, thereby endorsing "a value system that preaches bodily perfection and deny [sic] women the right to age."[37]

The women in this study often expressed their reasons for cosmetic surgery in terms of a desire to "look better" rather than a longing to be "beautiful." For Amy (23), "looking better" involved reshaping the tip of her nose to achieve the perfect proportion in order to emphasize all her best features. A number of women noted that their surgery did not change the way they looked; rather, it improved the way they looked. Sharon (35) explained that the surgery "didn't really change the way I looked in the first place. But I would say it improved the way I looked." Lillian (73) said that her facelifts greatly improved the appearance of her face and that a lot of women with "wrinkles" could really improve their appearance by having cosmetic surgery. The women in this study were influenced by cultural images of aging and beauty in such a way that they evaluated themselves — and other women in general — with a critical eye. Their judgements were based on standards stemming from the larger social/cultural context.

The four older participants in this study (age 57 and older) often expressed their motives for cosmetic surgery in terms of dissatisfaction with particular facial parts or features, rather than dissatisfaction with the aging process. As Rachel (58), who underwent eyelid surgery, remarked, "I was really unhappy with these bags under my eyes. I've got lots of other lines and I can live with those, but these, I could not live with the bags." For Marlene (57), who at the time of undergoing a facelift was in therapy dealing with child abuse issues from her past, the bags under her eyes and her facial lines were an outward sign of the agony she was going through, rather than as a result of aging. She knew she would get through the agony part, but she did not want to be left with the evidence of the agony staring her in the face every single day of her life. The older women often referred to how these signs of aging (such as bags under their eyes, wrinkles and lines) made them look ravaged or tired. However, overt references to these characteristics as a sign of aging was not made.

The women's accounts revealed conflicting references to the role of aging. On the one hand, older women did not see cosmetic surgery as an age-concealment technique, citing, for example their non-dyed grey hair as supporting evidence. These women denied trying to defy the aging process and denied masking their chronological age. On the other hand, many women interviewed expressed fears of looking older than their chronological age. The social pressures on women to maintain a "youthful appearance" did not escape these women, even though by their own account, they looked younger than their age-peers (even before their surgery).

The six younger women (ages 23 to 35) often expressed concern over the physical signs of aging. When asked whether she's noticed changes in her appearance over the last few years and how she viewed these changes, Tamara (30) responded:

> I've got wrinkles on my neck now. I never thought I would, but I've noticed I've got wrinkles on my neck and around my eyes ... I don't like them. I don't like them at all. No. I feel that if I could age without them I'd be all the better for it. No, I really don't enjoy these changes at all. I don't see these wrinkles as a sign of wisdom, I see them as wrinkles.

Amy (23) saw her nose-reshaping surgery as a preventive measure since she comes from a family where members' noses grow in size as they age. She explained, "My aunt stayed single most of her life and she had a very, very, very large nose. So, I think I was influenced by that ... I was scared that it was going to get bigger and everything, I guess."

The younger women's concerns about age-related changes suggest that they may resort to having more cosmetic surgery in the future and, by their own accounts, a number confirmed this possibility. Sharon (35), for instance, who had recently seen a dermatologist for age spots, explained that she would not rule out the possibility of having a facelift when she is 50 or 60 and that her decision "depends on how horrible it [her face] looks." The younger women were also more receptive to the idea of having more cosmetic surgery than were the older women. Even Amy (23), whose surgery left her disfigured, explained that she would consider having more surgery in the future. She said, "I know what happened to me was rare. I know there's a lot of good things that come out of surgery."

The inclusion in this study of both younger and older women reveals clear age-group differences in these women's acceptance of aging and their physical appearance: older women generally felt better about aging and their physical appearance than did younger women. The primacy of appearance in the younger women's lives suggests that as the next cohort of elderly women, they will continue to be plagued with concerns over their appearance and the physical signs of aging. Younger women are also likely to resort to having more cosmetic surgery in the future. The more that cosmetic surgery is seen as acceptable, attainable and affordable, the more likely women of all ages will be willing to undergo it.[38] With the aging of the "baby boomers" and the continual increase in the number of women who are electing to have cosmetic surgery, further research exploring the relationship between aging and cosmetic surgery is needed. A longitudinal study would allow us to disentangle age and cohort effects.

As an increasingly greater number of women choose to have cosmetic surgery, more information needs to be available to equip them to make an informed decision. The stories of the women recounted here clearly explicate the urgent need for the dissemination of information and education about the realities of both the positive, and the negative, effects associated with facial cosmetic surgery. Facts about the realities of cosmetic surgury will challenge some women's reverence for it only if the facts speak to and respect women's desires to transform their bodies in their efforts to meet cultural requirements of youth and beauty.

While cosmetic surgery is clearly an individual choice at an individual level, it can be a rational action for women to increase their social power in a patriarchal culture that gives women few avenues to power. However, at the socio-cultural level, cosmetic surgery is disempowering in that women may be seen to be collaborating in the dominant discourses and ideologies that disadvantage them.

Notes

1. Diane Lefebvre, "The Beauty Fix," *Homemakers* (March 1995), 42–51; Deborah Sullivan, "Cosmetic Surgery: Market Dynamics and Medicalization," *Research in the Sociology of Health Care* 10 (1993), 97–115; and the American Society of Plastic and Reconstructive Surgeons, *Statistics* (Arlington Heights, IL: ASPRS, 1994), 1–12.

2. Kathy Davis, *Reshaping the Female Body: The Dilemma of Cosmetic Surgery* (London: Routledge, 1995), 1–38; Marcene Goodman, "Social, Psychological, and Developmental Factors in Women's Receptivity to Cosmetic Surgery," *Journal of Aging Studies* 8 (1994), 375–396; and Marcene Goodman, "Culture, Cohort, and Cosmetic Surgery," *Journal of Women and Aging* 8 (1996), 55–73.

3. Sharon McIrvin Abu-Laban and Susan McDaniel, "Aging Women and Standards of Beauty," in Nancy Mandell ed., *Feminist Issues: Race, Class, and Sexuality* (Toronto: Prentice Hall, 1995), 108.

4. Chris Shilling, *The Body and Social Theory* (London: Sage Publications, 1993), 1.

5. Goodman, "Social, Psychological, and Developmental Factors in Women's Receptivity to Cosmetic Surgery," 376.

6. Davis, *Reshaping the Female Body: The Dilemma of Cosmetic Surgery*, 14; and The Centre for Cosmetic Surgery, "The History of Cosmetic/Plastic Surgery." <http://www.electro-source.com/~centcosm/index.html>. January 25, 1999.

7. Lefebvre, "The Beauty Fix," 48.

8. Davis, *Reshaping the Female Body: The Dilemma of Cosmetic Surgery*, 15–16.

9. Diana Dull and Candace West, "Cosmetic Surgery: The Accomplishment of Gender," *Social Problems* 38 (1991), 34–70.

10. Ibid., 51.

11. Ibid.

12. Irving Zola, "Medicine as an Institution of Social Control," *Sociological Review* 20 (1972), 487–504.

13. Ibid., 494.

14. Thomas Pruzinsky and Milton Edgerton, "Body-Image Change in Cosmetic Plastic Surgery," in Thomas Cash and Thomas Pruzinsky, eds., *Body Images: Development, Deviance, and Change* (New York: The Guilford Press, 1990), 217–233.

15. David Harris, "The Benefits and Hazards of Cosmetic Surgery," *British Journal of Hospital Medicine* 41 (1989), 540–545.

16. Efrat Tseelon, *The Masque of Femininity* (London: Sage Publications, 1995), 84.

17. McIrvin Abu-Laban and McDaniel, "Aging Women and Standards of Beauty," 97–122.

18. Naomi Wolf, *The Beauty Myth* (Toronto: Vintage Books, 1990), 259.

19. Goodman, "Social, Psychological, and Developmental Factors in Women's Receptivity to Cosmetic Surgery," 375–378.

20. C. McKie, "Population Aging: Baby Boomers into the 21st Century.," *Canadian Social Trends* (Summer 1993), 2–6.

21. Susan Bordo, "The Body and the Reproduction of Femininity: A Feminist Appropriation of Foucault," in Alison Jagger and Susan Bordo, eds., *Gender, Body, Knowledge: Feminist Reconstruction of Being and Knowing* (New Brunswick, NJ: Rutgers University Press, 1989), 13–33; Kathryn Pauly Morgan, "Women and the Knife: Cosmetic Surgery and the Colonization of Women's Bodies," *Hypatia* 6 (1991), 25–53; and Wolf, *The Beauty Myth*.

22. Davis, *Reshaping the Female Body: The Dilemma of Cosmetic Surgery*.

23. Bordo, "The Body and the Reproduction of Femininity: A Feminist Appropriation of Foucault," 13–33; Pauly Morgan, "Women and the Knife: Cosmetic Surgery and the Colonization of Women's Bodies," 25–53; and Wolf, *The Beauty Myth*.

24. Davis, *Reshaping the Female Body: The Dilemma of Cosmetic Surgery*, 165.

25. Ibid., 153.

26. Ibid., 180–181.

27. This quote and all following quotes are drawn from interviews that were held during October 1997 and March 1999 in Winnipeg, Manitoba.

28. Mike Featherstone, "The Body in Consumer Culture," in Mike Featherstone, Mike Hepworth, and Bryan Turner, eds., *The Body: Social Process and Cultural Theory* (London: Sage Publications, 1991), 170.

29. Davis, *Reshaping the Female Body: The Dilemma of Cosmetic Surgery*, 104–114.

30. Goodman, "Social, Psychological, and Developmental Factors in Women's Receptivity to Cosmetic Surgery," 380.

31. Jane Hyman, "Who Needs Cosmetic Surgery? Reassessing Our Looks and Our Lives," *Ourselves, Growing Older* (Boston: Boston Women's Health Book Collective, 1987), 37–45.

32. Janine O'Leary Cobb, *Understanding Menopause* (Toronto: Key Porter Books, 1988), 167.

33. Deborah Lupton, *Medicine as Culture: Illness, Disease and the Body in Western Societies*, (London: Sage Publications, 1994), 38.

34. Sullivan, "Cosmetic Surgery: Market Dynamics and Medicalization," 97–115.

35. Wolf, *The Beauty Myth*.

36. Goodman, "Social, Psychological, and Developmental Factors in Women's Receptivity to Cosmetic Surgery," 390.

37. Ibid., 376.

38. Ibid., 392.

CHAPTER SEVEN

POLLUTED BODIES
INUIT IDENTITY AND THE
ARCTIC FOOD CHAIN

Chris Egan

∞

"WE'D BECOME *Qallunaat!*" was a not uncommon response of Inuit women to my question "How would you feel if you were not able to eat Inuit foods anymore?" *Qallunaat* is Inuktitut for "white people." For many Inuit ("the people"), the lack of access to their traditional foods would result in a total loss of identity. If they had to eat Qallunaaq foods, they would become Qallunaat. As expressed in the adage "You are what you eat," there is a tendency in contemporary Inuit society to recognize food as central to a person's sense of identity.[1] For example, traditional food is a marker of identity for Inuit in Clyde River who assert that by choosing to eat hunted animals, their Inuit identity is maintained.[2] Eating Inuit foods contributes to the making of a genuine Inuk (*Inummarik*) — an individual who holds a cumulative knowledge derived from her/his direct contact with the environment.[3]

Originally, I set out to determine Inuit women's views on the potential consequences of a decrease in traditional foods due to contamination. However, when I conducted a pilot study in an Inuit community in northern Québec (Nunavik), I was informed by several Inuit women that they were not particularly concerned about contaminants in the food chain; they had more urgent issues to worry about, namely, drug and alcohol abuse. This information was pivotal in the reformation of the study I subsequently conducted in Nunavut. I decided to focus on how Inuit women understand perceptions of risk in consuming potentially contaminated foods — not only because women are usually responsible for the preparation and distribution of food but because historically, women everywhere have been marginalized in the discussion of environmental concerns.

I wanted to identify Inuit women's specific concerns regarding contaminants and pollution because their interests have not been considered. Previous studies on contaminants have focused on the opinions of hunters and on chemical analyses of their catch. In these studies, assessment of risk is usually assumed to be a gender-neutral practice as it focuses on the scientific identification of probabilities and health hazards, but since risk perception is a social process, it is necessarily gendered. A feminist analysis begins with the understanding that environmental problems, such as contamination of the food chain, derive from the exercise of power and the struggle of vested interest groups. Hence it must address the social, cultural and political institutions that are responsible for any type of environmental distress, including contaminants in the Arctic food chain.[4]

The feminist methodology I used for my project required a close connection with local women and I was fortunate in having these ties already established in a community of 700 Inuit in Nunavut. As is the norm in ethnographic fieldwork, this single community was the main focus of data collection for this case study. I had worked there both as a community health nurse and as a researcher over a period of fourteen years, and felt that I was reasonably well accepted. Indeed, I was told by many women during the research process that if they had not known and trusted me for a number of years, they would not have granted me such lengthy interviews (and I would not have obtained such rich information).

I spoke with forty-seven women, who ranged in ages from eighteen to sixty-three. All were mothers of adopted or natural-born children, or were pregnant at the time of the interview; ten were employed outside the home; fifteen did not speak English. Since my skills in Inuktitut are somewhat limited, I engaged an interpreter I had worked with in the past to translate when necessary. All of the explanations/associations I discuss in this chapter were presented to me by my research participants, but the interpretations are mine.[5] I did not solicit specific answers to my questions, though I have sifted through many hours of transcribed conversations in order to highlight the elements presented here.

A feminist enquiry is an appropriate choice for ethnographic community studies as it emphasizes the experiential and values engagement with all those participating in the research process. Although the ethnographic approach I use allows for a reciprocal relationship between researcher and participant, it is, however, necessarily subjective. Gwen Reimer characterizes Inuit female consciousness as being specifically appropriate to the Inuit cultural context as it refers to "women's recognition and acceptance of the culturally defined gender role they are expected to fulfil."[6] In recognizing Inuit women's lived experience in history and culture, their female consciousness becomes salient; this is demonstrated in their ongoing commitment to act as caretakers in the home and community. It was in listening to their responses to my questions about pollution that I realized that, for Inuit women, identity is integrally tied to the maintenance of uncontaminated Inuit cultural norms and mores.

IDENTITY

Personal identity can be understood as a web characterized by strands of competing tensions, many of which are culturally conditioned, and of overlapping environmental influences, including the physical and the social.[7] Collective or cultural identity is more than the combination of all the personal identities of the individuals who make up the collective, or of the combined aspects of their shared characteristics; its formation often involves a group or community struggle. Among the Inuit, it seems that a symbiotic relationship develops between the individual's identity and that of the collective as each is affected by the other in a reciprocal process. In contrast, the individualization of the body in Canadian popular culture is usually seen as an expression of personal identity, rather than of ethnic identity. However, the body as "garment," the outer layer, conceals as much as it reveals. For the Inuit, it is not merely the surface of the individual body that symbolizes the self, it is from the very depths of their all-encompassing beings that they instinctively and unquestioningly know who they are. (I avoid using the dichotomous terms "mind and body" or "body and spirit" so that a hierarchy is not suggested.) They are Inuit — "the people." If they became Qallunaat, they would be reconstructed into another form. It would be a human form, but one accompanied by a dreadful loss — that of the former self.

During her many years of association with the Inuit, anthropologist Jean Briggs learned that when cultural traits (such as hunting, preparing skins, eating Inuit food) are threatened, they are accorded emblematic status.[8] For the Inuit, their traditional food is heavily invested with symbolism — it is associated with love and the sharing of food with family and friends. When their food is not available, Inuit crave the food that symbolizes affection. Like their traditional foods, other visible Inuit traits such as the sewing of skins become emblems or markers of Inuit identity and serve to strengthen their "sense of ethnic rootedness."[9] It is important also that these emblems, which arise out of emotionally charged personal experience, are visible to and recognized by Qallunaat. Some emblems may be used differently by different members in Inuit society, but food appears to be a consistent and significant emblem of identity.

ARCTIC POLLUTION

For some years now it has been known that harmful environmental substances, including organochlorines such as PCBs (polychlorinated biphenyls) and heavy metals like mercury, have been carried to the Arctic by the atmosphere and ocean currents from distant areas around the globe. These pollutants are deposited in the land, air and bodies of water in the Arctic where they are ingested by benthic organisms, biomagnified up the food chain and finally consumed by humans.[10] Benthic organisms are the plants and animal forms found at the bottom of the sea. Known as the benthic zone, the sea bottom has been used as a dumping ground for radioactive materials and sewage with heavy metal content.[11]

My concern about the contamination or pollution of Inuit food stemmed from accounts in the literature portraying sociocultural disruptions in Northern communities subsequent to various types of environmental contamination.[12] For example, in areas affected by mercury-contaminated rivers, radioactive fallout or oil-slicked beaches and oceans, it was evident that more than the immediate physical environment became polluted; pollution of the social body of the community also occurred. As a result, women's and men's work was affected when a dramatic decrease in traditional hunting and fishing pursuits occurred. In addition to the loss of the actual foods and the pride of being able to feed one's family, important sociocultural elements, such as the camaraderie of the hunt (for men) and the sharing of the fruits of the hunt (women's task), were also lost. In these cases, women continued to be immersed in childcare and household responsibilities, but some men with empty time on their hands instigated family violence, and drug and alcohol problems escalated. Women became victims of abuse from their jobless men and, in addition, suffered from feelings of uselessness and of becoming burdens on the already stressed resources of the community. How could a woman find a substitute for such activities as the drying of fish or the preparation of animal skins — skills that no longer belonged to her? With what could she now identify? Many hardships were endured, and one would hope that lessons could be learned from such situations.

For example, if significant quantities of contaminants are found in the Canadian Arctic, and traditional subsistence activities of the Inuit are no longer possible, I believe that both anticipation and recognition of potential problems in a timely manner can help alleviate stress and allow any issues to be dealt with before they become intractable. Hence, I asked Inuit women what aspects of hunting activities they would miss the most if they experienced a similar situation. I expected to be told that they would miss the social aspects of communal hunting and the traditional sharing of food (which, to some extent, they did). However, their answers were more profound than I anticipated — many told me that they simply would not survive.

The Inuit still depend on the land and sea for about 50 percent of all food they consume.[13] If they were unable to access their traditional foods from the sea, they would experience great loss. Some of the women told me that "a lot of bad things would happen," or "maybe I wouldn't be normal any more," or " we would die right away," and "I wouldn't have any more strength." Several women in their thirties expressed it this way:

> We would be very sick — our bodies are so used to eating it. When my kids haven't had native food for a while they start craving for it and ask when are we going to have some.

> I would feel very sad. I have to have Inuit food every second day or else I seem to be craving for something. Even if I have Qallunaq food, I feel I don't want anything if I can't have Inuit food. When I'm in the South I find something similar, like pork ends, or spareribs that have fat on them.

> I would feel terrible. I don't think I would last long — too used to eating it. There would be hundreds of crazy Inuit running around looking for cached food. The hunters would get bored. We crave Inuit foods worse than wanting a cigarette.

If it were necessary to substitute Qallunaaq food for Inuit food, the very essence of Inuit existence would be diluted. After eating Inuit food, people tell me that they feel warm and full (and I must admit to feeling the same when I eat seal and walrus), because the blood of the animal is consumed along with the meat and fat. However, when Qallunaaq food is eaten, Inuit feel cold and are soon hungry again. For them, store-bought Qallunaaq food has no association with family or affection, and, in addition, it violates the important Inuit value of sharing food.[14]

Much respect is accorded to the animals who offer themselves as food and clothing for the Inuit, and, most importantly, these animals have souls which are then incorporated into the Inuit themselves. For some groups of Inuit, all metaphysical entities (known as *inue* or indwellers) such as rocks and snow are respected because, although they do not possess souls, they are manifestations of the vitality of nature.[15] Indwellers are, in fact, "the powers that constitute nature."[16] To the Inuit, all nature is to be revered and should be protected from any kind of contamination or pollution.

PERCEPTIONS OF POLLUTION

I asked women what the word "pollution" meant to them and they described it in various terms, both in English and in Inuktitut. Women

said that pollution "is like smog"; "is like something you're not supposed to have — like drugs"; "is mostly sewage that's dumped on the
ground"; that "drugs and alcohol are pollution for the body"; and
that "taking drugs is like pollution of the brain." Many Inuit women
described pollution as an invasion (in various forms) from the
outside. This is close to the concept of contamination or pollution
characterized by the anthropologist Mary Douglas, who discusses
pollution as a state of disorder in a naturally ordered universe.[17]

The Inuit cultural community boundary was crossed when outsiders brought in such pollutants as alcohol (*immialuk*, literally "fire-
water"), drugs (*aangajaarnaqtuq*, something that makes you high),
tobacco (*supuuqtugaq*, something to smoke) and, more recently,
PCBs. It is interesting that two terms used to describe non-specific
contaminants (explained as possibly representing PCBs) were
sourunatuq, meaning "wants your body," and *nungoojuituq*, meaning
"something like the atomic bomb that will not go away." Members
from within the community often regard these pollutants as potential
threats to their usual activities of daily living. To many, it seems that
the strength of their society's boundaries are being tested. Their
cultural borders' resistance to the invasion of unwanted pollutants is
beng challenged. Endurance of age-old beliefs and customs, as well as
the very survival of the Inuit, then comes into question.

I examined various philosophical and theoretical paradigms that
might help articulate these various interpretations of pollution. For
example, ecofeminism develops connections between feminism and
ecology, but some see it as being essentialist in nature, and I, among
others, regard it as somewhat utopian.[18] The notion of the body, too,
could be deemed essentialist, but I see it as having great metaphoric
flexibility. By linking somatic concepts with those of pollution —
starting with the individual body, expanding to the social body and
extending to the body politic — we witness the influence of a host of
factors. For example, a few Inuit women told me that their fears
concerning health risks to individual bodies were associated with pollution problems highlighted by the media. One such problem is the
proximity of their communities to the abandoned generators of the
stations and army bases along the old DEW (Distant Early Warning)
line.[19] The DEW line was constructed along the 55th parallel after the

Second World War to protect North America from Soviet attack by providing an impenetrable radar shield.[20]

Although the media does report on Arctic pollution, not all women are aware of these reports. For example, in the 1980s, Inuit women in a community on Baffin Island who consumed large amounts of fatty sea mammals were found to have high levels of PCBs in their blood. The potential of these women transferring PCBs to their fetuses and to their infants during lactation was high.[21] PCBs are lipophilatic, that is, they accumulate in the fatty tissues and organs of animals, particularly in sea mammals such as seal, narwhal and walrus. The meat, blubber and organs of these animals are consumed by Inuit. These findings were shown on television and were published in Northern and Southern newspapers. Although many women with whom I spoke had heard the word PCBs, no one knew what PCBs really were.

The women occasionally suggested that unexplained and unexpected illnesses of the recent past could be possibly related to pollutants, even though they admitted to being unfamiliar with PCBs or, indeed, with any types of invisible contaminants. They did not doubt the scientists in detecting some types of contaminants in the animals; however, many women told me that until they actually saw people fall ill or die because of eating food that was proven to be contaminated, they could not accept that their traditional foods would harm them. One fifty-year-old woman told me:

> I've not heard of contaminants in food around here. I would believe scientists, but I know better. I have lived on the land longer and I know what it's like and of any changes. Pollution is dangerous for your body. We know if animals are sick, we don't eat them.

The Inuit, as a people, have been hunting these animals for thousands of years and they feel secure in their own judgement regarding the safety of their consumption. Inuit recognize if an animal should not be eaten, for example, if it were skinny or if the fat had a strange odour or colour. Inuit feel that they are not to blame for the contamination of Arctic animals, they have committed no offense that would render Arctic animals unfit for consumption; however, they are not closed-minded to other ways of knowing (such as western science), particularly ways that could be used to conserve all components of

Inuit identity. When asked, Inuit women suggested that the Canadian and US army, the Canadian government, Russia or simply "the South" were responsible for pollutants invading the Arctic food chain.

The question of whom to blame for the occurrence of unexpected disasters is approached differently by various peoples. For example, some explain misfortune by attributing it to the work of individual adversaries, but community members do not arbitrarily decide on a particular pattern of blaming; blaming becomes culturally acceptable.[22] The Inuit are well aware of taking responsibility themselves for mistakes they have committed and for the amending of wrongdoings. There is an Inuit folktale that echoes biblical warnings of the withdrawal of blessings when transgressions have been committed in society. All of the women I interviewed claimed to follow the Christian religion. In Deuteronomy, it is stated that when (social) order is created, women are made fertile and food becomes plentiful. However, in the chaos of disorder, the fruits of the body as well as the hunting grounds are cursed. Sedna (also known as *nuliajuq*) is the prominent Inuit goddess (or indweller) of the sea who controls access to food. When social order is maintained and people (Inuit) are conforming to the proper ideals, Sedna wears her hair in neat braids and provides food in the form of sea animals for the Inuit to hunt and consume. However, if anyone engages in improper behaviour, Sedna's hair becomes entangled in the rough waters she creates, and food is withheld from the whole community. Only when the transgressor publicly repents is order restored.[23]

This parable-like account may seem to have an orientation whereby social order is fundamental to sociocultural norms. Sociocultural beliefs regarding pollution may be seen as coercive in that they help maintain social solidarity and the concept of shared values. Anachronistic explanations usually ignore social change whereas traditional beliefs and folktales such as the Sedna story continue in their influence and relevance to a community coping with constant, and in some cases, escalating change. It is also noteworthy that even though the roles of women in Inuit society are changing, there is still a recognizable continuity of the female role as "keeper of the camp."[24]

IMAGES OF THE BODY

Concepts such as the authority of an individual mythical body, for example Sedna, or of bodies of agents representing authority, were not in the specific narratives of the women with whom I spoke. And, although I did not consciously look for bodily metaphors during the research process, they became apparent to me during the analysis phase because, as aptly depicted by Emily Martin, women's bodily processes go with them everywhere, forcing women to "juxtapose biology and culture [and] glimpse every day a conception of another sort of social order."[25] For many years, images of the body have been an important area of analysis in health research and the social sciences. For example, in 1978 Mary Douglas talks about the western concept of two bodies: the physical (individual) body and the social body that constrains and modifies it; it is the tension between the individual and social bodies that allows for an elaboration of meanings. Margaret Lock, however, asserts that the body is "no longer portrayed simply as a template for social organization" and that mind/body dualities are collapsed and dialectical interpretations are now privileged.[26] Elizabeth Grosz insists that human bodies cannot be understood as either ahistorical or as natural objects in any simple way because they are "not only inscribed, marked, [and] engraved by social pressures external to them, but they are the products, the direct effects, of the very social constitution of nature itself."[27] The body is thus not merely a physical representation but is also produced by historical and social factors.

Douglas also identifies four distinct social systems of natural symbols in which the body image is used to reflect and enhance each individual's experience of society.[28] These four bodies are present in the understanding of pollution in Inuit society. The first is a social/political body — that of communication, which emanates from the head down to ancillary parts of society. I recognize a similar system in the Inuit situation where it is apparent that there are unclear lines of commucation between the scientists involved in contaminant research, the media reporting their own interpretations and those Inuit who may be affected by their findings.

The next system characterizes the body as a vehicle of life: the body is seen as being permeable or vulnerable, as it may fail to control the quality of matter it absorbs through its orifices. Douglas elaborates by explaining that "sometimes bodily orifices seem to represent points of entry or exit to social units."[29] In Inuit culture this poses a threat to the boundaries of the physical body because various types of pollutants may be absorbed or consumed.

In the third system, the body rejects wastes and controls physiological processes, including addictive behaviours. This can be likened to the interpretation of pollution as "being stoned" (ujarasimajuq). Women told me they felt that they were losing their children to drugs and that these young people were becoming strangers to their families — they were losing their identities.

In the fourth system, the body can be seen as a symbol of evil. This form represents an unworkable system of society and embodies the corruption of power and organization. Interestingly, some women told me that they suspected that contaminants could have been deliberately placed in Arctic animals so that Inuit would be compelled to buy food from the store. This would benefit local shopkeepers and Southern suppliers; such collaboration could be, I was told, government-inspired. Inuit would then become weakened and diseased. The threat of disease is a threat of disorder, "metaphorically, literally, socially and politically."[30] And disorder, Douglas reminds us, represents a state of pollution.

For many years the Inuit have lived harmoniously and co-operatively without interference. They have never transferred their individual or collective rights to the state and a consensus government structure has been established in the Northwest Territories. This political body helps provide a framework for the real human bodies within its geographical boundary, a boundary which changed with the establishment of Nunavut in 1999. Such a durable cultural boundary will enhance resistence to invasion from the outside.

In this chapter I have presented Inuit women's perceptions of pollution based on the explanations they presented to me, that is, in a three-part somatized form: 1) the individual or personal body is phenomenally experienced, insomuch as it is palpable to the senses; 2) the social body is seen as a natural symbol for expressing relations and relationships; and 3) the body politic is one artificially contrived in order to control the first two bodies.[31] Individual bodies in the North are being contaminated by drugs and alcohol (and possibly, through their traditional foods); Inuit families are losing younger members to illicit substances; and, to many, the body politic appears impotent (or in a state of disorder). However, we should also acknowledge that the body's characteristics are potentially open to reconstruction.[32]

Inuit women shared with me their own explanations of body and identity and, although the analysis is mine, I have strived to report accurately and emphasize sufficiently the potential loss of identity that could occur in Inuit society through environmental pollution. Paradoxically, one woman told me that compared to Inuit, who monitor their food from the kill to the kitchen, Qallunaat are more at risk of pollution because their food goes through many machines and is touched by so many people, and chemicals are added to the food. An elder said, "Pollution in the world, I think, is made by Qallunaat." Because culture is rooted in nature,[33] any loss of nature converts into loss of culture and identity. The Inuit women with whom I spoke understand this concept well, and are anxious to retain their identity as "the people."

Notes

1. C. Shilling, *The Body and Social Theory* (Thousand Oaks, CA: Sage, 1993).

2. K. Borré, "Seal Blood, Inuit Blood and Diet: A Biocultural Model of Physiology and Cultural Identity," *Medical Anthropology Quarterly* 4 (1991), 47–62.

3. J. O'Neil, B. Elias and A. Yassi, "Poisoned Food: Cultural Resistance to the Contaminants Discourse in Nunavik," *Arctic Anthropology* 34 (1997), 29–40.

4. J. Seager, *Earth Follies: Coming to Feminist Terms with the Growing Environmental Crisis* (New York: Routledge, 1993).

5. The quotations from the women throughout this chapter are taken from my interviews with them.

6. G. Reimer, "Female Consciousness: An Interpretation of Interviews with Inuit Women," *Études/Inuit Studies* 20 (1996), 79.

7. M. Griffiths, *Feminisms and the Self: The Web of Identity* (New York: Routledge, 1995).

8. Jean Briggs distinguishes between *trait* and *emblem*: an emblem is born when the symbolic loading is conscious and paramount in determining our use of the act or

artifact. "From Trait to Emblem and Back: Living and Representing Culture in Everyday Identity," *Arctic Anthropology* 34 (1997).

9. Ibid., 229.

10. E. Dewailly, P. Ayotte, S. Bruneau, C. Liliberté, D. Muir, and R. Nordstrom, "Inuit Exposure to Organochlorines through the Aquatic Food Chain in Arctic Québec," *Environmental Health Perspectives* 101 (1993), 618–620.

11. G. Jones, A. Robertson, J. Forbes, and G. Hollier, *Environmental Science* (Glasgow: Collins, 1990).

12. See H. Beach, "Perceptions of Risk, Dilemmas of Policy: Nuclear Fallout in Swedish Lapland," *Social Science Medicine* 30 (1990), 729–738; S. Miller, "In a Faraway State," *Environmental Science Technology* 24 (1990), 1286–1289; J. Kidd, "Mercury Alert: Grassy Narrows and Whitedog Anti-Mercury Campaign," *The Archivist* 20 (1993), 26–29; and L. Palinkas, M. Downs, J. Petterson, and J. Russell, "Social, Cultural and Psychological Impacts of the Exxon Valdez Oil Spill," *Human Organization* 52 (1993), 1–2.

13. Chris Egan, "Nutritional and Sociocultural Advantages of Consuming Traditional Foods in an Innuit Community" (master's thesis, McMaster University, Hamilton, Ontario, 1990).

14. Briggs, "From Trait to Emblem and Back."

15. K. Birket-Smith, *The Eskimos*, 2nd ed. (London: Methuen, 1959).

16. D. Merkur, *Powers Which We Do Not Know: The Gods and Spirits of the Inuit* (Moscow, ID: University of Idaho Press, 1991), 29.

17. Mary Douglas, *Purity and Danger: An Analysis of the Concepts of Pollution and Taboo* (London: Routledge and Kegan Paul, 1979).

18. See, for example, Y. King, "The Ecology of Feminism and the Feminism of Ecology," in J. Plant, ed., *Healing the Wounds* (London: Merlin, 1989), 18–28.

19. T. Phillips, "Fire Near PCB Shacks Sparks Fears," *Nunatsiaq News*, 9 June 1995, 4.

20. K. Coates, *Canada's Colonies: A History of the Yukon and Northwest Territories* (Toronto: Lorimer, 1985); and D. Purich, *The Inuit and Their Land: The Story of Nunavut* (Toronto: Lorimer, 1992).

21. H. Kuhnlein and D. Kinloch, "PCBs and Nutrients in Baffin Island Inuit Food," *Arctic Medical Research* 47, Supplement 1 (1988), 155–158.

22. Mary Douglas, *Risk and Blame* (London: Routledge, 1994).

23. Merkur, *Powers Which We Do Not Know.*

24. Reimer, "Female Consciousness," 77.

25. E. Martin, *The Woman in the Body* (Boston: Beacon Press, 1987), 200.

26. M. Lock, "Cultivating the Body: Anthropology and Epistemologies of Bodily Practice and Knowledge," *Annual Review of Anthropology* 22 (1993), 136.

27. E. Grosz, *Volatile Bodies: Toward a Corporeal Feminism* (Bloomington: Indiana University Press, 1994).

28. Mary Douglas, *Natural Symbols* (Harmondsworth: Penguin, 1978).

29. Ibid.

30. B. Turner, *The Body and Society: Explorations in Social Theory* (Oxford: Blackwell, 1984), 114.

31. N. Scheper-Hughes and M. Lock, "The Mindful Body: A Prolegomenon to Future Work in Medical Anthropology," *Medical Anthropology Quarterly* 17 (1987), 137–140.

32. Shilling, *The Body and Social Theory.*

33. Scheper-Hughes and Lock, "The Mindful Body."

CHAPTER 8

WITNESS
TESTAMENT OF A JOURNEY

Addena Sumter-Freitag

∽

I JUST DON'T UNDERSTAND

How come Santa Claus
Is only brown at *my* church?
And Carolyn tells me
We can't be Angels
Or Saints.
How come "Flesh-Coloured" is kinda Whitey-Beige?
And so is "Skin-toned"!
Some how that don't seem right.
It's like being in a "Black mood" means stormy or hostile.
Most Blacks I know
Are kinda fancy-free.
What's with "Black Comedy"
When all the actors aren't!
It's kinda really "whack" ya know
And very ...
Tiresome.

I WAS CHEATED

I'm not blaming
I'm identifying ...

I was cheated
Of the very best parts

Wounded
      And broken
            In fragments

And scattered
      And shattered ...
            And tattered ...

I ache
So deep

You took my song
You took my dance

I ache
So deep

They're missing
      My roots ...
            My essence ...

Forever dishonoured

How crazy
I'm mute
Yet

I'm screaming
      Can't you hear me?
            Can't you see me?

You say I'm so "visible."

I was robbed!
Call a cop
Put out an APB

'Cause 'alla' me is missin'!

Look
You left me naked
      And cold ...
            And migrant ...

Let me in!
Let me out!
See me!

These soft hands ...
      These full lips ...
            These Brown breasts ...

See me!
Tell me
I'm beautiful.

DIS'ED

When I rise above it, it's easier to see it all clearly.
I was "dis'ed" you know ...

Disinherited, disrespected, discriminated
And disregarded.
It left me disillusioned, disgusted
And disenchanted.

Honest to God
It was many, many years
Before I realized
You'd snatched my name away!

You'd already taken my language
From my mouth
And my rhthym
From my bones.

I miss my name!
So many times it's been replaced:
Bitch,
Nag,
N-e-g-r-o
"Person of Colour" ...

I've kept all of my anger
Locked away
In a little box,
Locked away
In here
So you couldn't see.

When I rise above it
It's easy to see it all clearly:
I have been dis'ed.

COLOURS

When she came home from her first day
At her job at the Steam Bath
My mother told us
> *They die their 'Floozies'!*
Shocking!
Terrifying.
> *Wouldn't the dye seep into their privates?*
Was my first thought on the matter
And then I tossed the thoughts out of my memory.

Years later,
In gym class
I learned first hand their hair was different ...
Brown
Black
Blonde
And even Red!
It looked silky soft
Both top and bottom!

And I'd "brush" quickly by them
Dress in the corner,
And cover my wiry "bush" in shame.

SELF-ESTEEM

Hey! What am I doing here
Holding on
to "this bag of self esteem stuff"?
Ain't nothin' wrong with me!
Fix the media!
Fix your sons!
Ain't nothin' wrong with me.

Hey!
Holdin' on to "this bag" must of give me some "muscle"
        'Cause I'm feelin' strong now
And I want my stuff back!
Yah, I know I gave it away
But I want it back now,
'Cause I know "right where" to put it!

I'm gonna lay it all out right here
So I can pick and choose
            ... a little of this
And an little of that ...
            O-oooooh! And a li ....
Here ...
You hold on to this "bag"!

Never

We have never known enough happiness
Never.
>I'm talkin' about the
>Black woman
>The wise woman
>Strong woman
>The lesbian woman
>The straight woman
>The weak woman
>The meek woman,

Never.

We have never known enough happiness,
>Joy
>Strokin'
>And soothin'
>And movin'
>And groovin'
>And writhing,
>Whoo-ooo-in'
>And takin' ya higher!

Never.

And you
Have never *really* known *us*
    Never had the privilege
    Of bein' real familiar
    And we were there
    For you to hold
    And touch
    And taste ...
    Inside
    And out
    We were there
    Raisin' you higher!
And you never really knew ...
You never.

BUBBLE GUM DOUCHES

It's bubble gum douches
'Cause ya gotta conform.
Can't smell of sweat
And lust
And the uniqueness of me,
Hot
And wet
And *wild* ...
Me.

Gotta don the Secret
Spray the Massingil
Stick my fingers down my throat
(keep those chips and gravy "offa' my hips")!

Thank *God* for these "big lips" I used to hate ...
Now they're "the rage" of white girls:
Big
"Pouty"
"Negro" lips.
(but they still got flat asses) ...
Honest to "gawd"
It's "silicone above the waist only"
That's the rule.

Below the waist,
It's "bubble gum douches"
"Wax"
"Neat"
And "sugar."
Wispy
Curly
Kinky
Shimmery
Pubic hair
Ain't sexy in anyone else's eyes
'Cept mine I guess.

In anyone's eyes 'cept mine.

INHERITANCE: INNER POWER

I own the moon
And the stars
The trees and the grass
The fire
And the rain.
I own my dreams
And my fears
And my hopes ...
And yah,
I own my pain.

I own my fate
And circumstance
And "Lady Luck" ... she's in my pocket
"Good Fortune," *watch my back*
So I can stride out in this world
With wisdom in my eyes
And laughter on my lips
And "pudge" around my waist
And "meat" upon my hips
'Cause ...

I own my body

I like it!
Like my mind, it is a precious gift
From "Spirit"... from "Universe,"
And yah,
Yah, I own it!

NATIONAL ANTHEM

It would seem you have succeeded
Your system of oppression has been
Internalized
In the minds of the people
So I live in a mental apartheid
In this ghetto of mine

In this ghetto of sexual
And ethnic politics
Where some people count more than others
That is the rule of this land
I have to deal with that

There is still a war raging here
And your armies came
And took away our defenses
Claiming your laws would protect us
Your laws
That condemn the physical assault
But allow you to beat the spirit to death

That is what haunts you
The spirits of the mothers
And fathers
And babies
That you brutally murdered

Snuffed out
And ordered my silence
Of your war crimes
With threats of exile
Rejection

I have to deal with that
So I take up the one weapon
You overlooked
My pen
And I write you
That you cannot reject me

I secede.

MEET ME AT THE AIRPORT

Island soul!
Salt fish and Akee
  To wash that Mc'donald's
  And Can-ay-dee-ian Food
  Ottah your mou-th.

    Let's see you got-an-nee rhythm left!

Girl! Don't you go 'tendin' y'all-fan-cee
'Cause you from Can-ah-da now.

    You still 'nappy-headed'

Had a 'Pickney'
Out of wedlock,

    And screwed ah-round
    And 'screwed up'

Like the rest of us

    Lookin' for 'Mr. Rye-ht'

Get your big-foot ashy-legged self

Move that round onion ovah here!

Give you' cousin a b-i-g kiss!

Yah girl, give you' cousins a big kiss!

Ah-hhh!!
I miss the Blackness
And the Browness
And the Blueness
All around me
Breathin'
Rhythm
And music
And laughter
Loud
Unabashed
Reggae music
Island music
To soothe my soul ...
Home.

© 1997 Addena Sumter-Freitag

PART II

OBJECTIFIED

BODIES

∽

CHAPTER NINE

REVISIONING THE BODY/MIND FROM AN EASTERN PERSPECTIVE

COMMENTS ON EXPERIENCE, EMBODIMENT AND PEDAGOGY

Roxana Ng

૭

NORTH AMERICAN SOCIETIES have become increasingly preoccupied with body size and shape. This has given rise to an industry based on dieting and body image, including health and fitness as a way of achieving the "ideal" body. Ironically, the so-called "fitness" industry is more oriented towards an ideal constructed by the media and the fashion industry of what women's (and men's) bodies should look like, rather than towards validating the diversity of bodies and experiences, and promoting health *per se*.

In this chapter, I share with the reader how I came to (re)discover the healing tradition of Traditional Chinese Medicine (TCM for short), which has helped me to reconceptualize body and health. This new understanding may help us to revision and reclaim women's bodies from an image that has been shaped by commercial interests of what constitutes fitness and health. I begin with my personal journey of regaining balance in my life, which transformed my teaching and raised questions about the foundation of western education. This education is premised on the separation between the mind (read intellect) and the body/spirit, and the superiority of the former over the latter. I then describe how I incorporate the insights and practice I gleaned from TCM into one of my courses in an education faculty. I end by describing a workshop I conducted in a feminist setting to show how TCM, although originating from a patriarchal society, may have utility for a feminist revisioning of women's bodies.

"The Personal is Political"

This well-used feminist phrase aptly describes the story I want to tell here. My chronic and non-specific health problems began around 1979 when I started my doctoral program after an intense and exciting period of activism in the women's movement and immigrant community in Vancouver.[1] One of my main goals in returning to school was to learn and develop a feminist sociology that would speak to women's experience and develop "immigrant women" as a legitimate field of scholarly inquiry.[2]

In the ensuing years, I threw myself relentlessly into my academic work, while participating in organizing activities with immigrant women, first in Toronto where I studied, then across the country as my academic jobs (many on a sessional basis) took me to Saskatoon, Kingston, Fredericton and eventually back to Toronto. I began to develop physical symptoms of stress, which at first manifested as frequent colds and flus, skin rashes and stomach cramps that came and went, but which culminated in several health crises such as pancreatitis by the mid-1980s and chronic fatigue in the late 1980s.

Although these conditions were serious to me (as I felt so ill at times that I could not work), they were never specific enough to warrant serious western allopathic interventions.[3] In fact, a fundamental weakness with drug-based allopathic medicine is its inability to successfully treat chronic non-specific, as well as degenerative, diseases. Since most of my ailments were unresponsive to allopathic treatments, I began to explore alternative medicines around 1980, at first mainly body work such as massage and shiatsu, and then homeopathy, with better results than those I experienced in my encounters with orthodox western medicine (allopathy).

In my heart, gut and mind, I knew that much of my ill health was the direct result of not only my academic work, but of my activism in the feminist movement. I joined other women of colour in anti-racism activities directed at the women's movement and at other hierarchical structures that marginalize and exclude us. It was (and still is) impossible for me to confine my work to either one of these spheres, because my scholarship is based thoroughly on, and inspired by, my activism. Indeed, my intellectual work is premised on the "standpoint of women,"[4] which posits the knower as an actor/activist fully located in the everyday world. Meanwhile, the relationship between our so-called public and private lives was and is not a subject for intellectual inquiry. Ironically, in spite of feminism's insistence that "the personal is political," we have yet to develop a language to speak of how our bodies embody our political and intellectual struggles.[5] Our preoccupation with our various activities that constitute the women's movement and feminist scholarship has prevented us from doing so. This bifurcation points to how fundamentally we have been influenced by Cartesian thinking — which posits a separation between the body and the mind,[6] and the privileging of mental over manual labour.[7]

For almost fifteen years, my professional and political work and my personal explorations on health and illness occurred in two separate and non-intersecting spheres. The success or continuation of the former depended on the latter; yet the latter remained submerged and unspeakable in a public forum.

In 1991, I had the opportunity to teach a course entitled "Health, Illness and Knowledge of the Body: Education and Self-Learning Processes" (hereafter referred to as "Health and the Body" — the course is now called "Health, Healing and Knowledge of the Body"). My colleague, who had initiated the course, moved into another field of study, thereby creating an opening for me to teach the course. This opportunity coincided with yet another personal and health crisis in my life. The only thing my allopathic physician could offer was a diagnosis of depression (much better than "it's all in your head"), a lot of sympathy and advice for psychotherapy. She was unable to treat the immobilizing fatigue I was experiencing. In addition to the therapies (Swedish massage, shiatsu, chiropractic and homeopathy) that I had integrated into my health regime, I turned to and (re)discovered Chinese medicine (since the other treatments offered temporary relief but produced little sustained effect). My experience with Chinese medicine was dramatic: within a week I regained much of my energy and in spite of physical weakness, I was able to function more or less normally. To understand my experience of TCM, I began to read about its principles and treatment modalities. As my interest in it grew, I took workshops and wrote literature reviews on TCM theories and research. My increasing knowledge gave me the confidence to incorporate TCM into my course on "Health and the Body." At last, here was an opening for me to bring the two seemingly unconnected spheres of my life together.

I use the word (re)discovered because, having grown up in the British colony of Hong Kong, TCM was not completely alien to me. There, as children, we were given herbal teas and soups in certain seasons; we learned to describe our bodies in terms of climatic conditions. We used terms such as hot, cold and damp to describe internal bodily states. However, these were considered our linguistic expressions. Allopathy was the dominant medical system in the colony and my paternal grandmother was an allopathic physician who firmly believed in the superiority of science. As a result of these influences, I did not realize that TCM was a rational healing system developed and refined in China over five thousand years ago. By "rational" I mean that it is a systematic medicine whose logic, diagnostic procedures and treatment modalities are internally coherent and consistent — albeit radically different from western notions of diseases and treatments. It is not *merely* a "folk" medicine — a derogatory term invented by anthropologists to describe the healing systems of other cultures. Like Ayurveda medicine, it is a systematic, rational medicine that is based in a formal scholarly tradition, in this case Taoism.[8]

In the ensuing months, I went through an intensive regime of TCM treatments consisting primarily of herbal therapy, acupuncture and later of exercises such as T'ai Chi Ch'uen (or Tai Ji Juan) and Qi Gong. I also began to read about the philosophical and theoretical foundation of TCM.[9] In this healing process I recovered a lot of the so-called "folk" knowledge that I had acquired growing up in the East, but that had been buried in my consciousness as I immersed myself in western educational systems. Through feminism and anti-racism, I discovered the colonizing effects of Eurocentric, male-stream thoughts.[10] I discovered through my body as my health improved over the next several years, the extent to which these thoughts have shaped the bifurcation of my consciousness. This journey, which is ongoing, has led to a profound psychic, philosophical and political shift that has ultimately reshaped the way I work, teach and relate to others — in short, it has transformed my life.

So, when I was developing the course on "Health and the Body," I intentionally juxtaposed TCM and allopathy. This method provided an opportunity to disrupt mainstream and male-stream knowledge in a way different than the standard scholarly pedagogical methods, which are based simply on the honing of intellectual and analytical skills. Studying TCM made me more fully appreciate the disembodiment of scientific knowledge and how feminist and post-colonial scholarship participate in the privileging of the mind over the body. TCM's philosophy of the unity of mind and body allowed me to explore ways of re-embodying the knower as subject in scholarly pursuit.

In the next section, I will describe briefly the premise, structure and content of "Health and the Body," drawing particular attention to how eastern philosophy, notably TCM, provides a way of knowledge construction and theory making that does not negate our bodily existence.

HEALTH, HEALING AND THE BODY

I designed "Health, Healing and Knowledge of the Body" as a course to disrupt western academic knowledge that privileges intellectual and critical thinking over other forms of knowledge construction. I did this in three ways: 1) by using course materials (readings, video and audio materials) with an emphasis on TCM. The purpose was to raise questions about prevailing assumptions in biomedicine and expose students to other healing systems; 2) by incorporating Qi Gong, a form of Chinese meditative and breathing exercises compatible with TCM, into the class; and 3) by using a reading notebook and health journal as key ingredients in the reflective and self-learning process. Since it is not possible to describe the course in detail, I will only highlight those elements in TCM and Qi Gong that pertain to my discussion in revisioning the body.

COURSE MATERIALS

To disrupt students' taken-for-granted assumptions about health (based on allopathy and the medical scientific view of the body), I introduce materials on health systems and healing practices from a variety of cultures, including those within western societies.[11] It is always surprising to me how little students know about other forms of healing practices outside of allopathy, even within western societies, such as osteopathy. For example, they are amazed to find that faith healing, like Christian Science, is a form of western healing practice. For many, these readings are a startling revelation. We also take a cursory look at healing systems in other cultures.[12] To avoid superficiality and what I call a "boutique approach" to the study of other healing systems, a great deal of time is devoted to an examination of Traditional Chinese Medicine (TCM). This approach gives students a deeper appreciation of the conceptual difference of the body from the perspective of a drastically different healing system through readings and through physical exercises known as Qi Gong (discussed below).

TCM is based on the central Taoist principle of unity of opposites — Yin and Yang. According to Chinese creation mythology, the universe was an undifferentiated whole in the beginning. Out of this emerged Yin-Yang: the world in its infinite forms.[13] In both Taoism and TCM, Yin-Yang is a symbolic representation of universal process (including health in the latter case) that portrays a changing rather than static process.[14] Kaptchuk puts it succinctly thus:

> Yin-Yang theory is well illustrated by the traditional Chinese Taoist symbol. The circle representing the whole is divided into Yin (black) and Yang (white).
> The small circles of opposite shading illustrate that within the Yin there is Yang and vice versa. The dynamic curve dividing them indicates that Yin and Yang are continuously merging. Thus Yin and Yang create each other, control each other, and transform into each other.[15]

The important thing to understand is that the two opposite states are not mutually exclusive or independent of each other; rather, they are mutually dependent and they change into each other.[16] Extreme Yang becomes Yin and vice versa. Health is seen to be the balance of Yin-Yang aspects of the body while disease is the imbalance between these aspects. This is a form of dialectical thinking, radically different from the causal linear thinking and logic of allopathy and positivist science. The body in TCM is seen to be a dynamic interaction of Yin and Yang; it is constantly changing and fluctuating.

Proceeding from this fundamental understanding of the nature of Yin-Yang and health as balance, TCM views illness not so much in terms of discrete diseases,[17] but in terms of patterns of disharmony. Thus, TCM goes on to outline eight guiding principles for determining these patterns of disharmony. According to Beinfield and Korngold, the eight principles are four sets of polar categories that distinguish between and interpret the data gathered by examination. These principles are Yin-Yang, cold-heat, deficiency-excess and interior-exterior.[18] Again, these are not mutually exclusive, but can co-exist in a person.

A major difference between biomedicine and TCM theory is the way in which the body is conceptualized. The Chinese body has no western anatomical correspondence. For example, Chinese medical theory does not have the concept of a nervous system; yet it can treat neurological disorders. It does not perceive an endocrine system; yet it is capable of correcting what allopathy calls endocrine disorders.[19] Although TCM language makes reference to what the West recognizes as organs such as lungs, liver, stomach and so on, these are not conceptualized as discrete physical structures and entities located in specific areas within the body. Rather, the term "organs" is used to identify the functions associated with them. Furthermore, TCM does not make a distinction between physical functions and the emotional and spiritual dimensions governed by the "organ" in question. Moreover, it does not only describe an organ in terms of its physiological processes and functions, but also in terms of its orb — that is, its sphere of influence.

For example, in TCM the Spleen is the primary organ of digestion. It extracts the nutrients from food digested by the Stomach and transforms them into what will become "Qi" and "Blood."[20] A way of expressing this is that the Spleen is responsible for making Blood, whereas the Liver is responsible for storing and spreading Blood. As such, the Spleen is responsible for transformation, transmutation and transportation — and these functions apply to physical as well as mental and emotional processes. At the somatic level, "weakness" in the Spleen[21] means that food cannot be transformed properly into nutrients that nourish the body. At the emotional and psycho-spiritual level, a weak Spleen affects our awareness of possibilities and disables us from transforming possibilities into appropriate courses of action, thereby leading to worry and confusion. Ultimately, it affects our trustworthiness and dependability.[22]

The body, then, is conceptualized not so much in terms of distinct parts and components, but in terms of energetics or energy flow (Qi). Qi, a fundamental concept in TCM and Chinese thinking, has no precise conceptual correspondence in the West (although it is frequently translated as "energy" or "vital energy"). Qi is what animates life. While there is Qi, there is life; when there is no Qi, life ceases. It is both material and immaterial. Qi is present in the universe in the air we breathe and in the breaths we take. It is the quality we share with all things, thus connecting the macrocosm with the microcosm. Qi flows in the body along lines of energy flow called meridians or organ networks.[23] Another way of conceptualizing disease is that it arises when Qi is not flowing smoothly, leading to blockage and stagnation, which, if persistent, will lead to disease (that is, pathological changes in the body). So, an important part of the healing process is to unblock and facilitate the free flowing of Qi. Different therapies (massage, acupuncture and herbology) are aimed at promoting the smooth flow of Qi and re-balancing disharmony.

To help students understand this different conception of the body and disease, as well as to integrate this new understanding into their own conceptualization and experience of the body, the course emphasizes reflections rather than focusing on a critical analysis of the structure and argument of the materials (as in other courses I offer). Students are asked to constantly reflect upon how the experience in the course (in terms of readings, lectures, discussions, films, audiotapes, physical exercises and so on) alters the way they think about health and the body — *their* body.

QI GONG (CHI KUNG)

Together with these notions of health and the body, the Chinese have developed exercise forms called Qi Gong (or Chi Kung, depending on the system of translation used). These exercises have been around for at least two thousand years. Again, it is impossible to provide a comprehensive description of what Qi Gong entails in this limited space. Briefly, they are exercises aimed at regulating simultaneously the breath, the mind and the body. There are literally thousands of forms of Qi Gong, from sitting postures similar to what the West recognizes as meditation to Tai Ji Juan, which, at its most advanced, is a form of martial art aimed at honing the body/mind to respond to external attack without force. Qi Gong is a recommended exercise form in TCM and is widely taught as a healing art in China.[24]

Practitioners of Qi Gong believe that by disciplining, activating and regulating the normally automatic, involuntary way of breathing, they are able to regulate and alter other functions of the body such as heartbeat, blood flow and other physical and emotional functions. Thus, Qi Gong is not *simply* a physical exercise. Nancy Zi, a professional vocal soloist who studies Qi Gong to enhance her singing in classical western opera, puts it concisely:

> The practice of *chi kung* ... encompasses the ancient Chinese understanding of disciplined breathing as a means of acquiring total control over body and mind. It gives us physiological and psychological balance and the balance of *yin* and *yang* ...[25]

Thus, Qi Gong is based on the same principles as TCM; they are complementary. In "Health and the Body," I use and teach Qi Gong exercises as a way of integrating the body/mind, not only in theory but in practice. For example, I start each class with gentle stretching and breathing. The purpose is to direct the students' attention to the parts of their bodies that are normally ignored in carrying out intellectual activities (such as reading and discussion). Then I introduce some simple Qi Gong exercises that activate most major meridians (lines and systems of circulation of energy in the body) and ask students for feedback regarding how they feel. I also encourage them to record their sensations and reactions in their notebooks and health journals and to observe physical and emotional changes over time as they practise the exercises. Here is an entry from a student's notebook:

> We moved our arms, as if holding a big balloon, until we found the position that was conducive to E[nergy] flow. My arms didn't make it far from my sides & I could feel a tingling sensation between my arms & body. There was a strange feeling of a magnetic field that kept my arms from moving further out & preventing them from

falling back towards my body. We kept that position for a while & allowed the chi to flow & warm our arms, hands.[26]

In addition to the exercises, I explain the Chinese view of the body in terms of meridian theory (which is explored through readings later on in the course) and the rationale for the exercises. For instance, to complement the readings on the Five Element Theory of TCM, I teach a set of Qi Gong exercises called the Five Seasons Exercise, which corresponds to the major meridians of Lung (autumn), Kidney (winter), Liver (spring), Heart (summer) and Spleen (late summer).[27] The exercise begins with autumn. The movements of the autumn exercise are aimed rhythmically at stretching and contracting the Lung meridian (that is, the line of energy flow that influences the function of the Lung). The Lung is the body's first line of defence against the external environment. Autumn signals the end of the summer and the movement into winter, when we are more susceptible to invasion by cold leading to colds and flus. Strengthening the Lung helps to reduce our chances of succumbing to these maladies.

I talk about acupuncture as a treatment modality in TCM, the anatomical location of selected acupuncture points and their functions, and show students how to find these points on their bodies in relation to the Qi Gong exercises. Through this kind of experiential learning, students obtain a different view of the body and are encouraged to acknowledge and value their physical and emotional experiences in addition to their intellectual experience. As well, they are asked to use their experiences in the exercises to reflect on the readings and discussions in an attempt to close the body/mind divide.

READING NOTEBOOK AND HEALTH JOURNAL

To facilitate and systematize the reflective process, the students use two tools. First, they are required to keep a reading notebook, which serves as a record of the readings, lectures and exercises. I give them three phrases to guide their personal entries: (a) what I see/read/experience; (b) how I feel; and (c) what I think. Second, the students are asked to keep a health journal, which is a record of their physical and emotional health during the course. I ask that journal entries be made on a weekly basis — or daily if students have a specific purpose in mind (for example, if a student wishes to use her journal to chart her menstruation cycle). Students can use either tool to record their experiences of the Qi Gong exercises and other thoughts that arise out of, or that are related to, the course.

I encourage students to develop a format for recording their observations that is most appropriate for their purpose. Over the years, I have read with interest the systems students develop to map their own health. One student used a series of codes that she developed to describe how she felt over her menstrual cycle and recorded the codes daily on a monthly calendar. Another student developed a series of symbols of faces (from smiling to downturn mouth) and coloured stars (red equals energetic; silver equals feeling tired) in relation to her daily entries. At the end of each week and month, she added up these symbols as a quick measure of how balanced her life had been. I must say this journal with faces and stars was fun to read and, I surmised, was fun to do as well. As a general rule, I do not read the journals unless a student wants me to; however, I glance through them at the end of the course to make sure that they are done.

I encourage students to use the materials recorded in the notebook and health journal as "data" for their term papers, especially if they wish to integrate their experiences into their scholarly inquiry or to explore writing as embodied subjects. For example, one student used the term paper to work through her experience of being sexually abused by her father and how she reclaimed her body as a result of Qi Gong. Her paper was subsequently published[28] and is now part of the reading materials for the course. In fact, I now specifically include a topic entitled "Learning to Write as Embodied Subjects" in the course content and use pieces of social scientific writing[29] to legitimize the form and to show how such an account can be written not merely as a self-absorbed autobiography.

Diana L. Gustafson provides another example of how students use their experiences as data in their writing. Diana's reflections on the course, written initially as her term paper, have become published papers. Her recording of how she experienced connecting body and mind is worth quoting at length, because it displays the interconnection between experience and learning that is grounded in the body:

> I felt my feet rooted to the floor. I sensed the movement of my limbs located in relation to the space I occupied. I sensed the

tension and relaxation of my muscles as a physical experience of my tissues. I felt the flow of breath that was at one moment a part of me, inside my lungs, and at the next moment, a part of the air that surrounded me. I experienced these things with my body, that physical part of my self.

There were times when I was so involved in the physicality of the experience that my surroundings faded from my vision. I was aware of the professor's verbal instructions and my efforts to translate those instructions into coordinated physical movement. I was aware of concentrating on the cycle of my breathing. I knew these and other things from the cognitive part of my being. At times it was as if I were an outside observer watching the experience of my body. My mind, my body, and my breath were connected yet separate entities engaged in qigong. It was like a revelation that day I was able to articulate a sense of body — my body — from those oppositional and interdependent positions. Through repetition of body movement which replicates the cycles of breath I was echoing the rhythms of life and nature ... Qigong training was embodied exploration of the invisible process of constructing knowledge of the body.[30]

APPLICATION FOR A FEMINIST
REVISIONING OF THE BODY

As I developed and reflected on the course, I began to call it "a pedagogy of embodiment" or "embodied learning." To conclude, I want to briefly discuss the implication and application of embodied learning, notably the practice of Qi Gong, towards a feminist revisioning of the body. I describe a workshop I conducted[31] in a feminist setting as an example of how we may adapt Qi Gong towards feminist goals of reclaiming the body from an ideal developed by the fashion and fitness industries. This discussion is not meant to privilege Qi Gong over other feminist attempts to deal with the problematic issues of body image — which has become a dominant preoccupation of women in our society.

Instead of privileging the mind over the body/spirit in our intellectual and political projects, embodied learning offers a means for knowledge construction that does not negate the materiality of our being, as Diana L. Gustafson asserted. She thought that this is a form of feminist pedagogy:

> Embodied learning offers women a way to learn new knowledge about the body, their body. Embodied learning actively engages women in the construction of that knowledge. The experience also validates women's embodiedness and the knowledge that comes from being an embodied subject.[32]

It is also a way for us to interrogate how our consciousness is developed and changed. Diana's journal entry is an example of how Qi Gong, like other forms of meditation, enables the practitioner to be *both* the active subject and the objective observer of her thought processes. This enables the practitioner/knower to examine her thoughts and behaviours, including disjunctures and contradictions in thought and action, without judgement. It offers a place from which the practitioner/knower can make appropriate changes should she desire them.[33]

At the workshop I offered on Qi Gong at the 1997 CRIAW[34] conference in Fredericton, I began by giving a brief explanation of the philosophical and theoretical basis of Qi Gong. I then asked the participants to assume the basic Qi Gong posture, which can be done by standing or sitting. In this basic posture, the practitioner stands (or sits) with feet parallel, shoulder-width apart (that is, the feet are aligned vertically with the hip and the inside of the shoulder joints). The spine of the practitioner should be straight "like a string of pearls" (that is, the practitioner should stand in such a way that the spinal column is straight with each vertebrae loosely connected from the tailbone to the top of the head so that the spinal column resembles a string of pearls). Finally, the Dan T'ien, an energy centre approximately two inches below the navel, should be aligned laterally with an acupuncture point in the lower back called the Ming Men. This is done by bending the knees slightly, thereby straightening the lower back. This posture is said to maximize the flow of Qi in the body.

While standing (or sitting) with the right body alignment, the participants were asked to move their arms until they felt a new or different sensation (as discussed by the student in the previous section). This gave them an experiential sense of what I meant by Qi and how we can direct the flow of Qi by intention (making the hands warm, for example). Based on my own experience of teaching Qi Gong in class and with cancer survivors,[35] I know that usually most, if not all, the participants feel something. They are asked to share their experiences. Apart from serving as a check point for me, I want to explore the diversity and uniqueness of the experiences and to emphasize that there is not a right or wrong experience. Experience simply *is*. And this should be honoured and respected both individually and collectively.

One thing I emphasized in the workshop was the primary energy centre of the body, the Dan T'ien. Interestingly, this is a critical area in both eastern and western religious and martial arts traditions (for example, yoga, tai ji juan, karate).[36] I asked participants to put their palms there once they felt warmth and to send warmth to this area. I then explained that the goal of martial arts and meditative practices is to open up and expand this energy centre; thus a rounded, protruding abdomen is desired. This is contrary to the contemporary North American ideal that women should have a flat abdomen. Indeed, most aerobic and calisthenic exercises are aimed at flattening or reducing the size of the abdomen! Looking at this ideal from an eastern perspective, I see it as robbing women of their power located in the primary energy centre of the body.

In the workshop, we discussed what the eastern view of the body might mean for the participants and how we might nurture this view through Qi Gong and other practices. Participants who were yoga practitioners also shared their knowledge with the group and discussed yoga as an alternative method towards revisioning the female body. I then taught a simple Qi Gong exercise to give the participants a flavour of what Qi Gong practice consists of. This exercise, called "The Rising Eagle," consists of six movements that are co-ordinated with breathing. It symbolizes our flight to freedom from the shackles of the ideal image imposed on women in contemporary society.

The six movements are as follows: first, the practitioner assumes the basic standing posture with straight legs, and arms close to the sides of the body. With an in breath, the practitioner raises her forearms while tugging in her elbows close to the waist and letting the wrists relax. This resembles the eagle getting ready to stretch its wings. With an out breath, the practitioner extends her arms in front of her until they are shoulder height, parallel to the ground. The palms should face forward, a position known as "sitting the palms." This movement resembles the first flapping of the wings and stretches the major meridians (lines of energy flow) that run along the arms to the finger tips. At this point, with an in breath, the practitioner flaps her "wings" overhead, with the backs of the hands facing each other directly on top of her head, stretching the same meridians further. She can roll her weight forward to the ball of her feet with this movement, but she should not stand on tiptoe. As she breathes out, she flaps her "wings" down until her wrists cross each other in front of her body. As she lowers her "wings," she sits down by bending her knees slightly, thereby straightening and stretching her lower back. With the next in breath, she extends her "wings" outwards along the sides of her body, with palms facing upwards. With the next out breath, she turns over her palms to face the earth and lowers her "wings." As she lowers her arms or "wings," she stands up (that is, she takes flight and visualizes pushing herself off the ground); she resumes the original standing position with legs straight, thereby completing the exercise. An important point about Qi Gong is that most, if not all, the movements are performed gently and gracefully, as if every joint in the body is a well-oiled hinge. Also, the mind of the practitioner should be "on the breath" and the breath should be "on the mind" (that is, with concentration and intention). In the Rising Eagle, as in other exercises, visualization is an important part of the exercise as the practitioner moves through the six major steps. Thus, Qi Gong is a form of moving meditation that calms the mind and regulates the breath at the same time.

Obviously within the time limit of the workshop (one and a half hours) and the space constraint of this chapter, it was and is impossible to explore the implications of embodied learning and revisioning of the body at length. However, the example given here of the principles of Qi Gong, based on Chinese medical theory and its application in a feminist context, shows that an eastern perspective has valuable applications in our reframing of the existing societal ideal of women's bodies. This perspective adds to our collective repertoire to help us work towards a feminist revisioning of the body.

Notes

1. Some of these activities have been recorded in Roxana Ng, "A Modest Beginning: My Work on and for Immigrant Women," *Canadian Woman Studies* 4 (1982), 61–64; and Roxana Ng, *The Politics of Community Services: Immigrant Women, Class and State*, 2nd ed. (Halifax: Fernwood Books, 1996).

2. This intellectual and political journey began when I worked with other feminists,to establish the Vancouver Women's Research Centre (WRC), which we envisioned to be a place outside the academy that would contribute to the development of feminist theories and research arising out of women's concerns in the everyday world. Dorothy Smith, a leading academic feminist sociologist, was a central figure at WRC at the time. I was so impressed by the feminist methodology she was developing that I left Vancouver, in 1978, to study with her at the Ontario Institute for Studies in Education (OISE).

3. I am using the term "allopathy" or "allopathic medicine" to refer to "mainstream" or biomedicine in recognition of the fact that western medicine is made up of two major branches: homeopathy (treatments based on the principles of "like cures like" and the administration of the minimal dosage) and allopathy (commonly known to be the totality of western medicine, which, since the turn of the century, is increasingly reliant on drug therapy and surgery). For an introduction of these systems, see Andrew Weil, *Health and Healing* (New York: Houghton Mifflin Company, 1983); and Ted Kaptchuk and Michael Croucher, *The Healing Arts: A Journal Through the Faces of Medicine* (London: British Broadcasting Corporation, 1986).

   As I acquire more knowledge of allopathy, I view the inability of allopathic physicians to treat me as my good fortune. It is now quite well known that many modern diseases and ailments are in fact iatrogenic, that is, caused by prolonged use of pharmaceutical drugs and other interventions such as surgery. In addition to the above authors, see Andrew Weil, *Spontaneous Healing* (New York: Fawcett Columbine Book, 1995).

4. This is the scholarship coined by Dorothy Smith as "the standpoint of women." See Dorothy E. Smith, *The Everyday World as Problematic: A Feminist Sociology* (Toronto: University of Toronto Press, 1987); and Marie Campbell and A. Manicom, eds., *Knowledge, Experience, and Ruling Relations* (Toronto: University of Toronto Press, 1995).

5. There are exceptions. See, for example, Marianne A. Paget, "Life Mirrors Work Mirrors Text Mirrors Life ..." *Social Problems* 37 (1990), 137–148; and Kathryn Church, *Forbidden Narratives: Critical Autobiography as Social Science* (Amsterdam: Gordon and Breach Publishers, 1995).

6. Susan R. Bordo, *The Flight to Objectivity: Essays on Cartesianism and Culture* (Albany, NY: Ballentine Books, 1987), especially Chapter 5.

7. Karl Marx and Frederick Engels, *The German Ideology* (New York: International Publishers, 1970).

8. By "rational," I refer to the fact that TCM is a text-based healing system with its own internal logic, albeit one that is drastically different from western positivism and empiricism, the basis of biomedicine. I avoid using the term "science" or "scientific" to describe other healing systems even though they are systematic because I want to locate the development of science in its historical and cultural context; its ascendancy is closely connected with the rise and dominance of capitalism in the West, and is by no means the *only* systematic way of understanding the world. For a fabulous discussion and critique of the epistemological basis of different medical systems, see Donald Bates, ed., *Knowledge and the Scholarly Medical Traditions* (Cambridge: Cambridge University Press, 1995).

9. I also kept a daily health log that detailed changes in my body as I took the herbs and received acupuncture treatments (and sometimes these changes were dramatic). Later, with the encouragement of my psychotherapist, I incorporated emotional and psychic changes in the log.

10. Mary O'Brien, *The Politics of Reproduction* (London: Routledge and Kegan Paul, 1981).

11. See Weil, *Health and Healing*, the text used for the course, and Kaptchuk and Croucher, *The Healing Arts*.

12. Margaret Stacey, *The Sociology of Health and Healing* (London: Unwin Hyman, 1988); and Lesley Malloch, "Indian Medicine, Indian Health: Study Between Red and White Medicine," *Canadian Woman Studies* 10 (1990), 105–112.

13. Harriet Beinfield and Efrem Korngold, *Between Heaven and Earth: A Guide to Chinese Medicine* (New York: Ballentine Books, 1991), 50–51.

14. Ted Kaptchuk, *The Web that Has No Weaver: Understanding Chinese Medicine* (New York: Congdon and Weed, 1983); Beinfield and Korngold, *Between Heaven and Earth*; and Giovanni Maciocia, *The Foundations of Chinese Medicine: A Comprehensive Text for Acupuncturists and Herbalists* (London: Churchill Livingstone, 1989).

15. Kaptchuk, *The Web that Has No Weaver*.

16. Maciocia, *The Foundations of Chinese Medicine*, 2–6.

17. Here I make a distinction between illness and disease following Kaptchuk's definition: "... illness is the state of a patient, beyond discomfort, but defined in the patient's terms. Disease is an objective condition, independent of the patient's judgement, which many medical models often assume to be the whole of illness." Kaptchuk and Croucher, *The Healing Arts*, 9.

18. Beinfield and Korngold, *Between Heaven and Earth*, 77–80; and Maciocia, *The Foundations of Chinese Medicine*, Chapter 18.

19. Kaptchuk, *The Web that Has No Weaver*, 2–3.

20. Note here that the organs belonging to western conceptualization are referred to in lower case; those in Chinese conceptualization are capitalized. Thus, for example, the Blood in TCM theory is both similar to and different from the western notion of blood, the red liquid, which is perceived to be the red fluid that circulates throughout our bodies in arteries and veins. Although it is true that the Chinese

Blood is a liquid that circulates through the body, where it is said to circulate is conceptualized differently. Again, the physical pathways are less important than its *functions*. The major function of Blood is to nourish, maintain and moisten the body. TCM also distinguishes different kinds of blood (see Kaptchuk, *The Web that Has No Weaver*, 57; and Maciocia, *The Foundations of Chinese Medicine*). For example, the concept of "stagnant blood," which can arise from blood stagnation in the body or result from injury, is foreign to the West.

21. This is a western characterization. In TCM terms, the two major disruptions pertaining to the Spleen are dampness and deficiency, which produce different problems in the transformation and transmutation process too complicated to explain here. But this example clearly indicates the conceptual differences between East and West.

22. This insight is derived from a seminar given by Ted Kaptchuk entitled, "Ladders of the Soul and Oriental Medicine: The East Asian [sic] Perspective on Psycho-Spiritual Issues in Therapy" (November 17, 1996).

23. See Kaptchuk, *The Web that Has No Weaver*; Beinfield and Korngold, *Between Heaven and Earth*, especially p. 30; and Maciocia, *The Foundations of Chinese Medicine*, 35–37.

24. See "The Mystery of Chi," the first in a six-part television series of "Healing and the Mind" narrated by Bill Moyers. Also see the companion book by Bill Moyers, *Healing and the Mind* (New York: Doubleday, 1993).

25. Nancy Zi, *The Art of Breathing* (New York: Bantam Books, 1986), 3.

26. Student Journal, September 23, 1996.

27. The Chinese calendar is divided into five seasons, with two summer seasons (early and late summer) and not four seasons as in the European calendar.

28. Si Transken, *Reclaiming Body Territory* (Ottawa: Canadian Research Institute for the Advancement of Women, 1995).

29. For example, Paget, "Life Mirrors Work Mirrors Text Mirrors Life ..."; Susan Wendell, "Feminism, Disability and Transcendence of the Body," *Canadian Woman Studies* 13 (1993), 116–122; and Transken, *Reclaiming Body Territory*.

30. See Diana L. Gustafson, "Embodied Learning about Health and Healing: Involving the Body as Content and Pedagogy," *Canadian Woman Studies* 17 (1998), 52–55. In this chapter I have not included materials on student resistance and negative experiences in the course, since they are not central to the discussion here. For these topics see Roxana Ng, "Toward an Embodied Pedagogy: Exploring Health and the Body Through Chinese Medicine," in George Dei, Budd Hall, and Dorothy Goldin-Rosenberg, eds., *Indigenous Knowledge in Global Contexts: Multiple Readings of Our World* (Toronto: University of Toronto Press, in press).

31. The workshop was conducted at the 1997 conference of the Canadian Research Institute for the Advancement of Women (CRIAW) in Fredericton, NB.

32. Gustafson, "Embodied Learning about Health and Healing: Involving the Body as Content and Pedagogy," 55.

33. Space does not allow me to expound on this point. For a fuller discussion, see Jon Kabat-Zinn, *Full Catastrophe Living: Using the Wisdom of Your Body and Mind to*

Face Stress, Pain and Illness (New York: Delta Book, 1990); and Roxana Ng, "Is Embodied Learning Critical Pedagogy?" Paper presented by invitation at the American Education Research Association, April 1998, San Diego.

34. CRIAW is short for the Canadian Research Institute for the Advancement of Women, a non-governmental feminist research organization aimed at linking academic and community-based research.

35. For the past three years I have been working as a volunteer with Wellspring, a cancer support group in Toronto that offers alternative therapies and support to cancer patients and survivors.

36. For a theorization of the seven major energy centres of the body in terms of health and healing, see Caroline Myss, *Anatomy of the Spirit* (New York: Three River Press, 1996).

CHAPTER TEN

SHATTERING THE MIRROR
A YOUNG WOMAN'S STORY OF
WEIGHT PREOCCUPATION

Kate Rossiter

IMAGINE A SOCIETY WHERE uncountable numbers of people live in quiet oppression. Imagine a regime so sneaky and powerful that the oppressors trick the oppressed into oppressing themselves. Imagine a culture where not only is there enough food for all but the starving ones willingly starve themselves. Are these images from some corrupt far away or long ago society? Hardly. These are images from our own society, a society which considers just a small few body shapes to be beautiful and acceptable. In so doing, society forces many into lives of self-oppression.

Like so many other forms of oppression, it is difficult and frightening to release one's self from the tyranny of body-hatred. Slowly, however, we are starting to witness the beginnings of a social movement that combats this type of oppression. This social movement is one which is relatively new, and I am proud to say that I am a part of it. The social activism of which I speak is a movement that accepts all types of body shapes and sizes regardless of the "beauty standard."

In this chapter, I want to talk about the effects of self-image on me, both positive and negative. I will tell my own story and share what is, in my belief, a common struggle for many women concerning their physical shape and self-image. I will also discuss how activism against body-hatred has helped me in battling my own "body oppression" and, hopefully, how it contributes to a growing social movement that rejects narrowly defined body images.

I am a second-year university student and I have struggled, in the last few years, to understand my personal experiences in political terms. I was always a large, stocky kid. I don't remember feeling this way my whole childhood, but I do remember becoming acutely aware of my body in a self-conscious, painful way as I entered adolescence. By the time I was fifteen, I was so anxious about my weight and so uncomfortable in my body that it seemed like a good option for me to join Weight Watchers. I understood Weight Watchers to be a sensible weight loss program; I knew of the program through my mother who had attended Weight Watchers when I was a small child. I went with the expectation that I would become simultaneously thin and self-confident and, as a result, become a happier, healthier individual.

Once I had joined Weight Watchers, weekly weigh-ins and pep talks (for a stiff fee) marked my supposed progression towards happiness. But as I grew closer and closer to my ideal weight, a strange thing happened: the thinner I became, the more unhappy I felt with myself. What once may have been my "dream" body now looked to me as lumpy and fat as my "old" body. I still wasn't quite perfect. Despite my weight loss I still had not learned to accept myself. In fact, the constant body/mind competition set out by Weight Watchers led me to further criticize my shape and size. In truth, it didn't matter what size my body was: I was stuck in an obsessionally self-hating mind frame which was supported by the world around me. After losing 30 pounds (13.6 kilograms), it seemed only reasonable to set my goal weight another 10 pounds (4.5 kilograms) lower. As a result, I was aware of everything I put in my mouth.

After nine months on the Weight Watchers program, I stopped going to my weekly weigh-ins. I had reached my weight loss goal. I had the Weight Watchers booklets and programs memorized back to front. The weight goal, set by the program, did not satisfy me, even though my weight loss had begun to slow down. While the Weight Watchers program had assigned reasonable weight goals, they had also created a mentality of self-loathing, self-betrayal and an unnatural "fear of fat." I was at war with my body. I began taking more extreme measures towards my weight loss. Skipping meals, counting calories, diet products, purging and constant weight obsession became my lifestyle. I was miserable. I felt trapped in an ugly, fat body, one which I presumed would only cause me grief and pain for the rest of my life. To me, living in a fat body felt like living with a chronic disease: it was both distressing and debilitating.

By the eleventh grade, I was completely obsessed with my food intake and with the maintenance of my body shape. The amount of food I consumed, or the lack thereof, became everything to me — a measure of my success. If I denied myself enough food, I could prove I was a good, strong person; any indulgence signified weakness of will. Proudly I gave away my lunches and denied myself "specialty items" such as my own birthday cake. Unfortunately, this also led to a feeling of isolation and despair. Food had always been a source of pleasure and comfort for me and the self-denial was tormenting. I don't know whether my peers and family noticed my secret obsession, although one friend commented on my routine of giving my lunches away. I did not talk openly about my continuing body-hatred to anyone, I simply wanted to be "normal" — I didn't want my struggles with my body to be obvious, although in retrospect I believe my self-hatred was blatant.

Looking back on the situation, I often wonder why no-one — parents, teachers, friends or family — was concerned with the state I was in. Why did I have to suffer alone for so long? The answer is simple. My parents, teachers, friends and family were all too busy being proud and envious of me to notice that my weight loss plan had turned into a twenty-four-hour-a-day, seven-day-a-week obsession because from the "outside," I looked great. I was thinner than I had ever been and, in the words of my close family members, "showed great strength of will and will power." Apparently, I had served as a weight-loss role model for other large family members. This is not to say that my community is shallow or unobservant. It was just that no one could understand how being thin could bring anything less than happiness. I had fulfilled a whole society's dream by "becoming beautiful." Nevertheless, I was sick and miserable.

At this point, I felt completely trapped. I could not give up and I could not let go because of the respect I gained through the weight loss. However, I could not go on being so unhappy. I remember clearly a moment of distinct shock when my mother's cousin approached me after seeing my "new body" for the first time. "You look fine now," she said, "but I have to tell you I thought you were beautiful before too." For me, this was a very powerful statement. I felt at once sad and angry. Could it be that I had gone through this whole process for nothing? Was I really as beautiful before as I was now (even though I still didn't feel beautiful)? I could not believe that anyone had found my old fat body anything but hideous. I dismissed the thought for another year or so and continued to slash and burn my sense of self. My cousin's belief in me was too tenuous and strange for me to act on. To believe that I had been beautiful before the weight loss meant that I had to completely give up a value system that equated thinness with happiness, a belief to which I adhered and had worked so hard to achieve.

This value system began to crack for me months later, in the middle of my twelfth grade year. One evening, while eating supper with my family, I, as usual, managed to deny myself half my dinner. Later in the evening, I trekked into the darkness for my power walk. During the walk I decided I had eaten too much at dinner. Subsequently I was nauseated and tried to throw up on my neighbour's lawn. I remember vividly a moment of stepping out of myself, looking down and being struck by the appearance of a pathetic creature trying to rid herself of the only nutrients she had permitted herself to eat all day. I went home and cried and cried, and knew that I could not continue this way. Slowly, I began to recognize and admit to my bulimic tendencies. I began finding allies in other women who suffered from similar ailments. Gradually, I began to talk to family and friends about the pain and hatred from which I was suffering — a scary and difficult process.

I look on this period of my life as "coming out of the closet as a fat person." I had the world convinced that I was indeed a good, thin girl but somewhere inside I knew this was a scam. First of all, I was not naturally thin and quickly gained back the weight I had lost. Second, being thin felt like a cover-up of my true self. The biggest problem with trying to find my "fat self" was the complete lack of social support, which I needed in two areas: overcoming my eating problems and accepting myself, whatever size that might be. I was addicted to terrible eating habits and low self-esteem. Unlike other addictions, there were no open arms, no loving family members who would say, "You look beautiful no matter what — finish that chocolate cake!" Instead, society worked against me to further my addiction. Every time I lapsed and admitted to feeling like a fat failure, the answer was inevitably: "Well, lose five pounds — you'll feel much better." An answer I did not want to hear.

I gathered support where I could. *Swim After Dinner*, a film made by ex-bulimic Stacy Dickerson, led me to understand I was not alone. I was also able to find a few people in my life struggling with similar issues. It was a difficult struggle though, because social norms seem to make it impossible for people in situations such as mine to be helped. Recovery from dieting and accepting my body shape seemed the right approach, yet social norms make it clear that letting go of the traditional ideals is dangerous and may lead, paradoxically, to a lack of acceptance.

Realizing this failure on the part of the world around me helped to politicize my decision to be "fat and proud." Instead of turning inward and feeling horrible about myself, I was finally able to spot the world around me as the real villain. Instead of feeling low and ugly, I felt strong and furious. How had I been roped into the lie that "fat is ugly"? As Dorothy in the *Wizard of Oz* says: "All I ever needed was in my own backyard to begin with." I always *had* the perfect body! I had spent years of my life being miserable for no reason at all!

I finally understood that in the eyes of the world, there was no perfect body. Conforming to society's "standards" means you will *never* be perfect. There will always be something wrong with your body. As an example, I recently found two advertisements, a page apart, in a hair magazine. One advertised a magic potion to burn fat away. "Say Goodbye to Fat Forever" the ad shouted out at me. A skinny woman beckoningly held the excess elastic of her old "fatty" pants in front of her taut new tummy. The next ad guaranteed immediate success in weight gain for those who are *too* slim. "Skinny Isn't Sexy!" the page screamed, modelling a slightly more curvaceous and definitely ecstatic bikini-clad gal next to a gaunt woman who looked like she was barely surviving. The message was obvious; there is not even a small window of perfection — there is no way of reaching the pinnacle of beauty. Looking for the zenith of beauty is like looking for the Holy Grail or the elixir of life; we spend countless amounts of physical, spiritual, emotional and economic energy on something which is mythical and does not, cannot exist.

Learning to live in a fat-phobic society is never a completed journey. At many points during this long struggle, I have felt like a failure for not keeping up my "strong will." I knew that some I knew whispered behind my back, wondering why I had "let myself go." I often chastised myself, telling myself that this political, anti-dieting stuff was just a cop-out — a way of letting myself be lazy or finding an excuse for letting myself go. In actual fact it was much harder work to get myself to stop feeling terrible after I stopped dieting than to continue dieting. In addition, what I was doing was not socially acceptable. Western society views fat as the greatest sin. Allowing one's self to be a natural size and shape is like being self-branded with the admittance that one is lazy, ugly, weak-willed and stupid.

However, the benefits of self-acceptance are huge. There are innumerable new things I can do now that I previously wouldn't have dreamed possible. I can try on a bathing suit without hysteria. I can eat a full meal without checking the fat content or Weight Watcher's food value equivalents. I can eat a full meal without feeling like a failure or like a pig. I can eat publicly. I can mention my size without cringing or feeling hideous. I can shop happily. I can look in the mirror and truly smile back at myself. I can willfully take up space. I can allow myself to be photographed and can look at the photographs without wanting to cry. I can dance. I can exercise for fun and health, rather than obsessively for shape and weight loss. I can think about other things beside my body.

Along with these newfound abilities has come an awareness of the immensely fat-phobic surroundings we live in. Fat-phobia does not simply concern one's own self-perception. Many people hold prejudices towards others, especially other women. I know that most people discriminate against those who do not try to conform to the "right size." While gay jokes, racist jokes and sexist jokes are not in fashion or acceptable anymore, a good fat joke will still "crack 'em up." Fat jokes still prevail because disdain of fat is still socially condoned through the media and through our general collective consciousness. For example, in one of the meal halls at the university I attend, large groups of males will moo and laugh if a female, particularly if she is the "wrong" size, goes for ice cream — a personal nightmare of mine. An entire women's residence, Huntom House, has been nicknamed the "Huntom Cows." This is, of course, an extreme form of silencing that ensures women know their place within the tight box of body-conformity.

The anger caused by the awakening to the widespread fat-phobia in our society led to many realizations in my life. I realized that this need to be thin was not *my* problem, it was the problem of a sick society. All I had to do was accept myself as I was. This, of course, was more easily said than done; self-acceptance was made extremely difficult by the lack of social support. In our society we provide more support to alcoholics and drug addicts, more "acceptable" forms of self-hatred, than those trying to battle dieting and body-hatred. Dieting is not seen as a punitive and destructive measure; the addiction to dieting not seen as a form of self-deprecation. I realized that the eventual acceptance of myself, at any size, threatened many people around me. I was challenging the status quo. I realized that by changing myself, I encouraged change in society as a whole.

Understanding this helped me to further overcome my body-hatred. The more I began to fight against body-oppression, the better I felt about myself: my personal beliefs had suddenly become an imperative political stance for me. I refused to tolerate the idea that I had suffered so much torment and subsequent work at rehabilitation to simply keep quiet and watch other girls and women in my life suffer the same fate. I found it extremely therapeutic to expose my personal struggles with dieting and body image. It was important to me to name these previous experiences as wrong and painful, and to allow others to share in the anger created by such pain.

Thus, I began to talk. My story became public knowledge. I found that whenever I spoke about my experiences, girls and women of all ages seemed to recognize their own painful experiences with personal body-hatred. This was not only surprising to me, but empowering as well. While it was disappointing and hurtful to find so many women battling similar problems, at the same time it was exciting to see women's perception of themselves and their attitudes towards their bodies change. It inspired me to want to talk more, to write and to fight harder.

In the last year, I have had the opportunity to continue this fight for social change in a formalized way. I was invited to help start a body image support and awareness group on campus, at Mount Allison University in Sackville, New Brunswick. This group was a challenge, at times both rewarding and difficult. The group's aim was to provide information and a forum for discussion of the issues, with a focus on time and space for personal reflection. Meetings took place every week with a set agenda, a certain amount of content from the leaders, exercises and discussion time. The group has helped solidify my own knowledge and feelings towards the issues. Creating a safe space for women (and men!) to feel angry and to turn that anger into empowerment was important to me. This aspect was perhaps the most rewarding.

The other form of social action that I have been doing is public speaking. In November 1997, I was a speaker at the Canadian Research Association for the Advancement of Women's conference on women's bodies and lives. I spoke quite simply on my personal experiences as a teenager surviving and overcoming an eating disorder. The response overwhelmed me. Some people thanked me; others asked if they could quote me. I had expected people to be uninterested in my story. I was surrounded by academic speakers, those who had researched and written about eating disorders. All I had to offer was my story, which was common to begin with. Once again, the understanding that my personal story does indeed have immense impact on people and the fact that I feel passionately about a new social movement is an important part of recovery. I came to understand at a profound level that the personal is indeed political. At the conference, for example, one woman thanked me by saying, "You don't know how much your story affected my daughter. She is fifteen, and you have given her hope."

I believe that the value in telling my story of private oppression publicly is that many women can relate to it. When members of the audience voice the commonalities between my story and theirs, we share a moment of understanding — that body image is a widespread, public oppression, rather than an individual, private concern. From such moments of understanding across similarities as well as differences, we can start to build a common political and social goal of resistance to body-oppression and fat-phobia.

I don't know where this struggle will take me. I look forward to furthur opportunities where I will be able to share my knowledge and story. I hope to find more like-minded women. However, one vital aspect of my struggle has been learning that sometimes people need to be dissuaded from traditional ways of thinking. Old ideologies do not disappear quickly or easily. As a result, I do not allow my close friends and family to act fat-phobic around me, and I try my best to encourage positive-body-image thinking in them. I know the fight is not over yet, though it gets stronger every day. I have realized that including my story in this book on body image is a form of social protest and action.

My journey towards greater self-acceptance was grounded in the desperate circumstances of my life. It helped that I was brought up in a family and a community where social criticism is acceptable and encouraged. While my family and friends had unwittingly supported my self-hatred earlier, they also worked to change their own behaviour and attitudes after they understood that the traditional conceptions of body image were dangerous and hurtful to me. I know that changing attitudes is difficult and at times painful for both men and women. Nevertheless, I know that there is hope, simply because I can discuss my story publicly.

In conclusion, with full acknowledgement of the many differences among women, I hope that my memories of my own struggles with body image have resonated with you. I believe that the strength of the activism that has begun rests on the sharing of our experiences of pain and oppression. I have told my story from my social location as a young, white female university student. I hope to strengthen my own resolve and gain an understanding of the experiences of other women in diverse social or cultural locations. To share our understanding and raise our consciousness on the many ways women's power is controlled through our bodies is an excellent starting place for a powerful social movement that can resist and fight the dominant ideas in society.

CHAPTER ELEVEN

ONE MOTHER AND DAUGHTER APPROACH TO RESISTING WEIGHT PREOCCUPATION

Gail Marchessault

ᡋ

MOST GIRLS AND WOMEN, even those who yearn for weight loss, express at least some resistance to the pressures on women to be thin and beautiful. This resistance to potentially harmful cultural ideals of feminine beauty is largely overlooked in both popular and academic discussions of weight. Even when the deliberation focuses on the unhealthy nature of women's obsession with weight, a topic which implicitly favours a consideration of resistance, it is seldom raised.

The centrality of weight in the lives of Canadian and American girls and women is a popular theme for newspaper, magazine and television stories. The academic literature on weight preoccupation concentrates on girls' and young women's ubiquitous dissatisfaction with their body shape and their acceptance of unrealistically thin weight standards, seemingly inspired by supermodels and actresses. A 1993 review by the Dairy Bureau of Canada concluded that restrained eating, binge eating and fear of fatness were the norm in middle-class girls.[1] Judith Rodin, Lisa Silberstein and Ruth Striegel-Moore, in their seminal paper, concluded similarly, that body dissatisfaction was a "normative discontent" for women.[2] Eating disorder expert David Garner reported in 1997 that 89 percent of respondents to a survey for *Psychology Today* wanted to lose weight, with almost one-quarter willing to sacrifice three years of their lives to achieve their desired weight.[3]

These studies, and others like them, create the impression that women passively internalize the multitude of messages encouraging the physically impossible, tall, thin and busty Barbie-doll stereotype. There is no doubt that the overwhelming and pervasive pressures to emulate a thin ideal create difficulties for many girls and women. But what of the 11 percent in Garner's study who didn't want to lose weight? Were they satisfied, and if so, why? Can we study the healthy impulse of girls and women to resist unrealistic weight goals?

Despite the lack of attention to resistance, it is not an uncommon reaction. Glimpses of resistance are evident in interview studies of women. Janet Davidson Allan studied Texan women's weight-related, self-care activities in 1988. She found women rejected both biomedical and cultural weight norms, adjusting their personal weight goals to protect their self-image and well-being, and that this was especially true in older women.[4] Carole Spitzack, in her book *Confessing Excess: Women and the Politics of Body Reduction*, cites women's statements that reveal their concern with weight.[5] These statements simultaneously reveal scepticism regarding the reality of media images, dissatisfaction with relationships based on looks and rejection of other people's judgements based on appearances. Marci Millman, in *Such a Pretty Face: Being Fat in America*, found that women sometimes gave social and political explanations for their weight, although personal and psychological reasons were much more common.[6]

These examples illustrate that acceptance of, and resistance to, narrow weight norms are often tightly intertwined. This has been eloquently discussed by Jill Tunaley and her colleagues in an analysis of interviews with two working-class teens in Sheffield, England. These interviews revealed a complex and contradictory simultaneous rejection and acceptance of the thin ideal. The girls had reflected and actively rejected the thin ideal, but ultimately accepted its importance in interactions with others. The authors present the girls' unsuccessful struggle as a demonstration of the power of the dominant cultural discourse about weight.[7]

Investigators with Tucson, Arizona's Teen Lifestyle Project reported that compared with white girls, the African-American girls had more flexible beauty concepts. White girls spoke of "being perfect," which they summed up rather formulaicly, as being 5'7" (1.73 metres) tall and between 100 and 110 pounds (45 and 50 kilograms), with long, flowing hair, usually blond. The African-American girls valued creativity and individualized style, which they spoke about as "making what you've got work for you." They said if one of their friends called herself fat, they would remind her that negative thinking holds you back. The white girls said they would reassure her she was not fat. The African-American girls de-emphasized the importance of appearance in popularity, in striking contrast to the white girls. If these differences stem from unique cultural ideals, they cannot properly be regarded as resistance. However, the investigators emphasized that the African-American community worked pro-actively to instil a strong identity in their daughters, to teach them to "project an image and attitude of power through the way they dress and carry themselves."[8] This is not to say that eating disorders do not exist in Black women. Others have reported that stereotyping Black women as having more relaxed attitudes to weight has blinded health professionals to eating disorders when they do exist.[9] However, finding alternative attitudes to appearance in young women merits further exploration for its potential to aid in efforts to prevent problems with eating and weight.

While there are only a few studies looking at how girls and women react to weight in their everyday lives, there has long been an active movement to educate women about weight preoccupation and eating disorders. As early as the 1960s and 1970s, Hilde Bruch and Susan Wooley linked weight preoccupation and eating disorders.[10] There are formal organizations to fight discrimination against fat people (Canadian Association for Size Acceptance) and to prevent eating disorders (National Eating Disorder Information Centre). There is Healthy Weight Week in January, Eating Disorders Awareness Week in February and No Diet Day in May. There are interest groups on the Internet. For example, the Healthy Weight Network at http://www.HealthyWeightNetwork.com, and National Association for the Advancement of Fat Acceptance at http://www.naafa.org.[11] University and women's health services often offer weight preoccupation support groups. Movies, television shows, talk shows, youth novels and teen magazines regularly run features on bulimia, anorexia and less severe eating problems. In 1981, Kim Chernin wrote about the "tyranny of slenderness," and in 1990, Naomi Wolf popularized the "beauty myth."[12] Even

Health Canada, after extensive reviews of weight issues, switched from promoting weight control and the prevention of obesity to the Vitality Program, which focuses on healthy lifestyle and positive body image.[13] In the 1990s, a growing number of writers and speakers began to educate about and advocate ways to avoid the psychological traps associated with weight. These writers offer a coherent critique of, and strategies for resisting, the forces pushing women to battle their bodies.

Consequently the focus on girls' and women's enslavement to the thin ideal, without attending to their strengths and resiliency in the face of overwhelming pressures, is a surprising omission. It's perhaps even more surprising given the feminist tradition of searching for and celebrating ordinary women who challenge the status quo. Feminist writers tend to focus on women's fight for their rights, not just how women are duped and defeated by the system. Examples abound, from the early feminist writings of Mary Wollstonecraft in the 1700s, to the consciousness-raising groups of the 1960s, to current fights for reproductive rights.

In this tradition, Susie Orbach, in her book *Hunger Strike: The Anorectic's Struggle as a Metaphor for Our Age*, has interpreted anorexia as a political resistance through over-conformity to the demands of femininity.[14] As feminist anthropologist Lila Abu-Lughod has pointed out, resisting against one set of circumstances often backs people into compliance with another.[15] It seems ironic that we can interpret the anorexic woman's self-destructive behaviour as unvoiced protest, while we do not see openly articulated opposition with pressures to lose weight (a strategy that risks weight gain or at least a lack of weight loss) as a similar protest. Orbach's earlier book, *Fat is a Feminist Issue*, promoted a feminist analysis of compulsive eating in order to achieve weight loss.[16] This approach, while progressive even today, does not present women as challenging the need for weight loss.

Ordinary women who fight weight tyranny in their own lives should be seen as champions by feminists, but this discourse is virtually non-existent. While feminists most often interpret women's weight-related actions as ways of coping with complex life problems, as Orbach does in both her books, it also seems worthwhile to look specifically at how resistance takes shape in everyday life.

In *Disruptive Voices: The Possibilities of Feminist Research,* Michelle Fine argues that pervasive but unacknowledged cultural narratives are important in structuring racial and gender oppression.[17] Being silent is an act of complicity in maintaining the oppression; speaking out challenges the imposition of social controls. Fine discusses how silence about domestic violence permitted it to remain unanalyzed and unchallenged. When people began expressing their concerns publicly, women were enabled to challenge the positioning of violence as their individual problem. Speaking out is clearly an essential step in understanding and resisting power relations.

This model of the importance of cultural narratives in structuring oppression can be extended to the thin ideal. Feminist authors, such as Naomi Wolf, Carole Spitzack and Patricia Fallon and her colleagues have argued that standards of beauty are a mechanism of social control.[18] Applying Fine's framework, silence about the role of the cultural ultimatum for thinness in oppressing women protects the dominant view by masking the power relations, allowing them to remain unanalysed and uncontested. Public discussion of weight preoccupation and the ways individuals resist it, positions women to challenge this social control and can itself be interpreted politically as resistance.

Resistance may be directed at changing the cultural imperatives regarding weight, but this may not seem practical to individuals. Under conditions where changing unjust societal structures is not a viable option, James Scott has argued that everyday resistance will be focused on preserving self-esteem and human dignity.[19] The expression of healthy resistance to societal pressure on females to be dissatisfied with their bodies may take this form.

The goal of this chapter is to open up this discussion, to explore the ways women and teens resist weight preoccupation. What does resistance to weight preoccupation look like in actual practice? How do women and girls express resistance to weight preoccupation? How does it fit into their lives? What are the difficulties they encounter? Why do some resist more strongly than others? What do they lose and what do they gain by resisting?

MOTHER AND DAUGHTER RESISTANCE

A number of researchers have suggested that young girls, racially oppressed and working-class women are most likely to resist social
norms.[20] The members of these groups would be likely candidates as
resisters, and their resistance might apply to our culture's weight norms.
This was a major rationale for interviewing inner-city adolescent girls
and their mothers, a population consisting of middle-aged women and
their young teenaged daughters from ethnically mixed and primarily
lower-income families.[21]

The ways in which weight concerns are articulated within a
mother-daughter pair are also of interest because it is widely believed
that mothers are a major, if not *the* major, influence on their daughters.
Although the family to be discussed next demonstrates the potential for
a mother to influence her daughter at a particular point in time, I do
not wish to imply that all resistance or, for that matter, weight preoccupation, is inspired by the mother. The interviews with twenty mother-
daughter pairs do not support this conclusion, and the few non-clinical
studies correlating mother-daughter attitudes to weight provide conflicting evidence.[22] The direction, intensity and extent of a mother's
influence on her daughter is complex and unquestionably linked to the
girl's developmental age. A thorough discussion of these factors is beyond the scope of this chapter.

Talking about weight with these primarily lower-income girls and
women elicited variable levels of concern.[23] As individuals explained
why weight was an issue (for girls and women generally, and often, for
themselves specifically) they invariably expressed resistance to these
influences to a greater or lesser degree. One mother and daughter were
both deeply committed to resisting weight preoccupation in their own
lives. I selected this pair as a case study because of the strength and consistency of resistance expressed in each of their interviews. However,
with the exception of the specific action taken by the daughter, the
strategies evident in their interviews were present in other interviews as
well. Focusing on these resistance-rich interviews allows an opportunity
to examine strategies used to fight weight pressures as practised in daily
life within the context of a single family.

Studying such resistance is inherently theoretically valuable. It
takes on added significance because weight dissatisfaction is reported as

pervasive, even epidemic, the "normative discontent" referred to earlier. Studying healthy reactions to weight preoccupation may suggest practical ways to influence preventative measures.

MOTHERS AND DAUGHTERS IN THE STUDY

It is important to understand the mother and daughter's comments in the context of the twenty mother-daughter pairs that I interviewed. I therefore will give a brief description of the sample and some of their insights. The sample was drawn randomly from the class list of Grade-Eight girls attending an inner-city school in Winnipeg, Manitoba, between October 1992 and March 1993.[24] The women in this group were middle-aged with an average age of forty-one (thirty-two to fifty-four). Their daughters were mainly thirteen and fourteen. Eleven mothers were single parents. The mother-daughter pairs came from different backgrounds. Nine families identified their ancestry as Native, seven as European and four were first generation immigrant families (from Latin America, Eastern Europe and Asia). Two-thirds of the families' incomes fell below the Low Income Cut Off, a measure sometimes equated with poverty. The average income was $23,527 for an average household size of 4.2 people.[25]

The women's educational backgrounds were diverse. One woman had attended university for nine years. Another grew up on a trap-line in northern Manitoba with no opportunity for formal schooling. Women's educational achievements frequently mismatched employment and income experiences, making the assignment of class problematic. Of the twelve women who had graduated from high school or attended college or university, eight were living below the poverty line. The majority of these women were or had been employed in positions such as cook, cleaner, store clerk or sewing machine operator. Six of the eight families that might have been classified as working class had no wage earner at the time of the interview. Four families could be described as middle class. Given the complications of class assignment, it seems preferable to rely on descriptive statistics to situate the sample.[26]

The mix of educational and occupational experience turned out to be serendipitous because, contrary to my expectations, it was the more "middle-class" women who expressed more resistance.[27] Five women consciously advocated political action to counteract the pressure on girls and women to be slim. These women cannot be characterized by size as two were "heavy," two were "average" weight and one was "thin."[28] They were university educated or had a long history of involvement with feminism or disability activism. Two of the women had lived in countries where the attitudes to weight were much more accepting of heavy people. Four were currently single, and one was living with her fiancé. This clustering suggests that single status, in particular a failed marriage, may play a role in inspiring examination of many assumptions, including weight preoccupation, although there were certainly single women in the study who did not question weight norms as extensively. The women expressing relatively more resistance to weight preoccupation seemed to be comparatively better off financially, even if incomes fell below the poverty line. This suggests a more complicated relationship between social class and resistance to cultural weight norms than originally suggested. The number of women expressing extensive resistance is small, and so these comments are offered speculatively.

Of the women who actively resisted applying societal weight norms to their own lives, only two of their daughters followed suit. Each mother and daughter in these two pairs stressed that she thought her own body was quite acceptable. One mother and her daughter both said other people perceived them as too thin. The second pair, whom I refer to as Irene and Izzy, said others perceived them as overweight or obese.[29] I focus on Irene and Izzy because being seen as large is both more common and more challenging. I begin with a summary of how weight was discussed by the two age groups and then discuss how Irene and Izzy coped with being seen as large women.

TALKING ABOUT INFLUENCES
ON WEIGHT CONCERNS

My key questions were intended to assist participants to reflect on why girls and women are concerned about weight. To this end, I asked the teens if weight was a problem for girls, and, if appropriate, if it was more of an issue for girls than for boys. I asked similar questions with slightly different wording of the women. As anticipated, most participants responded affirmatively, and this allowed a discussion of the influences on weight concerns, and particularly why these influences varied for girls and boys, for women and men, and for overweight and underweight people. These questions brought into focus a number of themes that were raised by most participants, although the two age groups emphasized them differently.[30]

The girls talked most extensively about the role of weight in attracting friends (especially boys) and avoiding teasing (especially by boys) about being too fat or too skinny. They said weight was important to be able to wear nice clothes and look good, and many noted the influence of models in setting the standards. The role of weight in health was frequently although briefly mentioned. This discussion emphasized problems associated with being underweight.

The women's discussion of their experiences with lovers and spouses sometimes reinforced and justified the perceptions of the girls that being overweight could have severe negative social consequences. One woman, for example, discussed how her husband had left her for a younger, "drop-dead gorgeous" woman. More frequently, women related experiences of intimacy that ameliorated pressures to be thin. In these instances, women related reassurances from their husbands of continued love regardless of size or appearance. Generally, the women talked about their own friends as being supportive, sometimes commenting that this was not the case for their daughter or her friends. The women said that appearances could affect a woman's employment opportunities. The importance of looking good was discussed more circumspectly by the women than the girls, but was an issue for both. Women talked more about the difficulty of finding clothing that fit and was comfortable, attractive and reasonably priced. They also talked about teasing, and how it affected them and their daughters. Some had vivid memories of intensely painful childhood and adult experiences. The women, in contrast to the girls, discussed health and social impacts largely in terms of being overweight. Some were experiencing health problems which they saw as caused by being heavy. They emphasized the issues of health and media representations of thin bodies more than the girls.

Although health was mentioned by almost everyone, both the girls and the women focused on specific social problems associated with weight. Both groups described a consistent pattern of external pressure to be a "perfect" weight, neither too fat nor too skinny, with rewards accruing to those able to approximate this narrowly defined standard. Discussion of teasing permeated the interviews and came across as a strong sanction against disregarding beauty standards.

While these pressures were universally recognized, there was a great deal of variability in the personal concerns about their own weight, especially amongst the girls. Few girls, but more than half of the women, were "heavy."[31] Similar to other reports, about half of the girls (twelve of twenty) and two-thirds of the women (fifteen of twenty) wanted to lose weight. About one-quarter of the girls were trying to gain weight, a finding not commonly reported in studies of girls' attitudes towards weight. Three girls and two women expressed little interest in weight issues, which is obviously difficult to interpret. Two girls and three women actively resisted applying weight norms to themselves. Even though the majority of both girls and women said they were concerned about being overweight, to some extent everyone reacted against idealized weight stereotyping.

While more women than girls wanted to lose weight, the women generally expressed more disagreement with the weight-related pressures they described, suggesting both more concern about their own weight and more resistance to externally imposed weight norms. This paradoxical juxtaposition may be accounted for by several factors. The acceptance of and resistance to body weight norms increases in complexity with maturity, which brings both increasing body weight and more life experience. While many of the women and girls expressed disagreement with idealized weight norms, Irene and Izzy — the mother and daughter in the case study — integrate intellectual challenges to weight preoccupation with a practical resistance to the pressures on them to attempt weight loss. Izzy and her mother, Irene, are both active resisters and are both dealing with similar weight issues in their own lives.

The Mother:
Pioneering Anti-Fattist Philosophy

When asked to describe herself, Irene said:

> [I'm] a single mother, two teenagers, which is important, who really struggles to live in a real ethical manner. And who really wants to not leave the planet worse than the way I came into it ... I describe myself as a feminist. It is important. It's central to my life ... And I often describe myself as an activist. And then I talk more about the work that I do.

Irene is a high-school graduate who works as a consultant out of her small, efficiently organized bungalow. Irene's ex-husband, a truck driver, provides some child support. Irene talked about being poor in the sense of not being able to provide her children all the opportunities she would like to give them. She had family and friends in the city she could draw on, and she was resourceful herself, making her seem well off compared with other families in this study.

Irene's long struggle with her weight provides a necessary background for her remarks. She said that someone comments on her size just about every day. She has been dealing with weight issues since her adolescence. She matured early and weighed about 150 pounds [68 kilograms] by age thirteen or fourteen. She said she was considered "very fat" by her classmates, and this affected who would be her friend. She recalled her school days as the worst period in her life. She described being "humiliated" into dieting in her teen years by her "fat-hating" family. Weight was not the reason for her marriage break-up, but she said deep down her husband did not approve of her size either.

Irene attended her first weight loss group at age seventeen and got her weight down to approximately 130 pounds (59 kilograms). Then she yo-yoed, going back up, losing it all again, and so on. In her early twenties, prior to her first pregnancy, she found herself gaining 20 and 30 pounds (10 and 13.6 kilograms) a month, and was diagnosed with a hypothyroid problem. She said, "I have tried my whole life to be smaller." She had stopped dieting nine years prior to the interview, at the age of twenty-nine.

Irene said life is improving as she gets older. People no longer judge her on the basis of her looks, but respect her personality, skills and abilities. Nevertheless, she indicated that her early childhood experiences continued to influence her: "I think that basically on some deep down level, I believe that I don't deserve certain things because I'm large ... This is just a carry over [from childhood]." Irene expressed these difficult feelings despite volunteer work on weight preoccupation in schools, with much time and conscious thought devoted to the issue.

She also expressed a strong awareness of weight biases. She articulated how tenacious these ideas about weight are, even in someone who has spent much time studying and actively challenging cultural attitudes to weight. She made an explicit comparison with racism:

> I know I do have fattist attitudes too. Like everyone does. It's sort of like that idea of racism. We all are racist, 'cause we're all raised in a racist society. We all are homophobic because we're raised in a homophobic society and we are all fattist. I have a bit more consciousness about it, 'cause I have to live in it ... I see it [fattist attitudes] even in close friends or family, and it's a real challenge because how do we discuss this in a way that we can all even talk about it?

Irene discussed how weight preoccupation permeates daily life, giving the way we conceptualize health as an important example. Health messages about weight create confusion, she said, "because we're told that there's only one way to be healthy and that's to be small." She cited actress Victoria Principal, "one of these stars that became an exercise guru," as an example of "sanctioned bulimia":

> And she said that she just would not be the size she was if she didn't exercise four hours a day. Well, maybe that's true for me too. I never even tried that. But to be healthy you don't have to exercise for four hours a day ... And it's all talking about health, but it isn't talking about health. It is talking about keeping her body a certain way, a certain size, shape ... And it's just all masked in that she's healthy.

Irene is drawing a parallel between bulimia (compulsive eating followed by purging) and compulsive exercising to burn off calories. Neither are healthy behaviours, but "sanctioned bulimia," as Irene refers to it, is not even recognized as a problem because our fattist attitudes lead us to equate skinny and healthy. This masks the behaviour. Irene pointed out that women in her aerobics class would start out by talking about being there to get fit and improve their health, but ended by discussing how many doughnuts they had burned off, an underlying motivation that parallels Victoria Principal's logic. This demonstrates again how health discussions can be a facade for the other motives, "the curtain that covers everything else," a smokescreen allowing us to delude ourselves and others about our reasons for pursuing thinness.

No one else discussed fattist attitudes and how thinking of skinny as a proxy for good health influenced us, possibly to the detriment of our health. Many respondents, although not all, indicated an awareness of weight preoccupation, usually as they discussed how the media's impossible standards caused some girls and women to think of themselves as fat when they were not. They also discussed people's obsessive focus on weight regardless of one's size, giving examples of how this could create problems.

While many women and girls emphasized that they did not judge other people based on what they looked like, few suggested that they too were entitled to similar respectful treatment. Fewer still insisted on this treatment for themselves. This is a difficult area for women. Irene comments on the disparity between how she treated others and how she treated herself: "I notice a whole bunch of incongruities in my life. I'm trying to learn how to be more accepting and tolerant of other people and then I notice that I'm not very accepting to myself. Generally I'd say I am, but I have times when I'm not happy with the way I look."

Size acceptance requires reflecting on and rejecting the standards people use in making judgements. When I asked Irene how she rates her body, she said, "Compared to what the world thinks I should be, I'm markedly overweight. I know that's how I would be defined. But you know, I think that I'm just about right because when I think about what we need to do on the planet, it doesn't have much to do with that." While she answered my question, Irene refused to allow herself to be defined by it, insisting on broadening the framework to terms that she found more acceptable.

Consistent with this philosophy, here is Irene's explanation of why she consciously chose to stop dieting:

So I thought, "Here I am trying to love myself but I'm dieting." And other people have described dieting as a way of self-care. I don't see it that way at all. Especially if you're going through starvation diets. You know, you're pretty miserable. I saw it really as an act of self-hatred. I was primarily motivated to diet because I hated the way I looked. Just hated it. And I thought, "Here I am trying to love myself and then at the same time I'm doing this thing." It doesn't fit.

Irene's opposition to "lifelong semi-starvation" did not mean she was uninterested in health issues. Elsewhere, Irene emphasized her efforts to eat healthily and maintain an active lifestyle. She was clear that health, not weight loss, was the goal.

Irene suggested that education is needed to help women see that this is "more than a personal problem ... most of all to become aware of how infiltrated we are with these weight messages." She emphasized that it takes ongoing effort to counteract the ongoing negative cultural messages, and this is difficult work. When asked what advice she gave her daughter about weight, Irene first promoted the use of caution when giving advice to teenagers, and then described her approach:

I really reinforce that she's just perfect the way she is, that she's a very wonderful young woman, and that she has very many gifts to offer the world ... I encourage her to be active in the world and well, it's just like me. Make sure that your body is healthy, take good care of it, that kind of self-care stuff.

She also discussed a more indirect influence on her daughter:

I've really talked about this being such a fat-hating culture. I don't talk just about it with my daughter but she hears it within other conversations and there's the fact that I'm so anti-diet or anti-starvation actually ... By this time many kids would have been [on] a few diets, and she isn't [like] that at all. So, yeah, I think it [my awareness] really has influenced her.

THE DAUGHTER: TAKING ACTION

Similar to her mother's history, Izzy also had a mature figure by age fourteen. She said she was often mistaken for a twelfth grader, even though she was an eighth grader. Despite this, almost all of Izzy's remarks were consistent with liking her body. She did not weigh herself on principle, did not have an ideal weight and did not diet. When asked if she was happy with the way she looked, Izzy replied, "People tell me I'm pretty all the time, so I'm finally beginning to believe it after a long time, and I wouldn't want to change anything about me. So I think I'm very happy [with my looks]." While expressed tentatively, Izzy's response was more positive than most of her schoolmates. Only four other girls answered this query positively, and two of them were trying to alter their weight.

When asked, Izzy rated herself as slightly overweight but indicated that she did not think of herself this way. Like her mother, she rejected the framework of the question. When asked if she was afraid of getting fat, Izzy said she wasn't because she would always have friends who would accept her. She said she didn't want to get too thin and described a book about a girl who had died from bulimia. When asked if weight could be controlled, she replied, "I think you should just be happy with the way you are."

Izzy recognized weight as a major concern for girls: "I think that's a big problem because everybody wants to be skinny and they're just not happy with the way they look. No one is. Well, maybe me." She echoed the other girls in observing that boys chose thin girls for girlfriends and that "girls who are slightly overweight don't have as many friends." These are important concerns, and Izzy addressed them early in her interview. She said girls are concerned about their weight because they want to be popular, "but you just got [to] be yourself. If you're very nice, like friendly, and stuff." I interpret this to mean that she considered character to be preferable to looks as the basis for friendship despite recognizing that girls and boys superficially relate on the basis of appearance. Unfortunately, we did not discuss this further, but her mother had volunteered a comment that reinforces, but doesn't confirm, this interpretation. Irene said that if her daughter thought weight loss was a good way to fit in, she'd probably try to lose weight, but she had decided to try "just being really friendly and reaching out to people."

Izzy also observed that girls are teased about weight. She attributed the negative effects of this to a girl's self-perception and self-esteem, rather than to the weight or being teased. She said, "If she thought she was [overweight], her self-esteem would go really low, and she might get in with the wrong crowds and start smoking and stuff like that and she might actually ruin her life." There's a fine distinction in Izzy's choice of words: "If she thought she was overweight" implies that everything hinges on a girl's interpretation. There's a difference between being fat and how you feel about yourself. By being clear about this distinction, she controls the major effects of the teasing. The way to protect your self-identity is not by relying on peer approval, which might lead you to engage in self-destructive behaviours. You must have good self-esteem and think for yourself. This is generally good advice that Izzy has applied to the weight issue.

This was not just a theoretical argument for Izzy, as she was currently defending herself from what most people call teasing, but what she referred to as "harassment." She said she had been "harassed" about her weight by a group of four or five boys for about a year. She referred to "Hank" as the "ringleader," noting that he constantly made rude comments about her weight, sometimes of an explicitly sexual nature. She described her treatment as sexual harassment, an explanation that she attributed to a recent conversation with her mother. She thought the reason for this harassment was because she looked older and more mature than everybody else.

Initially, she tried to ignore Hank, but she found his rudeness upsetting. On her own initiative, she had called Hank's mother to discuss his inappropriate behaviour. This did not result in any improvement and she was now using the informal student-conflict manager system at her school. She had gone through the process with one of the other boys and it went well. He reported not knowing that the teasing upset her and his behaviour had improved. She was planning to discuss the problem with Hank and two student-conflict managers the next day. She was understandably nervous about this meeting, reporting sleepless and tearful nights. She was worried her actions might backfire and increase the harassment. If this occurred, she was considering changing schools the next year, a decision she was reluctant to make because she didn't want to leave her friends.

Her meeting with Hank was initially successful. His behaviour improved, but only briefly. Izzy's actions worked to some extent, but the ending was ambiguous. Hank changed schools before we could learn whether he would have continued his intimidation. Consequently we do not know if Izzy would have continued to resist or switched schools. Protest does not ensure success, however, and the easier resolution was no doubt welcomed by Izzy.

Izzy's experience with teasing may seem trivial; however, politics are built on trivia. Almost every study of schoolgirls records similar incidents, which are typically dismissed as "boys will be boys" or "it means he really likes you." Hank's harassment of Izzy is a blatant attempt to control her behaviour. His use of sexual innuendo to question her morality is a time-honoured tradition adopted by some men to keep women in line.

To appreciate why Izzy's actions are acts of resistance it is helpful to consider the other interviews. The almost universal reaction of the other girls and women to even the possibility that someone might *think* they were fat was to attempt to lose weight or to turn their anger inward to self-loathing. Izzy did neither. She refused to redefine herself as fat. She refused to feel bad about herself and to attempt to correct an alleged defective body by dieting. Although she verbally considered that she might change schools in the future, she did not actually run away from this difficult situation. She did not dismiss Hank's behaviour as "just teasing." She named it harassment and challenged her harassers to examine and change their behaviour. She expected to be treated with respect, and requested such treatment when it was not forthcoming.

Stating the problem as harassment shifts the focus from fixing the body to dealing with rude behaviour. Rather than individualizing the issue, with its tendency to self-blame, Izzy's approach is politicized action. If girls were able to do more of this, their acts of resistance would improve their everyday lives. And boys would learn that sexual harassment is unacceptable behaviour, an important lesson for the adult world they will soon be entering.

FURTHER REFLECTIONS

Surveys that focus on weight preoccupation gloss over the ways that women and girls disagree with societal weight norms. This chapter has focused on one mother-daughter pair in more depth than is possible in a survey. As stated previously, these interviews were atypical, not in the modes of resistance employed but in the extent of resistance expressed. My interpretation of this unique mother-daughter example is offered, not to generalize, but to contribute to a fuller understanding of existing and potential resistance. It is offered in the context of women's complex and varied reactions to multiple pressures promoting unrealistic body shapes. Studying healthy reactions to unhealthy pressures, within the context of a specific family, may offer insights useful in working with other teens and their families.

Attitudes to weight are complicated. As groups, the girls and women interviewed discussed the influence of friends, boyfriends, teasing, the media and their own desire to be attractive and healthy as issues that shaped their attitudes to weight. Noticeably absent was any discussion of family influence, even when specifically queried. While this mother had an obvious influence on her daughter, there were other families where a daughter was extremely weight preoccupied but her mother was unconcerned about her own weight. This was particularly obvious in several of the immigrant families. There was no instance where both mother and daughter demonstrated extreme concern about weight. As mentioned earlier, some studies have found a relationship between mothers' and daughters' attitudes to weight, while others have not.

The overall mother-daughter relationship and similarity of body shape and life experiences are potentially important factors in determining a mother's influence on her daughter. Irene articulated a well-thought out political position on weight. This presumably guided her weight-related communication with Izzy. It seems obvious that Izzy's resistance results from her mother's influence. It seemed equally obvious, in both the mother's and her daughter's interview, that they had a good relationship. Irene, then, is able to communicate her love and understanding to her daughter. She is sensitive in providing educational instruction on occasions when Izzy might be receptive. She teaches indirectly, respecting Izzy's search for autonomy, knowing that her daughter needs to experiment and learn for herself. The mother's memory of her own treatment as a child and adolescent positions her to share her experiences around weight in a way that can assist her daughter in understanding her own situation. Irene's reflection and subsequent education inform how she now handles weight issues and what she can pass on to Izzy. While the daughter at age fourteen and sixteen expressed ideas similar to her mother's, the mother's own evolving philosophy is a reminder that weight perceptions are not static.

Understanding how the mother learned to resist weight preoccupation is problematic. Irene did not learn her resistance to weight preoccupation from her own mother. By her own report, her mother's body shape, experience and philosophy were radically different from her own. The widespread condemnation that she describes from her childhood is tragically common, but does not commonly result in this degree of resistance. It may be that the long and unsuccessful struggle to conform, combined with activist tendencies, primed Irene to be attentive when she encountered alternative views on weight. While these alternative views exist, they are continuously undermined by messages promoting slenderness from media, friends and family. The mother discusses how difficult and tiring it was, and still is, to continually reinforce counter-culture views. Nonetheless, she realizes that this alternative viewpoint is critical to her mental health and social well-being. While being heavy does not seem to be a prerequisite or a predictor of resistance, failed efforts at weight loss and the experience of prejudice may play a role in inspiring resistance to conventional ideals.

The preservation of individual identity, self-esteem and dignity is basic to the resistance examined here. The major gain in taking this stance is the retention of a positive view of self that allows the individual to live a fuller life. Relegating weight to an irrelevant status frees people to pursue realistic goals more directly, such as health, friendship and personal achievement. For example, Irene focuses on healthy lifestyle rather than weight loss. Izzy tries to make friends by being friendly, rather than attempting popularity through a superficial focus on beauty.

Resistance might have been somewhat easier for Izzy if there had been more visible support for her to tap into, a broader public discussion of the rightfulness of her actions. But there is no widely shared talk that counters the publicly expressed social norms. Izzy was one of the few girls who said she does not talk about weight with her friends, possibly an indication that she does not expect them to understand or support her position. Being different entails effort and courage. The cost was evident in Izzy's anxiety over her position. She was well aware that not everyone will admire the oppositional stance she took.

Irene explicitly compared fattist attitudes to racism. The strategies elaborated here resemble strategies developed by African-American parents to innoculate their children against racism, as reported by Janie Victoria Ward. Ward found that African-American parents incorporate daily lessons of critical consciousness and resistance to prevailing negative images and evaluations of Blacks. This can be as simple as sharing personal experiences of discrimination, daily affirmations of the value and uniqueness of differentness (for example, regularly complimenting a child's kinky hair) and practise in analyzing racism by constantly critiquing media messages. Ward discussed how awareness of prejudice facilitated children's ability to understand how images shape perception and mask reality. Politically informed children were better able to resist internalizing negative messages and stereotypes and to create a self that included Blackness as positive and valued. Children confronted racism instead of blaming themselves for others' attitudes.[32] This is often cited as the reason black girls are better able to withstand the conventions of femininity, including the emaciated model stereotype. Niobe Way also found urban, poor and working-class girls to be outspoken (except with boys) and theorized parents socialized their girls to speak up, knowing it would be critical to survival.[33]

Surveys of girls' and women's weight-related behaviours continue to indicate that weight preoccupation is prevalent and has negative implications for physical and psychological health. Longitudinal studies are needed to delineate the changing influences on girls as they develop. Further research into healthy resistance to weight preoccupation is needed to discover the conditions that elicit resistance, the strategies used and whether vulnerable girls and women can usefully adopt such strategies.

The resistance discussed here included straightforward observations of weight-preoccupied behaviours, statements rejecting the application of unrealistic weight norms to others and — the greater challenge — to oneself, verbally defending self and others, a call for education and, finally, some politicized action. Building this discourse can itself be viewed as a political action, one that builds a foundation for further political action. These strategies recognize and reject weight norms in favour of more individualized goals. They are literal refusals to identify with cultural ideals of feminine beauty that can be damaging to both women and girls.

Notes

I am very grateful to "Irene and Izzy," the anonymous mother and daughter, for their extensive participation in this paper. Besides the interviews, they also read and commented on draft manuscripts. I also thank the girls and women who generously shared their thoughts with me, and to the school personnel who facilitated the interviews. I appreciate the guidance of Drs. Linda C. Garro, Patricia Kaufert and Karen Grant during my master's program. I also thank Pat Martens, Chris Egan, Tina Marchessault and Morley Walker for comments on the paper prepared for the CRIAW conference. Drs. Patricia Kaufert and Manly Spigelman, an anonymous reviewer and the editors of this volume, including Beth McAuley of Sumach Press, helped improve this chapter. I gratefully acknowledge financial support from the Canadian Home Economics Association, Canadian Dietetic Association and the University of Manitoba during my master's, and from Health Canada through a National Health Research and Development Program (NHRDP) Research Training Award during the writing period for this chapter.

1. Dairy Bureau of Canada, *Myths and Malnutrition: A Growing Problem. A Summary of Clinical Papers and Recent Studies* (Toronto, ON: Author, 1993).

2. Judith Rodin, Lisa Silberstein, and Ruth Striegel-Moore, "Women and Weight: A Normative Discontent," in I. B. Sonderegger, ed., *Nebraska Symposium on Motivation* (Lincoln: University of Nebraska Press, 1985), 267–307.

3. David M. Garner, "The 1997 Body Image Survey Results," *Psychology Today* (February 1997), 30–44, 75–84. For a summary of these influences, see also Gail D. M. Marchessault, "Weight Preoccupation in North American Culture," *Journal of the Canadian Dietetic Association* 54 (1993), 138–142.

4. Janet Davidson Allan, "Knowing What to Weigh: Women's Self-Care Activities Related to Weight," *Advances in Nursing Science* 11 (1988), 47–60.

5. Carole Spitzack, *Confessing Excess: Women and the Politics of Body Reduction* (Albany, NY: State University of New York Press, 1990).

6. Marci Millman, *Such a Pretty Face: Being Fat in America* (New York: W. W. Norton, 1980).

7. Jill Tunaley, Paula Nicolson, and Susan Walsh, "Young Women, Self and the Thin Ideal," paper presented at the Qualitative Health Research Conference, June 1994, Hershey, Pennsylvania.

8. Sheila Parker et al., "Body Image and Weight Concerns Among African American and White Adolescent Females: Differences that Make a Difference," *Human Organization* 54 (1995), 111.

9. Becky W. Thompson, *A Hunger So Wide and So Deep: A Multiracial View of Women's Eating Problems* (Minneapolis: University of Minnesota Press, 1996); L.K. George Hsu, "Are the Eating Disorders Becoming More Common in Blacks?" *International Journal of Eating Disorders* 6 (1998), 113–124.

10. Hilde Bruch, *The Golden Cage: The Enigma of Anorexia Nervosa* (Cambridge, MA: Harvard University, 1978); Orland W. Wooley, Susan C. Wooley, and Sue R. Dyrenforth, "Obesity and Women — II. A Neglected Feminist Topic," *Women's Studies International Quarterly* 2 (1979), 81–92.

11. Frances M. Berg is founder of *Healthy Weight Network* and editor of Healthy Weight Journal, and I am associate editor.

12. Kim Chernin, *The Obsession: Reflections on the Tyranny of Slenderness* (Toronto, ON: Fitzhenry and Whiteside, 1981); Naomi Wolf, *The Beauty Myth* (Toronto, ON: Vintage Books, 1990).

13. Health and Welfare Canada, *Promoting Healthy Weights: A Discussion Paper* (Ottawa, ON: Author, 1988).

14. Susie Orbach, *Hunger Strike: The Anorectic's Struggle as a Metaphor for Our Age* (New York: W.W. Norton, 1986).

15. Lila Abu-Lughod, "The Romance of Resistance: Tracing Transformations of Power Through Bedouin Women," *American Ethnologist* 17 (1990), 41–55.

16. Susie Orbach, *Fat is a Feminist Issue: A Self-help Guide for Compulsive Eaters* (New York: Berkley Books, 1981).

17. Michelle Fine, *Disruptive Voices: The Possibilities of Feminist Research*, 4th ed. (Ann Arbor: University of Michigan Press, 1995).

18. Patricia Fallon, Melanie A. Katzman, and Susan C. Wooley, eds., *Feminist Perspectives on Eating Disorders* (New York: Guilford Press, 1994). See also Spitzack, *Confessing Excess*, and Wolf, *The Beauty Myth*.

19. James C. Scott, *Domination and the Arts of Resistance* (New Haven: Yale, 1990).

20. See for example, Michelle Fine, "Passions, Politics, and Power: Feminist Research Possibilities," in Michelle Fine, ed., *Disruptive Voices: The Possibilities of Feminist Research* (Ann Arbor: University of Michigan Press, 1995), 205–231; Carol Gilligan, "Joining the Resistance: Psychology, Politics, Girls and Women," *Michigan Quarterly Review* 24 (1990), 501–536; bell hooks, *Feminist Theory: From Margin to Center* (Boston, MA: South End Press, 1984); Emily Martin, *The Woman in the Body: A Cultural Analysis of Reproduction* (Boston, MA: Beacon Press, 1987).

21. Other investigators have suggested that working-class women value thinness less than other women. For example, Sobal suggests lower socioeconomic status (SES) cultures in the US "are often more accepting and even desiring of obesity in women." Jeffery Sobal, "Obesity and Socioeconomic Status: A Framework for Examining Relationships Between Physical and Social Variables," *Medical Anthropology* 13 (1991), 238. It has also been suggested that women from a variety of

minority groups have relaxed weight goals. This would be interesting, but would not be resistance. There is also some evidence for comparable weight concerns across SES groups. See P. Leichner et al., "An Epidemiologic Study of Maladaptive Eating Attitudes in a Canadian School Age Population," *International Journal of Eating Disorders* 5 (1986), 969–982. See also Allan, "Knowing What to Weigh." One of the goals of this research was to investigate such claims in this understudied segment of society.

22. Two studies that provide support for this hypothesis include Ilana Attie and J. Brooks-Gunn, "Development of Eating Problems in Adolescent Girls: A Longitudinal Study," *Developmental Psychology* 25 (1989), 70–79; and Andrew J. Hill, Claire Weaver, and John E. Blundell, "Dieting Concerns of 10-year-old Girls and their Mothers," *British Journal of Clinical Psychology* 29 (1990), 346–348. Studies that find more mixed results include Kathleen M. Pike and Judith Rodin, "Mothers, Daughters, and Disordered Eating," *Journal of Abnormal Psychology* 100 (1991), 198–204; Gail Marchessault, "Urban Aboriginal Mothers' and Daughters' Expressed Concerns about Weight: An Interview Study," in Jill Oakes and Rick Riewe, eds., *Issues in the North* (Winnipeg, MB: Canadian Circumpolar Institute, 1998), 3–12.

23. While the women and girls are mothers and daughters, it is only when the data is paired that this relationship is relevant. I refer to the women as mothers only within the context of family relationship in order to avoid a potential ecological fallacy, that is, women and girls may be similar, but this does not mean individual mothers and daughters are similar. Applying group norms to individual pairs can create an ecological fallacy.

24. The school principal mailed information about the project to the mothers. Subsequently, I phoned or visited to explain the study further and request the mother's participation. If the mother consented, I interviewed her and then requested permission to approach her daughter. All of the mothers interviewed provided this consent. I then approached the daughter in the same way. The sample consisted of twenty of the twenty-five eligible families contacted, a response rate of 80 percent. The primary method of data collection was in-depth interviewing. A qualitative approach was considered appropriate given the exploratory intent. I used an interview guide, but asked more questions to follow up interesting leads and to clarify meaning, as is standard procedure in qualitative research. Close-ended questions were asked to measure concern over weight. Mothers were asked for background information. All but one interview was tape-recorded and fully transcribed. The initial interviews and selected portions of all interviews were coded line-by-line to systematically generate themes based on the interviewees' open-ended responses. Version 2.0 of Gofer (Microlytics, 1989) was used to search, find and retrieve text.

25. Descriptive statistics are based on a sample size of twenty families, except for income. Income calculations are based on eighteen women who gave their household income to the nearest $5,000. The midpoint of the range or actual income was used according to the method outlined by Statistics Canada, "Income Distributions by Size in Canada" (Ottawa, ON: Author, 1990). The Low Income Cut Off is referred to as the poverty line by the Economic Council of Canada, "The New

Face of Poverty: Income Security Needs of Canadian Families" (Ottawa, ON: Canada Communication Group, 1992).

26. Further details about the education and employment backgrounds of the women in the sample are as follows: of the twenty women, five had a post-secondary certificate, diploma or university degree; four had some post-secondary education; four had some secondary education; three had completed high school; and four had less than eight years of schooling. At the time of the study, three women were enrolled in adult education programs and one was at university. Nine households had no wage-earner, seven had one and four had two. Ten women classified themselves as employed (two were part-time), four as homemakers, four as students, one as unemployed and one said she was a "full-time volunteer."

27. This also seems to be the case with inner-city and suburban families that I am currently interviewing.

28. A person's size is a relevant factor in understanding their weight-related reactions. The body mass index (BMI — weight in kilograms divided by height in metres squared) was developed to assess health risks associated with adiposity (Health and Welfare Canada, *Promoting Healthy Weights*). It is used here for descriptive purposes. A BMI between twenty and twenty-five is considered a healthy weight for most adults (referred to here as "average"). A BMI above twenty-seven is considered to increase health risks due to overweight ("heavy") and less than twenty may be considered underweight ("thin"). The BMIs are based on self-reported data and should be considered approximate. The BMI terminology implies a value judgement that is irrelevant to my purpose. "Thin" and "heavy" are not parallel in meaning, but people do not speak of women as being "light," and while "fat" is appropriate and politically correct to those fighting for fat acceptance, it usually is interpreted as a negative value judgement. Therefore, the admittedly unsatisfactory categories of "thin" and "heavy" are used.

29. All names are pseudonyms, and some details have been changed to protect confidentiality. Quotes have been edited to improve readability. All quotes that follow are taken from these two interviews.

30. These themes are drawn from Gail D. M. Marchessault, "How Mothers and Daughters Talk about Weight" (master's thesis, University of Manitoba, 1993).

31. Two women had BMIs less than twenty; seven were between twenty and twenty-five; one was between twenty-five and twenty-seven; and nine were greater than twenty-seven. Eight girls had BMIs less than twenty; seven were between twenty and twenty-five; and one was greater than twenty-seven. Two women and five girls did not provide their height and weight. The women clearly had BMIs greater than twenty-seven.

32. Janie Victoria Ward, "Raising Resistors: The Role of Truth Telling in the Psychological Development of African American Girls," in Bonnie J. Ross Leadbeater and Niobe Way, eds., *Urban Girls: Resisting Stereotypes, Creating Identities* (New York: New York University Press, 1996), 85–116.

33. Niobe Way, "'Can't You Hear the Courage, the Strength that I Have': Listening to Urban Adolescent Girls Speak about their Relationships," *Psychology of Women Quarterly* 19 (1995), 107–128.

CHAPTER TWELVE

WOMEN, WEIGHT AND APPEARANCE SATISFACTION

AN AGELESS PURSUIT OF THINNESS

*Michelle N. Lafrance, Marilyn T. Zivian
and Anita M. Myers*

໑

IN RECENT DECADES, EATING DISORDERS have become more prevalent in North America. They occur primarily among adolescent and young adult women and can have serious health consequences. According to a recent US report, approximately five million Americans, 90 percent of whom are women, are affected by the eating disorders of "anorexia nervosa" and "bulimia nervosa." Only half of those suffering from anorexia nervosa are expected to recover fully; and over the next decade, more than 5 percent of those with this disorder are expected to die as a result. Thirty percent of those currently suffering from bulimia nervosa are expected to have recurring symptoms of the disorder during their lifetime. The average age of onset for anorexia nervosa is around seventeen years (with some studies suggesting two peak ages for onset, fourteen and eighteen, respectively), while bulimia nervosa first occurs in late adolescence and early adulthood.[1]

It is not surprising, therefore, that attempts to understand the development of anorexia and bulimia nervosa, and the extreme dissatisfaction with body weight and appearance that accompany these eating disorders, have focused almost exclusively on girls and young women. Concerns about weight occur at a young age. Girls as young as three to five years of age have been found to express worry about their weight. With the onset of puberty and the associated increase in fat tissue, female adolescents become increasingly dissatisfied with their body image and appearance.[2] An alarmingly high proportion of adolescent girls report being dissatisfied with their bodies — and a great many are willing to use methods of weight loss with potentially dangerous consequences for their health. Findings of studies in recent years suggest that body dissatisfaction is endemic among female high-school students, with approximately 60 percent expressing a desire to lose weight. Many young women believe that being thinner would have a positive impact on their lives; the use of extreme methods of weight loss such as fasting, vomiting, crash diets, diet pills or laxatives is common in this age group. However, body dissatisfaction in adolescent girls seems to be unrelated to actual body size, with many girls desiring to lose weight although their weight is within (or even below) the range considered normal and healthy for their height and build.[3]

A similar pattern of findings with respect to body dissatisfaction has emerged from studies with older adolescent and young adult women. For instance, among female university students, most report being dissatisfied with their appearance and perceive their current shape to be larger than ideal — and larger than the shape they believe to be most attractive to men. So many North American women are dissatisfied with their weight that some researchers have referred to such findings as reflecting a "normative discontent." Moreover, dieting is so widespread among women that it can now be considered "normal" eating behaviour.[4]

Only a few studies have investigated weight and appearance dissatisfaction among women older than university age and these studies find that although older women may be less interested in their appearance and body shape, they are as dissatisfied as younger women with their weight. Such findings indicate that the desire for thinness is not limited to younger women. For instance, one study asked women over the age of sixty-two their views about aging and found that weight gain was a major concern. In fact, the only thing that concerned these older women more than gaining weight was loss of memory.[5]

Studies of weight and appearance satisfaction have rarely included participants who represent a wide variety of ages. Where such studies have been conducted, they have typically involved surveys by magazines. Three surveys have been conducted by the magazine *Psychology Today*, the most recent in 1997. This survey found that 66 percent of the female participants, who were aged thirteen to ninety, were dissatisfied with their weight — a figure representing a significant increase from the 48 and 55 percent who reported being dissatisfied with their weight in the previous 1972 and 1985 *Psychology Today* surveys.[6] These lifespan surveys, together with findings of studies with older women, suggest that the desire to be thinner is not something that is limited to young women. And, the increase in the rate of weight dissatisfaction that appears to have occurred since 1972 indicates that women of all ages may be influenced by the current — very thin — standard of female beauty regardless of the cultural ideals of female beauty that were fashionable when they were young women.

From the late 1800s to the early 1900s (when the oldest respondents in the three *Psychology Today* surveys would have been in adolescence and young adulthood) the female ideal was the "Gibson girl": a woman with a slender bodyline, large hips and a large bust. During this period, women were likely to worry about being too thin. They tried to gain weight, weighed themselves frequently and used padding and bustles to make their bodies appear fuller. This fashion was reversed for a short period of time during the 1920s when the ideal female body type was almost boylike in shape. Padding was removed, corsets were abandoned and brassieres were used to bind women's breasts and flatten their silhouettes. During this period, bust-waist-hip measurements of the average Miss America contest winners were 32-25-35.[7] No winner had a bust size larger than her hips. Women used rolling machines, iodine, starvation diets and strenuous exercise to reduce their weight. In 1920, a conference of the New York Academy of Science was convened to study the "outbreak" of eating disorders.

In the 1930s, female beauty ideals shifted again and larger breasts once more became fashionable. During this period, the average Miss America contest winners' bust measurement increased to 34 inches, and the breast size of contest winners continued to increase. During the 1960s, nearly all Miss America contest winners had a larger bust than hip measurement. Within the entertainment and fashion worlds, women with large bosoms were favoured. Thus, for the older women in the *Psychology Today* surveys, larger, heavier-breasted women were "the fashion" for most of their adult lives. Following the late 1960s, however, the fashion norms shifted again; with a taller, thinner and smaller-breasted body becoming a more desirable shape for women. Whereas in 1894, the typical fashion model was 5'4" tall and weighed 140 pounds, by 1975 she was 5'8" tall and weighed only 118 pounds. During the 1980s, when the youngest participants in the 1997 *Psychology Today* survey were in their teens, a more muscular, healthy-looking but still thin body became the ideal. Bodybuilding became more acceptable for women, and women's fashions accentuated the more athletic look with the use of shoulder pads.[8]

The results of the *Psychology Today* surveys suggest that the desire to lose weight is characteristic of women regardless of their age or cohort.[9] If this is the case, it indicates that social and historical factors operating at the time when these surveys were carried out may lie behind the contemporary finding that weight dissatisfaction is widespread among women. One such influence is the unrealistically thin female body ideal that has been promoted within the media and popular culture since the 1970s. The extremely thin body size of fashion models depicted in magazines, the "thin" standard of female attractiveness promoted in the mass media (movies and television), the profusion of features on dieting and advertisements promoting weight loss products in women's magazines and on television in recent decades have been well documented.[10] Fallon suggests that the development of the mass media has been accompanied by an increased uniformity in standards of beauty and fashion in the West. And women themselves report that the greatest source of pressures to be thin come from the media.[11]

We designed the 1995 study to evaluate the hypothesis that women's desire to lose weight is primarily influenced by the current standard of female beauty being promoted by the media, rather than by their age or cohort. Neither the *Psychology Today* surveys (which did not directly investigate women's weight satisfaction in relation to their age) nor studies that included only older women allow for a direct test of this hypothesis. We asked women from a wide range of ages, from young teens to women in their late seventies, to rate how satisfied they were with their appearance and weight. They were also asked how many pounds they would like to gain or lose.[12] In addition, participants' height and weight were measured. If, however, women's satisfaction ratings are not related to their current weight or age, then cohort (past historical events), as well as age, can be ruled out as explanations for current body dissatisfaction. If, however, women's dissatisfaction with their weight and appearance is related to influences operating at the time of testing, the most likely reason is the current extremely thin standard of female beauty promoted in the media.[13]

TRACKING PRESENT-DAY STANDARDS

One hundred and ninety-nine women, ranging in age from 13 to 79 years took part in our study. The women were visitors to the Ontario Science Centre, a participatory science museum in Toronto, Ontario. Fifty-seven percent of the participants were Canadian and 43 percent were from the United States. The Ontario Science Centre tends to attract visitors who are slightly more educated and who have a higher socioeconomic status than the average person living in either the US or Canada; and the women in the present study were no exception. Most had at least one year of university education and could be classified as middle class.[14]

We solicited volunteers for the study by means of a sign placed near the museum entrance that invited women to take part in a study concerned about physical appearance.[15] The participants first completed a questionnaire in which they reported their age, height, weight, whether they wanted to lose or gain weight and how many pounds they wanted to gain or lose. They were also asked to rate their current level of satisfaction with their appearance and weight on 5-point scales. With regard to their appearance, participants indicated whether they were 1) greatly dissatisfied; 2) moderately dissatisfied; 3) neither satisfied nor dissatisfied; 4) moderately satisfied; or 5) greatly satisfied. With regard to their weight, participants indicated whether they were 1) greatly underweight; 2) slightly underweight; 3) at a desired weight; 4) slightly overweight; or 5) greatly overweight. After completing these ratings, participants were taken individually behind a screen where their weight and height were measured.

The women's weight and height measurements were converted to Body Mass Index (BMI) scores. BMI is a weight-to-height ratio score that provides an index of relative weight and takes into account individual differences in height. Because many of the younger participants probably had not yet reached their full adult height and since height is lost beyond midlife, BMI scores are more appropriate for comparing participants' weights. Overall, the older women tended to be somewhat heavier than the younger women.[16]

Based on the Statistics Canada guidelines,[17] BMI scores were grouped in the following way: individuals with BMI scores less than 20 were considered to be "underweight"; those with BMI scores between 20 and 25 were considered "normal weight"; those with BMI scores between 25 and 27 were classified as "slightly overweight"; and those with BMI scores over 27 were characterized as "overweight." Using these guidelines, a majority (75 percent) of the women who took part in the present study would be considered normal weight or underweight (BMI below 25).[18]

We next calculated the difference between what the women reported their weight to be and what they actually weighed. A large number (58 percent) of participants reported that they weighed less than was actually the case (an average of 6.5 pounds less). In contrast, only a quarter of the participants (26 percent) reported that they weighed more (an average of 3 pounds more) than their actual weight. Interestingly, the difference between the participants' reported and actual weight was unrelated to their age;[19] older women were as likely as younger women to under- or overestimate their weight. Whether such "errors" represent a "wish" on the part of a majority of the women to weigh less or a misperception of their actual weight, the older women did not differ from the younger women in this respect.

The older women also did not differ from the younger women in the number of pounds they wanted to lose; age was not related to the number of pounds the women wanted to gain[20] or lose.[21] Most of the women (77 percent) wanted to lose some weight (an average of 18 pounds). Only seven women (3.5 percent) wanted to gain weight (an average of 11 pounds).[22] In addition, the older women did not differ from the younger women in their satisfaction with their current weight; age did not predict whether a woman thought she was over- or underweight.[23] Regardless of their age, most women (69 percent) considered themselves to be overweight to some degree. Although three-quarters of the women were at or below a "normal" weight (BMI below 25), only a quarter of the participants reported being "at their desired weight."

We also found that there was a difference related to age in women's satisfaction with their appearance. Older women reported being less satisfied with their appearance than the younger women.[24] A majority of the women (63 percent) reported being at least moderately satisfied with their appearance, while only 28 percent reported being either "moderately" or "greatly" dissatisfied with their appearance.

For the most part, responses of the older women did not differ from those of the younger women. They were equally inaccurate in reporting their weight, they wanted to lose as much weight and they were just as dissatisfied with their weight. This striking lack of any age-related differences enables cohort, as well as age differences, to be ruled out as possible explanations for the dissatisfaction with their current weight. Instead, we interpreted these findings as pointing to the cultural and historical context of women's lives at the time of the study as a source of explanation for their discontent with their weight. The most likely candidate here is the thin female body ideal that is vigorously promoted in the mass media in conjunction with the heavy emphasis on dieting and weight loss products in recent years.

The older women did differ from the younger women, however, in two important ways: they were somewhat heavier and they were also less satisfied with their appearance. It is hardly surprising that the older women would be less satisfied with their appearance, given the dominance within a western cultural context of a youthful body shape as the ideal defining female attractiveness. What is surprising to us is that the oldest women did not want to lose *more* weight and that they were not less satisfied with their weight than were the younger women. One implication of this finding is that the larger, bustier standards of female beauty prevalent when the oldest women were themselves young women may still have some relevance to how they view themselves. But, whatever the influence of standards in place when these older women were themselves young, it does not appear to play a large part. Although over three-quarters of the women, including many of the older women, were either normal or underweight (BMI below 25), a large majority (69 percent) thought they were overweight and even more (77 percent) wanted to lose weight. Another alarming finding is the amount of weight these women wanted to lose — an average of 18 pounds. By any standards, this represents a significant amount of weight, especially among a group of women who, for the most part, would not be considered "overweight."

The findings of our study indicate that, among a sample of primarily middle-class, educated women, differences in age and cohort appear to play a very minor role in their desire to be thinner. Current social pressures reflected in the exceedingly thin female ideal portrayed in the current media appear to play a much larger part in women's desire for thinness. Further research, including a more diverse sample of women and specific questions about the role of the media, would allow a more direct exploration of the supposition that the apparently ageless pursuit of thinness among women today is linked to the pervasive influence of the contemporary "thin ideal" of female beauty.

Notes

1. See T. DeAngelis, "APA Co-Sponsors Briefing on Anorexia," *APA Monitor* (September 1997), 51; American Psychiatric Association, *Diagnostic and Statistical Manual of Mental Disorders-IV*, 4th edition (Washington, DC: American Psychiatric Association, 1994).

2. See R. Sheinin, "Body Shame," *National Eating Disorder Information Centre Bul-etin* 5 (1990), 1–3; and J. Wardle and L. Marsland, "Adolescent Concerns About Weight and Eating: A Social-Developmental Perspective," *Journal of Psychosomatic Research* 34 (1990), 377–391.

3. See J.C. Rosen and J. Gross, "Prevalence of Weight Reducing and Weight Gaining in Adolescent Girls and Boys," *Health Psychology* 6 (1987), 131–147; S.J. Paxton, E.H. Wertheim, G K. Gibbons, G.I. Szmukler, L. Hillier, and J.L. Petrovich, "Body Image Satisfaction, Dieting Beliefs, and Weight Loss Behaviours in Adolescent Girls and Boys," *Journal of Youth and Adolescence* 20 (1991), 361–379; and M. Grigg, J. Bowman, and S. Redman, "Disordered Eating and Unhealthy Weight Reduction Practices Among Adolescent Females," *Preventative Medicine* 25 (1996), 748–756.

4. See P. Pliner, S. Chaiken, and G.L Flett, "Gender Differences in Concern with Body Weight and Physical Appearance Over the Lifespan," *Personality and Social Psychology Bulletin* 16 (1990), 263–273; M.M. Hetherington and L. Burnett, "Aging and the Pursuit of Slimness: Dietary Restraint and Weight Satisfaction in Elderly Women," *British Journal of Clinical Psychology* 33 (1994), 391–400; J.C. Gustavson and C.R. Galbaldon, "Body Image Dissatisfaction Among American

Male and Female College Students: A Computer Based Graphical Approach," *Perceptual and Motor Skills* 76 (1993), 147–151; A.E. Fallon and P. Rodin, "Sex Differences in Perception of Desirable Body Shape," *Journal of Abnormal Psychology* 94 (1985), 102–105; J. Rodin, L. Silberstein and R. Striegel-Moore, "Women and Weight: A Normative Discontent," *Nebraska Symposium on Motivation* (1984), 267–307; and J. Polivy and P.C. Herman, "Diagnosis and Treatment of Normal Eating," *Journal of Consulting and Clinical Psychology* 55 (1987), 1–10.

5. See T.F. Cash and P.E. Henry, "Women's Body Images: The Results of a National Survey in the USA," *Sex Roles* 33 (1994),19–28; Pliner, Chaiken and Flett, "Gender Differences in Concern with Body Weight and Physical Appearance Over the Lifespan," 263–273; and R.H. Striegel-Moore, L.R. Silberstein, and J. Rodin, "Toward an Understanding of the Risk Factors for Bulimia," *American Psychologist* 41 (1986), 246–263.

6. See D.M. Garner, "Body Image," *Psychology Today* (January/February 1997), 32–84.

7. Bust-wait-hip size is represented in Imperial measurement.

8. See A. Fallon, "Culture in the Mirror: Sociocultural Determinants of Body Image," in T.F. Cash and T. Prozinsky, eds., *Body Images: Development, Deviance and Change* (New York: The Guilford Press, 1990).

9. While age is implicated in the idea of cohort, cohort refers to the notion of cultural and historical context in which a group of people are born.

10. See A.E. Anderson and L. DiDomenico, "Diet vs. Shape Content of Popular Male and Female Magazines: A Dose-Response Relationship to the Incidence of Eating Disorders?" *International Journal of Eating Disorders* 11 (1992), 283–287; C.V. Wiseman, F.M. Gunning, and J.J. Grey, "Increasing Pressure to Be Thin: 19 Years of Diet Products in Television Commercials," *Eating Disorders* 1 (1993), 52–61; D.M. Garner and P.E. Garfinkel, "Sociological Factors in the Development of Anorexia Nervosa," *Psychological Medicine* 10 (1980), 647–656; D.M. Garner, P.E. Garfinkel, D. Schwartz, and M. Thompson, "Cultural Expectations of Thinness in Women," *Psychological Reports* 47 (1980), 483–491; A. Morris, T. Cooper, and P.J. Cooper, "The Changing Shape of Female Fashion Models," *International Journal of Eating Disorders* 8 (1989), 593–596; L. Kurman, "An Analysis of Messages Concerning Food, Eating Behaviours, and Ideal Body Image on Prime-Time American Network Television," *Dissertation Abstracts International* 39 (4A) (1978), 1907–1908; and B. Silverstein, L. Perdue, B. Peterson, and E. Kelly, "The Role of Mass Media in Promoting a Thin Standard of Bodily Attractiveness for Women," *Sex Roles* 14 (1986), 519–532.

11. See L. Irving, "Mirror Images: Effects of the Standard of Beauty on the Self- and Body-Esteem of Women Exhibiting Varying Levels of Bulimic Symptoms," *Journal of Social and Clinical Psychology* 9 (1990), 230–242.

12. Although metric is the standard for expressing weight in Canada, we chose to use pounds as participants tended to be more familiar with this standard.

13. See K. Riegel, *Psychology Mon Amour: A Countertext* (Boston: Houghton Mifflin, 1978); and K.W. Schaie, "A General Model for the Study of Developmental

Problems," *Psychological Bulletin* 64 (1965), 92–107.

14. See B.R. Blishen and H.A. McRoberts, "A Revised Socioeconomic Index for Occupations in Canada," *Canadian Review of Sociology and Anthropology* 13 (1976), 71–79.

15. Reported here is a subset of the data collected, portions of which have been previously presented. See A.M. Myers, M.T. Zivian, S. Kirkland, and L. Zager, "Body Image: Cohort and Age Differences Across the Life Span," paper presented at the 1985 Annual Meeting of the Canadian Psychological Association, Halifax, NS.

16. We found a significant relationship between age and weight. That is, weight increased with increasing age. Pearson Product-Moment Correlation (r (196) = .32, p<.01).

17. See Statistics Canada, "Social Status and Health Risks in Canadian Adults: 1985 and 1991," *Health Reports* 5 (1993), 143–156.

18. BMI scores ranged from 15.12 to 39.99 (SD = 4.47) with an average score of 23.17.

19. Using a linear regression procedure, we determined that age did not significantly contribute to the difference between participants actual and reported scores (F (1,191) = 0.21, n.s.).

20. Linear regression analysis revealed no significant contribution of age to the number of pounds women wanted to gain (F (1,5) = 0.28, n.s.).

21. Linear regression analysis revealed no significant contribution of age to the number of pounds women wanted to lose (F (1, 151) = 0.60, n.s.).

22. The number of pounds women wanted to lose ranged from 2 to 99 (SD =16.92). The number of pounds women wanted to gain ranged from 5 to 20 (SD = 5.35).

23. Using a linear regression procedure, we determined that age did not significantly predict women's weight satisfaction (F (1, 196) = 2.93, n.s.).

24. Using a linear regression analysis, age was found to be a significant predictor of women's appearance satisfaction (F (1, 195) = 4.60, p<.05).

CHAPTER THIRTEEN

CONTOURS OF EVERYDAY LIFE
WOMEN'S REFLECTIONS ON EMBODIMENT
AND HEALTH OVER TIME

Pamela Wakewich

ᘓ

Written on the body is a secret code only visible in certain lights; the accumulations of a lifetime gather there. In places the palimpsest is so heavily worked that the letters feel like braille. I keep my body rolled up away from prying eyes. Never unfold too much, tell the whole story.

— Jeanette Winterson, *Written on the Body*

People have to inhabit their bodies, and their physical identity is part of themselves. Particularly as they grow older, they have a need to account for this identity, to draw together all that they have experienced. This body is their inheritance, it is the result of the events of their life, and it is their constraint.

— Mildred Blaxter, "The Causes of Disease: Women Talking"

WHILE EFFORTS TO INCORPORATE the body into social theory have become prolific in the past decade, it is only recently that writers have begun to explore the ways in which people actively constitute and experience the body in everyday life.[1] Analysts have tended to focus upon representations of the female body in the professional discourses of medicine and science or the popular discourses of media and advertising, and to presume a direct link between these representations and women's experiences of the body.[2] Even where authors seek to present alternative frameworks, their analyses generally remain framed by the scientific and biomedical categories and language that they wish to challenge. Body and identity are presented as static notions with the presumption that they remain fixed and homogenous through time and place.

However, recent historical and social science analyses suggest that the significance and impact of the "authoritative visions" of science and medicine (and one might also add media and advertising here) must be critically analyzed within a broad social, political and cultural context.[3] Writings by historians and anthropologists, such as Barbara Duden[4] and Margaret Lock,[5] provide us with case studies of radically different perceptions of the body and embodied experience among historical and contemporary European and Asian women. Research by Emily Martin on women's perceptions of reproduction reminds us that it is equally important to explore the possibilities for, and limitations of, discourses of resistance. Her now classic book *The Woman in the Body* has heralded the need to critically analyze how the professional discourses of medicine and science are interpreted and responded to by women themselves.[6]

Vivienne Walters makes a similar argument in her critique of approaches to women's health research and health policy in Canada.[7] She points out that laywomen's perspectives on health and illness remain largely absent from the "data" gathered for healthcare decision-making and planning. Rather, policy development relies on the expertise of healthcare professionals on the one hand, and key informants such as community organizations and women's groups on the other hand. While each of these brings important information to the dialogue, their perspectives are necessarily partial — reflecting only the experiences of those with whom they come into regular contact. They can't be presumed to reflect broader perspectives or concerns of the lay population. Ironically, even efforts to incorporate more community-based and participatory action research into the study of women's health has not ensured the recognition of *women themselves* as "key informants" with regard to their own health.

A similar limitation is evident in much contemporary feminist literature that addresses the relationship between media and women's body image dissatisfaction. Largely influenced by writers like Foucault, analysts have carefully documented the ways in which media and advertising serve to promote and normalize disciplinary practices of the female body towards the achievement of unhealthy ideals. Susan Bordo's much cited essay "Reading the Slender Body" brilliantly deconstructs the pathologized, individuated image that both medicine and media present us with — the woman who "succeeds" in achieving these ideals only to damage her own health and perhaps risk her life in the process. Bordo's analysis clearly shows the importance of seeing the "everyday-ness" of these disciplinary practices and how they inscribe on the surface (and increasingly the interior) of women's bodies the "bulimic personality" of contemporary American capitalist society. This society requires, at one and the same time, unrestrained consumption to achieve health and happiness, and intense repression of desire and body boundaries to meet narrowly prescribed moral and cultural standards.[8]

Yet Bordo's analysis, along with those of many others who address this topic, leaves us with little, if any, indication of how women "read" and respond to — or perhaps even resist — these dominant ideals. We get little sense of the extent to which these dominant ideals may or may not be significant or predominant in women's identity construction and how this may shift over time and in different social contexts, as well as in relation to other aspects of the multiple-subject positions women hold (such as class, ethnicity, age, sexuality, regional identity and so on). Thus the potential contributions of Bordo and other feminist scholars to articulate alternative discourses on the female body and embodiment are impoverished by the ways in which they tend to reinforce, rather than critically assess, conventional medical and scientific assumptions about women's bodily experience.

STUDYING HEALTH AND BODY PERCEPTIONS
IN NORTHWESTERN ONTARIO

These concerns were the points of departure for a research project that I conducted in northwestern Ontario between 1996 and 1999. Comparing the experiences of white working-class and middle-class women and men, I explored how ideas about health and the body are shaped and reshaped over time, as well as how identities of gender, class, sexuality, culture and region (in this case "northern-ness") are constituted within and through discourses on health and the body.[9] The decision to interview both women and men was in part motivated by my desire to "de-problematize" the female body, a problem that is evident in many current medico-scientific and feminist analyses. In keeping with the focus of this volume, however, this chapter concentrates on the findings relating to women's experiences of health and embodiment.

In conducting this research, I used techniques of feminist oral history to elicit what Barbara Duden calls "bio-logies," or body stories, in order to bring into view the everyday processes and social relations through which ideas about health and the body are constituted and experienced.[10] Several writers have pointed out that oral history is particularly suited to feminist research as it enables us to focus on women's perceptions and interpretations of the world around us and it provides a means to supplement and challenge dominant representations.[11] This technique is particularly suited to revealing the multilayered textures of peoples lives, or the bodily palimpsest that accumulates through the course of a lifetime. It allows us to hear how people articulate the complex intersections of culture, gender, class, sexuality and other key dimensions of their lives.

Oral history is not merely the representation of a life, but rather an active process of re-collection — a re-collecting or gathering together of aspects of our history in which we make and re-make sense of who and what we are. In this sense, the memories recounted are not seen as discrete *things*, but rather as *acts* and *imaginings*, "the products of a conscious being bringing to mind what is not present."[12] And while oral history interviews are always somewhat idiosyncratic (they begin with individual experience), "a person's self reflection is not just a private, subjective act. The categories and concepts we use for reflecting upon and evaluating ourselves come from a cultural context."[13] Thus oral histories provide an entrée to both the individual and the social body and illuminate how they are constituted in relation to one another.

My research was carried out in the city of Thunder Bay, in northwestern Ontario, a community whose own identity is in many ways negotiated and liminal.[14] By "liminal," I mean it is at once northern (officially considered part of the provincial north), and yet not northern (being located only 50 kilometres from the American border). It is urban (having a population of some 120,000), and yet rural (being physically isolated from other large centres by at least a full day's drive in either direction). It is an important regional business and service centre, and yet residents feel largely ignored and insignificant in provincial terms. Its population is culturally diverse, comprising a mix of various Northern and Eastern European roots, a significant First Nations population as well as recent migrants from Latin America and South East Asia, and yet conformity of style, speech and even behaviour is valued and remarked upon. As several of the women interviewed noted, straying too far from the accepted norms of dress and appearance may meet with social sanctions such as public commentary or ridicule. Although the primary resource industries (such as the paper mills and grain elevators) are no longer as significant to the local economy as they once were, and even though women make up an increasingly large share of the city's labour force, the city maintains an image in the eyes of both residents and outsiders of being a "lunch-bucket" or "working-man's" town.[15]

Interviews were conducted between 1996 and 1997 with forty women and men between the ages of thirty and sixty-five. In choosing this age range, I anticipated that participants would be old enough to have a "history" of body experiences to reflect upon, and yet young enough to not be preoccupied with significant gerontological concerns. To address the dimension of social class, equal numbers of working-class and middle-class women and men were included. For the purposes of my research, I followed the definitions of class developed by Wright.[16] As the "debate on classes" illustrates, the class structure of advanced capitalist nations has become very complex; and feminist and cultural critics have soundly critiqued androcentric and economistic class definitions.[17] Wright's analytical definitions served merely as a "starting point" for the identification of the sample.[18]

As Robert Crawford's research on working-class notions of health and white middle-class discourses on AIDS has suggested,[19] attentiveness to class enables a comparison of both gender and class discourses on the language and representation of health and the body, and the extent to which they are invoked in the constitution of identity. For working-class women, I expected that there might not be a distinctly positive association between the nature of work and body image. The exigencies of work, family and limited income experienced by working-class women might be seen as antithetical to the possibility of "cultivating" the ideal female body promoted by popular cultural representations. My interest here was to examine whether working-class women define their health and body experiences in relation to the middle-class norms represented in popular culture and medico-scientific discourse on the "healthy" body, or whether alternative identities are constructed.

The twenty women interviewed ranged in age from thirty-three to fifty-three, with a median age of forty-three. Sixteen of the women were currently married, one was living common-law, another was single and two were divorced. All but five of the women had children or dependents living at home. Some of these children were in their late teens and early twenties; however, the women still thought of them as dependents financially, emotionally and in terms of household labour. The working-class women's occupations included clerical work, grocery clerk, letter carrier, homemaker, babysitter, kitchen worker, union representative and diploma nurses. The middle-class women's occupations included nurse administrators, lawyer, teacher, university professor, homemaker, small business owner/workers and office administrator. Four of the women combined part-time work with primary childcare responsibilities, while the remainder were employed full-time, and most reported some additional responsibility for children or dependents. Nine of the women had more than one paid occupation — either a combination of part-time jobs, or a full-time job and a part-time job (such as union representative).

In broad terms, the interviews focused on the participants' past and current perceptions of health and embodiment with particular attention to the ways in which these have changed or remained stable through the course of their lives. Interviews explored the role of body image in the women's perceptions of health and well-being, construction of self and "other," and the significance attributed to popular culture, family socialization, employment, medical interactions and other aspects of the social environment in shaping ideas about health and the body.

The interview schedule focused on five main themes: 1) background information on family, education, employment and social class; 2) definitions of health and health protocols; 3) gender, work, family and leisure, and their relationship to health and identity; 4) ideas about body and body image, and their relationship to gender, work, family, health and identity; and 5) regionality or "northern-ness," and its relationship to health, body and identity. Throughout the interviews, the women were asked to give specific examples and provide a "historical" context to their comments through questions such as "Have you always defined 'health' in this way?" "Can you think of a time or a specific occasion when you thought about your body differently than you do now?" "Was there something specific going on in your life at this time that might have affected your perception of health?"

DEFINING HEALTH AND HEALTHINESS

For the majority of the women interviewed, ideas about health and body image are intimately interlinked and have changed over their lives. For many, ideas about health and healthiness have evolved from a more conventional biomedical notion of health as the absence of disease (adhered to at an earlier age), to the assessment of well-being in more environmental or holistic terms. The women's notions of health discuss levels of physical energy, comfort in carrying out and balancing multiple roles, satisfaction with quality of work and family relations and concerns about time for self and leisure.

When asked whether her idea of what it is to be healthy had always been the same, Carol, a forty-one-year-old university professor, responded this way: "No. I'd say now, getting older that ... there is no doubt that my sense of health is becoming much less separate from how I *look*, and much more to do with how I *feel*." Laura, a forty-three-year-old nurse administrator and part-time graduate student, said: "Probably as I have grown older my expectations for being healthy have actually increased rather than decreased ... To me *now*, being healthy does not just mean being free of disease or not on any medication, but being in the best state I can be in, mentally *and* physically." Janet, also forty-three and a teaching administrator, agreed that her notions of health had changed over time. As she notes: "I used to think before that you had to be like five foot five, 120 pounds [and] go to the gym everyday. That was my image of what it was to be healthy. I think now it's more like how you feel on the inside. Mentally, as well as physically.

The two kind of go together." Similarly, Debbie, a forty-four-year-old clerical worker responded: "I don't think that I thought about stress when I was [younger]. I don't think that I thought about assessing my health in that way. It is different now."

The women generally evaluated their health in terms of coping with multiple roles and the quality of family relations.[20] In contrast to many of the men who discussed the importance of physical endurance and a perceived sense of strength when evaluating their own health, the women were more likely to comment on outward appearance, and several expressed a sentiment of being "overweight" even though they generally felt healthy.

Behaviours associated with staying healthy had also changed over the course of the women's lives. Many indicated that they did little consciously to stay healthy when they were younger, but now were much more conscientious about eating well, getting regular exercise and rest. For most, time was the most important constraint to achieving optimal health. They cited the difficulties of finding time for themselves (for leisure or exercise) while juggling multiple work and family roles.

Reflecting on her past and present health practices in response to my question "Do you consider yourself a healthy person?" Mildred, a forty-nine year old co-owner/worker in a small family business, replied:

> *Sigh* ... well, I would like to think I was. There certainly was a time when I had a lot more time to spend on getting myself that way, [such as] all the time [we were] raising the children and everything. I still make all our own bread and pastries, cookies and those things. I think that counts. I buy meat from the farmer that I know doesn't use steroids or penicillin. We raise our own chickens, eggs and stuff like that. I *try* working at it. I *try* to get exercise. Years ago I got tons more than I do now. I would have to say the working thing has just cramped my style considerably. I'm overweight, of course, and I don't get as much exercise as I should. Years ago when I was home I would walk for three hours a day. I love walking. I love being outside. I also feel at times, I've narrowed it down, I know what it is — it is nature deprivation. I feel nature deprivation

if I don't get outside enough — you know, the less you do [exercise], the less you can do it. You get home and you're tired. You don't feel like going out.

I asked Mildred, "When would you say you used to do more? Was it when your kids were younger?" and she replied:

Yeah. And I babysat, and I was at home. We had the business out of the house for a while too. When we started doing it [establishing the business], that transitional period, I could just be out more. It was easier to do it ... If I could afford somebody full time [to help with the business], I would be out of here in a flash. I would be home feeding the chickens and raising the pigs and things like that. Because that's what I enjoy doing.

Several of the women indicated that they didn't have a sense of entitlement to "time off." Women with younger children generally built their own leisure pursuits around activities that could include their children. Terri, a professional who had been very athletic in her youth, expressed frustration at trying to get a "workout" for herself while doing activities with her children. Having recognized that the desires to spend time with her children and to exercise for herself were working at cross-purposes, she temporarily "resolved" the issue by putting her own needs on hold until the children were older.

Class differences were also apparent in the women's definitions of health over the life course. Many middle-class women identified with current "healthist" discourses that emphasize health as an individual phenomena, and blamed themselves for failing to live up to the the ideals of dietary and exercise regimes promoted in public health rhetoric. Ironically, even those who were professionals identified structural elements such as the exigencies of the double-work day and an unequal division of labour in the home as the major impediments to self-care. Working-class women tended to evaluate and discuss their own health in relational, rather than individual, terms. They assessed their own health in terms of their self-sufficiency and their ability to serve others (their family members, for example).

Body Image/s and Embodiment

In general, the women were attentive to, and aware of, body image issues through the course of their lives, yet the importance and meanings attributed to them had changed significantly for most.[21] Many had previously dieted and monitored their weight carefully as adolescents and in their early twenties, yet most had abandoned these practices, either due to a sense of frustration with their lack of success, or explicitly as a form of resistance to what they perceived as inappropriate medicalization and monitoring of their bodies by parents, doctors, partners and others.

Laura, a fifty-year-old clothing store owner and mother of two grown children, described how her ideas of body image and being healthy have changed over time in this way:

> I guess I was, as a baby boomer, probably on the leading edge of anorexia and bulimia and all that kind of stuff. I never had bulimia, but I'm sure I was one of the first anorexics [and this] was never diagnosed. Just from trying to starve yourself because society said you should be a thin person. If you weren't [thin] you felt you should be, so you tried anything to get there. That has changed for me drastically. *I'm not unhealthy and I'm certain my body image is no longer an issue [for me]. If somebody doesn't like me because I am heavy that's their problem, not mine.*

When I asked Laura whether there was something specific that changed her notion of health, she said:

> I think it was just finding out just after having my son that I couldn't starve myself every day. And why the heck should I have to — to be somebody else's image of what I should be? As long as I'm a good mother and a good person. Being in the [business of running a clothing store for large women] has certainly helped that too ... if you're clean and your makeup's on and your clothes are nice and you keep yourself looking good, that's what people see.

Most of the women talked about having multiple body images. They emphasized the fluidity and contextualness of their own perceptions. Body image was different at home and in public spaces, in the company of friends and with strangers, at times of healthiness and during illness episodes, and often between work and leisure. Karen, a thirty-three-year-old health administrator, described body image in the following way: "It's how you perceive yourself. How I perceive myself is not just my physical being. It's whether I am confident in a certain situation or feeling secure. It does change if you are in a situation that you don't feel as confident [in]."

Debbie pointed out that her consciousness of body image is affected by whether she is in the company of women or of men. She states: "I think I am more aware of what I look like and how I am perceived when I am with a bunch of women. Men are, even though you like to think men are fussy — they aren't fussy, they don't care. Women are much more critical. I think I worry about it more when I am with a bunch of women." Marg, a forty-five-year-old office administrator, similarly observes: "I think it's different in different settings ... Okay, for instance when I'm dressed in a suit or whatever, I call them my power clothes, I feel better about the way I look. I feel better, more confident when I'm dressed nicer and I look good. When I'm dressed in sloppy clothes around the house ... I don't feel too powerful."

For many of the women, different body images were also related to the quality of relationships with their partners or their peer group. Rita, a forty-three-year-old small business owner who had divorced and remarried, described a very different sense of body image with her new partner whom she described as "comfortable with me as I am." Laura indicated that comfort with her body shifts in relation to contact with a group of female friends who are extremely physically active and concerned about appearance. Louise, a thirty-eight-year-old homemaker with three school-age children, described herself as a "borderline" anorexic in adolescence, but had overcome this during her early twenties. She found the weigh-in and fundus[22] measurement during routine pregnancy checkups very anxiety-provoking; it created for her a negative shift in body image that has taken many years to resolve.

The women's notions of body image were fluid and changing over time. Often defined as body shape or physical appearance in adolescence, for some, body image expanded to a larger sense of "presentation of self"[23] as they aged. For professional and business women this incorporated not only appearance and styles of dress — or "dressing for success" as many described it — but also a sense of self-confidence, a feeling of accomplishment or skill in their field of work and an improved sense of healthiness over time. For many of the working-class women, being successfully relied upon by others and being seen as coping were important aspects of the assessment of body image. Some of their responses expressed a kind of idealization of a "northern" (almost akin to pioneer) woman for whom strength and endurance were key dimensions of a positive body image.

Consciousness of the body was also described as situational and, again, varied along class and gender lines. Many of the women indicated that they were not conscious of their bodies on an ongoing basis. A few women who were particularly concerned about weight described their bodies as constraints (as the opening quote from Blaxter suggests),[24] which they had difficulty transcending. However, most others indicated that body consciousness was situational, brought on by a particularly serious or sudden illness episode, by concerns about what to wear to a particular social event (for example, a class reunion or family gathering), by travelling to a large urban centre like Toronto where consciousness and monitoring of appearance seems more evident, or by shopping for clothing — especially the painful annual new bathing suit ritual. For many of the women, body consciousness and anxiety were also heightened by medical encounters (even routine checkups) that frequently raised concerns about unhealthy weight, independent of a woman's own assessment of her state of healthiness.

MEDIA AND OTHER REPRESENTATIONS
OF THE FEMALE BODY AND HEALTH

Responses to predominant media images of the idealized female body had also changed in the women's reflections. They differed on opinions about the extent to which ideals of slenderness and feminine beauty were more predominant or widely circulated today than when they were younger. Many remembered routinely reading or "studying" the teen magazines of their youth, such as *Seventeen,* often with a sense of regret that the products and fashions advertised were not readily available in the North. While many continue to be avid magazine readers, the choice of magazines has changed from teen magazines to ones such as *Canadian Living* or *Woman's Day*, and the appeal cited was as much the recipes and advice columns as the clothing and fashion images.

When asked how they respond to or whether they "see" themselves in the images of women presented in these magazines, most indicated a strong sense that the images were largely unreal and sometimes almost amusing in their absurdity. A few noted an increased representation of "real" or average women in the magazines in recent years. They found this trend appealing and felt they paid much more attention to these ads or pictures because they could get a sense of how clothes might really look on them.

Medical information and advice columns in the magazines were frequently read by the women and taken much more seriously than fashion layouts. Many of the women found these columns to be an important source of personal and family health information and said they discussed them with friends. But even this information could be dismissed or resisted if the women didn't feel that it matched their own perspectives.

The women recognized different body and appearance norms between residents of the north and the south (a euphemism for the large urban centres and their surrounding communities within the Niagara triangle of Toronto, Hamilton and Niagara Falls). The north was variously described as more relaxed: less style-conscious and preoccupied; more healthy due to access to the outdoors, better water and less pollution; less stressful because of its slower pace of life. By contrast, the north was also viewed as less healthy because of the limited availability of fresh fruit and vegetables; less healthy because it is easier to hide an "overweight" body in all of the clothes worn for cooler weather; and more stressful because of a lack of tolerance for diversity or heterogeneity among northern residents.

Body and body image were seldom discussed in individual terms, but rather almost always constituted in relational terms. Constructing the self was done in relation to a constructed "other." Thus, themes of northern-ness were discussed in terms of an imagined or real South; norms or expectations of femininity were contrasted with norms of masculinity (and vice versa); middle-class concerns about presentation of self and success were presented as opposite to stereotypes of a working-class lack of care or lack of discipline; and working-class concerns about the lack of time and money to pursue idealized health and body images were construed in relation to the presumption of generic middle-class investment in, and resources available to, achieve those ideals. The homogeneity of northern styles and ideals presented largely ignored or "othered" the obvious ethnic and cultural diversity of the city and region.

Contemporary senses of health and body image were referential to past notions and ideals and often made efforts to present an integrated or coherent history of embodiment. In some instances, where particularly troubling experiences of violence — such as sexual abuse or social stigma — were part of a woman's past, her efforts at providing an integrated narrative were contradictory or incomplete. The strong resonances of past experiences showed through the narrative surface, giving a texture much like the "palimpsest" that Winterson's opening quote to this chapter so eloquently describes.[25]

These observations suggest that women's ideas about body and body image are fluid and contextual. They are shaped and re-shaped over time and placed in relation to other aspects of identity and subjectivity. Ideas about the body are interlinked with notions of health and well-being and evolve in relation to both individual and collective experiences. Science, medicine and media may play an important role in shaping and normalizing our ideals and behaviours — particularly in our younger years — but they are often ignored or actively resisted when the images they present us with fail to match our own evolving sense of health or well-being. Thus the analysis and incorporation of body and embodiment in social theory and feminist research must attend to the fluidity and contextualness of women's experiences, and explore their constitution and reconstitution in specific times and places with particular attention to the quality and nature of the social relations in which they are shaped.

Notes

1. See, for example, Kathy Davis, ed., *Embodied Practices: Feminist Perspectives on the Body* (London: Sage, 1997); Frigga Haug, ed., *Female Sexualization* (London: Verso, 1987); Nicole Sault, ed., *Many Mirrors: Body Image and Social Relations*

(New Brunswick, NJ: Rutgers University Press, 1994); and Sue Scott and David Morgan, eds., *Body Matters* (London: The Falmer Press, 1993).

2. See Diane Barthel, *Putting on Appearances* (Philadelphia: Temple University Press, 1988); Susan Bordo, "Reading the Slender Body," in Mary Jacobus and Evelyn Fox Keller, eds., *Body/Politics: Women and the Discourses of Science* (London: Routledge, 1990), 83–112; and Susie Orbach, *Hunger Strike: The Anorectic's Struggle as a Metaphor for Our Age,* (New York: W.W. Norton, 1986).

3. Ludmilla Jordanova, *Sexual Visions: Images of Gender in Science and Medicine Between the Eighteenth and Twentieth Centuries* (Madison: University of Wisconsin Press, 1989), 159, and "Natural Facts: A Historical Perspective on Science and Sexuality," in Carol MacCormack and Marilyn Strathern, eds., *Nature, Culture, Gender* (Cambridge: Cambridge University Press, 1980), 42–69.

4. Barbara Duden, *The Woman Beneath the Skin: A Doctor's Patients in Eighteenth-Century Germany* (London: Harvard University Press, 1991).

5. Margaret Lock, "Cultivating the Body: Anthropology and the Epistemologies of Bodily Practice and Knowledge," *Annual Review of Anthropology* 22 (1993), 133–155; and *Encounters with Aging: Mythologies of Menopause in Japan and North America* (Berkeley: University of California Press, 1993).

6. Emily Martin, *The Woman in the Body: A Cultural Analysis of Reproduction* (Boston: Beacon Press, 1987), "Science and Women's Bodies: Forms of Anthropological Knowledge," in Mary Jacobus and Evelyn Fox-Keller, eds., *Body/Politics: Women and the Discourses of Science* (London: Routledge, 1990), and "The End of the Body?" *American Ethnologist* 19 (1992), 121–140.

7. Vivienne Walters, "Women's Views of Their Main Health Problems," *Canadian Journal of Public Health* 83 (1992), 371–374.

8. Bordo, "Reading the Slender Body," 97.

9. This paper is drawn from portions of my PhD dissertation, "Contours of Everyday Life: Reflections on Health and Embodiment Over the Life Course" (University of Warwick, UK, 2000). To study the ways in which ideas about health and embodiment change over the life course, I conducted in-depth interviews with forty working- and middle-class women and men in northwestern Ontario. Interviewing both women and men allowed a close comparision of the similarities and differences of women and men's experiences of health and embodiment, and the extent to which these were a potential source of gender consciousness.

All but two of the respondents were "white." I use the term "white" here as a social construct following Richard Dyer, *White* (London: Routledge, 1997) and Ruth Frankenberg, *White Women, Race Matters: The Social Construction of Whiteness* (Minneapolis: University of Minnesota Press, 1993). While the research sample reflects the ethnic diversity of the region, as other analysts have noted, the primary distinction recognized by local residents is that between First Nations, or Aboriginal Peoples, and "whites." See, for example, Thomas Dunk, *It's a Working Man's Town: Male Working-Class Culture in Northwestern Ontario* (Montreal: McGill-Queen's University Press, 1991). The dissertation includes an analysis of the terrain and interpretations of "whiteness" as it is both visible and invisible in the participants' narratives of "healthy selves" and "unhealthy others."

While participants did not explicitly name their sexual orientation, it was clear from the interviews that all were currently, or had been in the recent past, involved in heterosexual relationships. The dominant, and yet largely unspoken, discourse of heterosexuality in the interviews is addressed in the larger project.

10. Barbara Duden, *The Woman Beneath the Skin*, uses the concept of "bio-logies" or body stories to describe the changing understandings and representations of the body evident in the narratives given to eighteenth-century German physician Johannes Storch by his clients over the course of his professional relationship with them.

11. See, for example, Gwendolyn Etter-Lewis, "Black Women's Life Stories: Reclaiming Self in Narrative Texts," in S. Gluck and D. Patai, eds., *Women's Words: The Feminist Practice of Oral History* (London: Routledge, 1991), 43–57.

12. Mark Freeman, *Rewriting the Self: History, Memory, Narrative* (London: Routledge, 1993), 89.

13. Kathryn Anderson and Dana C. Jack, "Learning to Listen: Interview Techniques and Analyses," in Gluck and Patai, eds., *Women's Words: The Feminist Practice of Oral History*, 11–26. See also Haug, ed., *Female Sexualization*.

14. Liminality is valued by postmodern researchers because studying liminal or "in-between" categories highlights the ways in which differences are marked by people and given "presence" or value within a particular culture or subculture. See Sonya Andermahr, Terry Lovell and Carol Wolkowitz, *A Concise Glossary of Feminist Theory* (London: Arnold, 1997) for a discussion of the use of liminality in post-modern research.

15. Dunk, *It's a Working Man's Town*.

16. Erik O. Wright, *Classes* (London: Verso, 1985).

17. For a discussion of the debate on classes see Andrew Sayer and Richard Walker, *The New Social Economy* (Cambridge, MA: Blackwell, 1991) and Erik O. Wright, *The Debate on Classes* (London: Verso, 1989). Feminist critiques of the use of class in social theory are provided by Pat Armstrong et al., *Feminist Marxism or Marxist Feminism* (Toronto: Garamond Press, 1985); Michelle Barrett, *Women's Oppression Today* (London: Verso, 1980); Wallace Clement and John Myles, *Relations of Ruling: Class and Gender in Postindustrial Society* (Montreal: McGill-Queen's University Press, 1994); Christine Delphy, *Close to Home: A Materialist Analysis of Women's Oppression* (London: Hutchinson, 1984); and Terry Lovell, "Feminist Social Theory," in Bryan S. Turner, ed., *The Blackwell Companion to Social Theory* (Oxford: Basil Blackwell, 1996), 307–339.

Recent writings by Diane Coole, "Is Class a Difference That Makes a Difference?" *Radical Philosophy* 77 (May/June 1996), 17–25, and Beverly Skeggs, *Formations of Class and Gender* (London: Sage, 1997) argue for the importance of maintaining a focus on class in feminist analyses while integrating postmodern insights into plurality and diversity. Both authors suggest that class should not be priviledged in feminist analyses, but rather seen as one important dimension of experience. My approach to class is informed by this perspective.

18. One of the issues that I explored in the interviews was whether such analytical definitions reflect the common-sense understandings of the women and men interviewed. In *It's a Working Man's Town*, 6–7, Dunk has argued that in Thunder Bay, male cultural perceptions of class designation vary in different contexts. He points out that in one instance, individuals will describe themselves as "middle class" — as distinct in terms of wealth from the very rich or the very poor; in another instance, they will use a dualistic conception of society in which they are "the average Joe" — in opposition to "the big shots" who are decision-makers; and alternatively, they use a language reflecting a certain type of work experience referring to themselves as "hard hats" or the "lunch bucket brigade" — which distinguishes them from white-collar workers.

19. Robert Crawford, "The Boundaries of the Self and the Unhealthy Other: Reflections on Health, Culture and AIDS," *Social Science and Medicine* 38 (1994), 1347–1365.

20. A similar point is raised by Nickie Charles and Vivienne Walters in their analysis of age and gender in South Wales' women's accounts of health. They point out, "women's accounts demonstrate that their experiences and explanations of health, while showing certain commonalities, vary with age and stage in the life cycle and are shaped by wider structural changes in employment patterns and gendered divisions of labour. Thus structural and cultural change shape the discourses that women call upon when talking about health and illness ..." "Age and Gender in Women's Accounts of Their Health: Interviews with Women in South Wales," *Sociology of Health and Illness* 20 (1998), 348.

21. By contrast, many of the men found it much harder to reflect on "body" history and required more prompting to make connections between a sense of embodiment and specific activities or instances of their youth. Most often, they talked about embodiment in terms of success or endurance in sporting activities, the ability to do physical labour (especially for working-class men) or in relation to illness episodes. In comparison to the women, fewer men made reference to presentation of self or appearance norms. Those who did were primarily middle-class men who discussed presentation of self in terms of their leadership image at work and their embodiment of corporate imagery.

22. The fundus is the top of the uterus. Its changing position is measured throughout the pregnancy to assess the growth and position of the baby.

23. Erving Goffman, *The Presentation of Self in Everyday Life* (Garden City, NY: Doubleday, 1959).

24. Mildred Blaxter, "The Causes of Disease: Women Talking," *Social Science and Medicine* 17 (1983), 69.

25. Jeanette Winterson, *Written on the Body* (New York: Vintage Books, 1994), 89.

CHAPTER FOURTEEN

NEGOTIATING SEXUALITY
LESBIANS IN THE CANADIAN MILITARY

Lynne Gouliquer

∽

This is me. I am out of the closet and don't try and stuff me back in!
— Fatima, thirteen years of service

HUMAN SEXUALITY IS a complex phenomenon involving notions and expressions of bodily desires, sexual practices and sexual behaviours. It is typically perceived as primarily biological and people often infer sexuality according to their perception of a person's gender. Sexuality is also felt to be an essential part of our human identity, and perceived as a personal and sensitive matter for each individual. Although it may be personal and private, sexuality pervades all areas of life — whether private or public. It is also forged through two general processes. On the one hand, our social and public structures institutionalize and structure sexuality according to their size, culture, goals and policies. On the other hand, it is an outcome, a negotiation, a struggle of human interaction, and often a contestation of different and conflicting social practices and values.[1] Michel Foucault insists that sexuality also involves issues and relations of power.[2] Arguably, only one sexuality dominates most workplaces and organizations: "male sexuality." Though never acknowledged explicitly, it is taken for granted that it is heterosexual.

In this chapter, I explore the social processes, negotiations and constructions of women's homosexuality (lesbianism) in the organizational context and culture of the Canadian Armed Forces. I base my analysis, in part, on the data from a study I conducted in 1997. In addition to observations and field notes, I interviewed nine gay women,[3] who at the time, were members of the Canadian military.[4] Because of women's particular position in society, feminist standpoint theorists believe that research from the perspectives of women's lives will create less partial and less distorted facts.[5] Using this approach, I specifically adopt the perspective of gay women to investigate how sexuality is structured by the military and how these women negotiated their sexuality within its confines.

Institutions manage sexuality for their own purposes: either to enhance production or the goals of the organization or to prevent interference with those goals. The organizational context in which sexuality is negotiated is usually gendered, hierarchical and heterosexual. Not only is heterosexuality a worldwide norm, but men and what is masculine are valued over women and what is feminine. In addition, men dominate most of the power positions in organizations and society and are supported by a tradition of male domination.[6] In effect, masculine identities dominate; in particular, heterosexual ones.

Catharine MacKinnon argues that sexuality is the basis of women's oppression and suggests that it is organized and expropriated for the use of men.[7] In the case of lesbians, however, Adrienne Rich points out that lesbians are sexually and emotionally independent of men.[8] Yet lesbians are not free from being oppressed; in fact, they suffer the additional oppression of a stigmatized sexuality. While most women are not lesbian, they may be stamped as such in certain situations; this constitutes a threat given the disparaged status of lesbians. For instance, if a woman at work is labelled homosexual for not being sufficiently feminine, this acts as a threat against her. She may be harassed by management and co-workers, coerced into acting in a traditionally prescribed gendered way for the benefit of the organization — and men specifically. Lesbianism, therefore, may be conceived as defiance by women who do not want to occupy the traditionally feminine heterosexual role of subordination. It can be argued that the sexual and emotional independence of lesbians from men, indeed their sheer existence, challenges the hegemony of heterosexuality and the patriarchal social order. The Canadian military is a long-standing conservative institution with an unending history of male domination. Consequently, lesbianism — and the challenge it represents — is intensified in the strongly heterosexual world of the military.

Sexuality and the Military

Traditionally, militaries have been institutions dominated by men who tend to be more socially conservative and traditional. The military still provides men the promise of and the means to achieve manhood, and as such is masculine and heterosexual to the core. The particular masculine identity inculcated here, however, is anti-woman, anti-feminine and anti-homosexual. The disparagement and subordination of women and homosexuality that underpin military traditions, culture and training are also the quintessential core of a cultivated, dominating and institutionalized male heterosexuality.[9]

Any sign of weakness, vulnerability or sensitivity by a male soldier is usually labelled as a sign of homosexuality and interpreted as failed masculinity.[10] Unlike men, women are not labelled "homosexual" for being sensitive or vulnerable because these attributes agree with the societal gender norms for women. For women, acting and looking "like a man" are gender-inappropriate behaviours and appearances that lead them to being called "lesbians" or "dykes." A scholar in the field of psychology, Rhoda Unger suggests that when a person's gender-attributes violate the social norms appropriate for her or his sex, discrimination is more likely to occur.[11] The military environment, therefore, represents a milieu par excellence for the discrimination against lesbians: it requires women to engage in non-traditional activities while maintaining traditional behaviours and it is dominated by men who, arguably, adhere to stereotypical views of women and lesbians.[12]

Women in the military do, indeed, negotiate contradicting demands. On the one hand, to "fit in" requires adopting desired values and behaviours typical for the soldiers' work role, which translates into acting like "one of the boys."[13] On the other hand, due to the derogation of women in general and the social construction of lesbianism as "butch and masculine," specifically, military women must adopt certain behaviours that advertise their femininity and heterosexuality. Women's higher release rates indicate that where the policies support their actions, military men use homosexuality to eliminate women from their ranks.

In general, the majority of the world's militaries deem heterosexuality essential to its institutional makeup and repress homosexuality through policies and laws — as is the case in the United States.[14] Some militaries, Israel and Canada for example, have adopted fewer discriminatory policies allowing homosexuals to serve more openly and with fewer restrictions. In these cases, however, an "atmosphere" of male heterosexuality is still adhered to and cherished. Consequently, while homosexuality is not officially persecuted in some militaries, it is by and large not welcome. Lesbians, therefore, are still unwilling to "come out" publicly.[15] Given their gender, lesbians endure the same contradictions, isolation, negative social attitudes and sexual harassment as heterosexual women. While heterosexual women need not hide or deny their sexuality to remain in the military, lesbians are forced to do so or accept the consequences of homophobia, heterosexism or relevant discriminatory practices and policies of the organization. The story of the negotiation of sexuality in the Canadian military is intricately linked to the place women have historically occupied in this institution. The following section looks at some of the particular historical events or changes concerning women and homosexuality that have occurred in the Canadian military over the past thirty years.[16]

THIRTY YEARS OF MANAGING SEXUALITY

Like all Canadians, military personnel are subject to Canadian laws and codes. In addition, they are subject to a parallel system of military justice. The military system, which is made up of the Queen's Regulations and Orders and the Canadian Forces Administrative Orders, is primarily disciplinary in function. Though its jurisdiction often overlaps with civilian justice when dealing with offences such as theft and murder, it usually prevails.[17] At the time the army, navy and air force integrated in 1967, the military established a single policy concerning homosexuality. This policy was known as the Canadian Forces Administrative Order 19-20 (CFAO 19-20) and it remained in effect until it was revoked in 1992. According to this order, homosexuality was a sexual abnormality and members found to be homosexuals were dishonourably released from the military.[18] Between 1968 and 1969, the Canadian Parliament decriminalized homosexual behaviour and same-sex relations between consenting adults: homosexuality was no longer a criminal offence. The military, however, maintained its discriminatory policy on homosexuality even though civilian laws did not support it.

The 1970s women's movement and the advancement of women's rights in different civilian sectors opened up women's employment opportunities in the Canadian Forces. The Royal Commission on the Status of Women in 1970 recommended that the military lift the restrictions prohibiting women from working in many of its technical fields. Accordingly, the Canadian Forces opened various technical trades to women.[19] However, women could not serve at sea or in combat or near combat trades and positions. Changes to the *Canadian Human Rights Act* and to the Canadian Charter of Rights and Freedoms as well as the completion of the Charter Task Force on Equality Issues in the mid-1980s garnered for women roles and occupations in near-combat positions and at sea on naval vessels, which had been revamped to accommodate them.

Women as acknowledged, official members of militaries, are a phenomenon of the twentieth century. As a consequence of the two World Wars, many nations have increasingly "allowed" women to join their militaries. Nevertheless, the total number of women soldiers in the world is less than 2 percent of the total military count. In the Canadian Forces, women comprise nearly 11 percent.[20] Because it is a male enclave, any woman who joins the military makes a non-traditional job choice; however, their jobs within the military are located predominately in the more traditional female sectors of medicine, dentistry and administration. This is also the case for women in the Canadian Forces.[21]

Until 1992, the Canadian military officially discriminated against members who claimed to be, or were found to be, homosexuals. Prior to 1992, the Special Investigative Unit (SIU) (a special arm of the military police) investigated, interrogated and recommended the release of many military members for homosexuality. The years 1980 to 1983, which were particularly active years for the SIU concerning lesbianism, are vividly etched in the minds of some Canadian Forces women. During this period, many women were investigated and interrogated, and some were released because they were suspected of being lesbians. Many servicewomen refer to this particular era in the military as the witch-hunt, a period when women were aggressively and ruthlessly interrogated for homosexuality. Five of the nine women I interviewed were investigated and questioned by the SIU, and five knew women who had been released for homosexuality.

Beth was twenty years old when she underwent SIU interrogations in 1982. She joined the military in 1980 and has since worked her way up into the senior ranks as a non-commissioned member.[22] She has been an aircraft technician throughout her career. Beth describes the investigative techniques of the SIU:

> When I went through the investigation, they never really had the "broom ball" stuff on me. In broom ball, the SIU knew exactly who was with whom by rooms and names from hotel registers. They really threw that in people's faces. But then they started in on my bosses. I would be working away and concentrating on something in the maintenance/repair shop and next thing you know, they would be in chatting with my bosses. I think I was lucky. Zell, my partner, got called in about three or four times and they really grilled her. I mean four hours later, they would be still in there grilling her. Finally she broke: she said "Okay, I am gay." It took them a month to get her out of the military.

Beth's experience illustrates the degree to which these women's lives were scrutinized; all areas of their lives were suspect. In particular, the SIU would focus on their leisure-time activities such as the sports they played or with whom they socialized. One particular winter sport, broom ball, was reported in most of the interviews. Women probably took up this sport because it would be easier to learn than hockey. Other than learning stick-handling skills, it does not involve the art of skating, only that of negotiating the ice on a pair of specially designed shoes. It is, however, nearly as rough as hockey since bodychecking is usually condoned in all military tournaments.

Georgie has been with the military for sixteen years and is now a non-commissioned member at the junior rank level. The same year that she joined the military, 1983, Georgie was interrogated by the SIU. Though not "out" previously, these investigations coincided with coming out to herself and the commencement of dating women. Her following disclosure highlights the personal and professional costs of being suspected of lesbianism in the Canadian military during the early 1980s:

I was called in a couple times a week before they made their big bust. The MPs, military police, even broke into one girl's room. Two women were kicked out and two others walked out of the military. It was really scary. You are just coming out to yourself after years of denial and it feels great, and then all of a sudden, you are called in and grilled; it was really scary.

Isabelle joined the military when she was twenty years old in 1983. She has sixteen years of service and is now a master corporal, a junior rank. In 1984, the SIU questioned her about the woman with whom she was living; although unbeknownst to the SIU, she was also in a relationship with this woman:

I had never been informed that lesbians were not allowed [in the military]. And it is only when I was transferred to my first base that I heard from people that some girls were released from Cold Lake and other bases because they were lesbian. So it scared me because I was living with a woman. And it so happened that the SIU called me in and questioned me about my girlfriend. He asked me what kind of person she was, if she was friendly, and if she had touched me. I was scared he was going to discover her identity, make the [connection] and kick me out. I hid myself. Like, I wouldn't go to parties because I had no boyfriend or I would invite my neighbour just so they would think I was with the guy.

Given the nature of the "crime" (being a lesbian), the SIU had no easy task of amassing evidence against women. Because it was extremely difficult — if not impossible — to observe the crime, the SIU depended on the reports and "confessions" elicited during interrogations as well as their observations and conclusions drawn about the women's activities (sports games, for example). The women I interviewed commented that the SIU would often make untrue allegations and threats or misrepresent testimonies of other women in order to evoke a confession or coerce a statement about someone else. Consequently, the witch-hunt era marks a particularly traumatic period for some servicewomen that is not generally known in military history.

The 1986 Charter Task Force on Equality Issues was a turning point. Even though the Task Force upheld the military's policy of excluding and releasing homosexuals, the military began to liberalize its policies and practices. Changes in society in general tend to be reproduced in the military. Thus, the increased equitable employment of women and more general acceptance of gays taking place in Canadian society in the late 1980s were probably affecting military policy and actions.[23] In addition, lost court cases and the ensuing payment for years of retributions probably also made the military more cautious. As Beth recalls, one woman who was released for homosexuality subsequently took the military to court for wrongful release. She was reinstated and paid for the time she was out.

Following the Charter Task Force in 1986, military members were no longer obliged to report to their commanding officers if they suspected a colleague to be homosexual. Again in 1988, the military introduced a provisional clause on homosexuality that allowed homosexuals to be retained in the military, but with career restrictions. This addition to the still-active policy, CFAO 19-20, meant that commanding officers were no longer obliged to release military members accused of, or claiming, homosexuality. Even though homosexuals would be retained, their promotions could be denied, their transfers withheld, their career courses cancelled and their re-engagements refused. Despite the provisional clause providing homosexuals limited protection, the dismissal of Michelle Douglas took place in 1989. A new security officer in training at the time, she was investigated for homosexuality by military police and was subsequently discharged on those grounds.[24]

In the same year Michelle was released, the last official discriminatory barrier to women in the Canadian military — the restriction to serve in combat roles and occupations — was struck down by a Human Rights Tribunal.[25] In the following year, the military directed the SIU to cease investigating members suspected of homosexuality. Also in 1990, Michelle Douglas filed a "wrongful discrimination" suit against the military. In 1991, the Federal Court of Canada declared that the Canadian Forces' policy concerning sexual orientation was contrary to the Canadian Charter of Rights and Freedoms.[26] Consequently in 1992, the Canadian military officially announced that joining or serving in the Canadian Forces would no longer be denied on the basis of sexual orientation.[27] Despite its simplicity and clarity, the new policy was ambiguous. Daffodil, a master corporal with nineteen years of military service, recalls that restrictions remained in place despite the new policy: "We heard that you were not allowed to be posted to Europe or the United Nations. You were basically not allowed to go anywhere outside Canada if you declared your homosexuality."

Although lesbians and gays could now serve officially without fear of losing their jobs, social benefits and privileges accorded to heterosexual couples were not granted to them. For example, gay women were still considered single when posted to a new base. Isabelle found herself in this situation in 1993. In addition to having financial implications for her and her partner, the ordeal was emotionally difficult. She recalls one particular transfer from Eastern Canada to a base in the West:

> When I came here on my house-hunting trip, I would have pre-ferred my partner to be with me. I was feeling a big load on my shoulders. I came here in 1993, no apartments at all, nothing was available. [The military personnel who managed postings] said, "Well, you are going to have to buy or live in barracks." Private Married Quarters were not allowed for single people, and I was considered a single woman. "Barracks?" I said, "No way," because I wouldn't have been able to bring my girlfriend, my partner. So I had no choice; I had to buy something. I chose the carpet and everything from the basement to the roof.

The gay women, however, found unofficial ways to take advantage of certain benefits and privileges. For example, the military usually assumed the cost to move service members and their heterosexual part-ner. Prior to her transfer to Western Canada, Isabelle's partner moved all her furniture and personal effects into Isabelle's apartment. Thus, they avoided the cost of moving her possessions because Isabelle claimed them as her own for the move. In another case, Daffodil and her partner, Riann, both in the military, were posted to the same base at relatively the same time. Due to an unexpected and unavoidable delay in Riann's posting, Daffodil asked her chief warrant officer to arrange to have her posting dates postponed. During a meeting with him she told him:

> I said, "I will not leave here until I know if Riann is going to have an operation here or not." He said, "Well, what will I tell the career manager?" I said, "You're the boss, tell him whatever you like. You

know that Riann and I are together, you know I will not leave here till I know what is happening with her and if she has an operation. I will not leave till she is okay." His big thing was, "What do I tell the career manager?"

Following her request, the base from where they were being posted arranged that they travel together not only for their house-hunting trip but also for their posting.

In Canadian society, the extension of social and family benefits to homosexual couples has been a legally controversial issue for years. Certain cases in the civilian courts have had an impact on military policies. For example, in 1995 Jim Egan and his partner, John Nesbitt, sued the government for equal spousal benefits under the *Old Age Security Act*. Though this particular court case was unsuccessful for the individuals involved, the Supreme Court recognized that discrimination on the basis of sexual orientation should be prohibited constitutionally.[28] Consequently, in 1996, the military announced that social benefits would be available to members in a same-sex relationship.[29] Privileges such as compassionate leave (during the illness of a spouse/partner or dependent) were immediately made available; however, other benefits could not be accessed until military policies were officially changed. Similar to the common-law policy for opposite-sex couples, members claiming same-sex status are required to sign a statutory declaration that they have been in a relationship for a minimum of one year. The wording of the statutory declaration officially labels the relationship gay or lesbian. In other words, gay military women and their partners have to state and sign a declaration either in front of a lawyer or their commanding officer that they are in a "lesbian relationship." The intent of the declaration is to provide homosexuals access to the same benefits as heterosexuals; however, the wording of the declaration suggests that the military, for no justifiable reason, is still strongly interested in sexuality. Hélène, who has been in the military for eleven years and decided not to make a declaration, highlights the issue: "I have never written that I am in a homosexual relationship. Why should I? Heterosexuals don't have to claim that they are heterosexual. I shouldn't have to go in and say that my partner is a female." The wording of the declaration signifies to these women that the military is still interested in their sexuality to the point of documenting it. Not one of the gay servicewomen interviewed has declared officially that they are lesbian. Given the military's history of chastising homosexuality, it is little wonder that lesbian servicewomen hesitate.

In mid-1997, the Canadian Forces notified its personnel that members could make a special application for same-sex benefits. Each claim, however, had to be considered and approved on a case-by-case basis by the National Defence Headquarters in Ottawa because formal amendments to military policies were still pending. Shortly thereafter, another message followed advising military members that a same-sex partner was a "dependent" and not a "spouse."[30] The significance of the wording in the obligatory statutory declaration (which is required to claim benefits) reveals the heterosexist and conservative core of the military and the values it upholds. Isabelle is acutely aware that the military is guarding the sanctity of "spouse" for heterosexuals: "There is less discrimination about gays, but there is still some discrimination to get rid of — paper wise, and stuff. Like right now they are emphasizing that your same-sex partner is your dependent and not your spouse. There is a big difference between spouse and dependent." Anyone can be a dependent (your mother or disabled sister, for example) as long as they live under the same roof as the service member and provided the service member has accepted responsibility for the person. Not everyone, however, can be a spouse.

The Canadian military's preoccupation over the years with controlling and regulating homosexuality demonstrates how the organization structures and institutes the sexuality of lesbians. Gay women in the Canadian Forces negotiate and live their sexuality in the context of these organizational policies and practices. Most other organizations have not documented or regulated sexuality as clearly and officially as the Canadian Forces has (except in the application of benefits). Yet unofficial practices, such as the organizational culture, customs and values of an institution, also tend to result in a homophobic, heterosexist environment within which gay women work. In the military milieu, wherever women tend to gather, whether it's playing sports or simply living together in military communal housing, they are accused of being, or associating with, "dykes." On her first posting in 1986, Hélène recalls, "I stayed in Barrack Block 48 a single female living quarters when I got posted there. It was called Dyke Hall." Fatima, in the military for thirteen years, remembers the comments made about women who played broom ball, "I kept hearing the guys referring to them as the dykes-on-ice." The dominance of heterosexuality and hete- rocentric assumptions marginalizes homosexuality despite official regu- lations. The ways gay women live and negotiate their sexuality within the Canadian military today is influenced by a past that is made up of discriminatory policies and practices, as well as a culture based on a hegemony of heterosexuality and the disparaging of homosexuality and femininity.

NEGOTIATING SEXUALITY

The gay women in my study have found different ways to negotiate their sexuality. Prior to the changes in military policies, these women lived their sexuality in hiding or paid the cost emotionally, financially and sometimes even by losing work. Though gay servicewomen are now living their lives more openly, they are not always completely out of the closet. In my study, the women's manner of being out at work — and to what degree — is related to when they enrolled in the military as well as to their relationship to, or experience of, the witch-hunts of the early 1980s. I have categorized them into three eras: 1) the witch- hunt era, 1980 to 1983; 2) the post–witch-hunt era, 1984 to 1987; and 3) the liberal era, 1988 and after, when practices and policies became liberalized.[31]

The women who were in the Canadian Forces during the witch- hunt era either directly or vicariously experienced the trauma of SIU investigations and subsequent releases from the Forces. In other words, they concretely felt and feared discrimination based on their sexuality. These women joined the military in the late 1970s or early 1980s. Cur- rently, they have more military status than the other two groups due to their rank and time served. They are in their late thirties to early forties and approaching early retirement age. These women cannot be offi- cially dismissed for being gay; however, there are other financial and career losses that could be incurred due to more subtle discrimination. The women in the witch-hunt group hesitate to declare openly and officially their homosexuality. Daffodil explains the dilemma and possible costs associated with coming out:

> Riann and I talked about it. Personally, I would like to wait till the twenty-year retirement mark. Nothing has come from the changes. After officially coming out, Barb [a friend also in the military] has not received any of the money due to her. I don't know how the uppers think. I know it's a cowardly way to act, but I think its going to take two to three years just to settle the issue. There are still things to lose career-wise; for example, extensions at the end of my twenty-year contract, promotions, money I could lose if I was denied to go on temporary duty to the United States. The United States doesn't have to let us in. We lesbians are illegal aliens.[32]

Talking about your private life and recounting the weekend or weekday events is part of the general socializing that occurs in most workplaces. During the 1980s, lesbians avoided talking about their private life at work. Beth remembers clearly that "if someone asked me how my weekend went, I used to say 'fine,' and it was the end of discussion." Today, like everyone else at work, these women talk about their private lives and mention their partners by name to their colleagues. Even though they cannot lose their job for being lesbian, they will not explicitly discuss the issue of sexual identity or partnership status. Daffodil sums up the transition that has evolved for these women: "In those days, the 1980s, if someone asked me what I did on the weekend, I would say I saw a movie or I did the vacuuming. Today, it is more 'Riann and I' this, 'Riann and I' that." Their way of accessing benefits involves tapping into the system at the local level with their colleagues and supervisors. They ask for the same privileges heterosexual couples receive (for example, time off to take their partner to the hospital), but unofficially. Their approach is non-confrontational and subtle. These women never say "Andrea is my partner" nor do they make an official declaration about their relationship status. Instead, they talk about their partner using her first name and assume and act as if their colleagues and supervisors know. This example from Beth highlights this style:

> Zell tore a knee tendon. So I had to take her into the hospital. I phoned work; I was working evenings. I said I had to drive Zell to

the hospital in the city to get evaluated. Next day I get back to work and my boss wants me to put in a leave pass [this represents one day of vacation] and I told him right to his face, "NO!" When Zell got back to work, she had a chat with the chief warrant officer, our big boss. She explained to him that I had driven her to the city and that my boss expected me to take annual leave. He had a discussion with my boss and my boss came back and said, "You don't have to take a day's annual leave." I sat down with him about an hour or so afterwards. I said, "Would you expect to take a day's annual leave if you had to take your wife to the hospital?" And he said, "No." I said, "I am not going to take a day's annual leave because I took Zell to the hospital." Now, I don't know if that was admitting to him that she is my wife but he shut up and got the point.

The period following the post–witch-hunt era is not distinguished by a marked sense of relief or relaxation for gay servicewomen. Military policy still sanctioned discharge for homosexuality and the SIU were still investigating. However, this period is differentiated by a drastic decrease in the intensity and number of investigations and discharges from the military for being gay. None of the gay servicewomen in my study were investigated during this period and only knew of a few sporadic cases. Despite a residue of fear from the witch-hunt period and an occasional story of someone being caught for homosexuality, lesbian culture survived and flourished. Typically, gay servicewomen became part of, or aware of, the gay underworld of the military through friends. In addition, nearly all the servicewomen whom I interviewed associated female sports teams as a potential meeting ground, whether they joined or only watched the sport. Indeed, this connection between sports and lesbianism was so strong that Daffodill recalls consciously avoiding associating with any "sports dykes" because she felt it would be detrimental to her job and would affect her career advancement.

Lesbians who joined the Forces in the post–witch-hunt era heard a lot about the witch-hunt interrogations and releases from other gay women or co-workers. These women were receiving explicit and implicit warnings about homosexuality and its consequences. Fatima had friends (a member of the military police and her partner) who had been investigated by the SIU. She recalls the warnings they gave her: "I would go visit and stay with them and talk. We talked a lot, but most of what we talked about was look out for the SIU, be careful of what you say at work, just be careful and that was that."

After finishing her occupational training at Canadian Forces Base Borden in the early spring of 1987, Hélène was posted to an air force base in Western Canada. It was her first posting and she did not know a soul except for the few people she had just met at work. Prior to her arrival, the military had sponsored the first-ever broom ball nationals for women. Given the military's general interest in the physical fitness of the troops, it regularly promoted internal sports competitions as an incentive to keeping fit. Hélène vividly remembers the rumours circulating at work and on the base surrounding this particular event:

> [The military broom ball nationals] were just over and there was this big kerfuffle about these dykes. [I heard that at one broom ball game] the base commander was there and apparently these two women just started kissing and necking. I remember thinking that took a lot of guts, and how stupid to do this in front of the base commander. [I thought,] they are going to be kicked out. [The word was out that] they were all over each other. I was not going to talk to anyone about this. I wanted to defend these people but if I opened my mouth, I was admitting guilt. Yah, that really put me in a shell, big time, when I was confronted, face-to-face with everybody around me and their point of view of homosexuality.

Hélène who had only recently come out at her previous posting was torn between defending these women, confronting the homophobic attitudes of her colleagues at work and the reality that she could lose her job. After she got to know more people, specifically a few gay servicewomen, she heard about the SIU, the investigations and the witch-hunts of years gone by. She recalls "my world was rocked terribly," and attributes these particular experiences to keeping her in the closet longer, even to the extent of dating men.

Today, the post–witch-hunt group of gay women seems less reserved than their predecessors (the lesbians who survived the witch-hunts). They are less concerned with who knows about their sexuality. With the passage of time as well as the changes to the regulations that now prohibit discrimination and secure benefits for gays and lesbians, these women have been coming out to their co-workers. Their strategy in coming out is similar to the witch-hunt group in that they are non-confrontational, remain guarded and are not out officially. Their attitude, however, is different. Unlike the gay servicewomen of the witch-hunt era, if the post–witch-hunt lesbians see the opportunity and need, they come out to their co-workers. For example, Fatima, who has been out to herself and other gay servicewomen for years but not at work, says, "I don't know whether I changed the way I acted or just don't care anymore. If somebody is going to ask me, I am going to tell them. And right now I am at the point where I am tired of pussy-footing around the people at work. And over the past two weeks, I have told about six people but I have been selective about whom I have told." She mentioned that the clarity of Canadian Forces anti-discriminatory policy regarding homosexuality was helpful in her process of coming out at work because it was not as washed out as the American policy of "Don't ask. Don't tell. Don't pursue." The American policy still condones discrimination if a person's homosexuality is discovered, whereas the Canadian policy clearly indicates no discrimination under any circumstances. Thus, the women of the post–witch-hunt group, like Fatima, have grown tired of being closeted at work and are taking the risk of being more explicitly open as lesbians.

By the end of the 1980s and early 1990s, the military environment was relatively more liberal because of changes in society and changes to the policies concerning homosexuality. In 1989, the military was not as quick to release gays even though they had the legal authority to do so. As well, the SIU had ceased investigating suspected homosexuals in 1990; and in 1992, the military ceased to release known homosexuals or prohibit them from joining. The women who joined the military during this time after 1988 did not endure the overt and covert discrimination that both the witch-hunt and post–witch-hunt groups did, nor did they experience the fear of losing their jobs. They also have less seniority than the two previous groups and possibly have less to lose concerning their career and status if they do come out. Hélène describes the attitude of her partner, Margaret, who was a military member of the liberal era: "She was just tired of having to live a sheltered life. There was a whole world out there that she wanted to see as Margaret-the-gay-woman."

One young lesbian who had joined in the early 1990s felt that it was important for her co-workers to know more about her. Jay came out to her boss when she was transferred to a new base. As a result of her disclosure, her and her partner's names were displayed publicly on an organizational chart thereby outing her to everyone in her unit and anyone who happened to read the chart. Any heterosexual service member in her unit who is married or common-law has her name and spouse's name publicly displayed in a similar fashion. Given that homophobia is still prevalent in society and the military, Jay's boss, whether unwittingly or not, carelessly exposed her to stress and possible danger. Considering that gay-bashing is still occurring today, outing someone to the general pubic is a genuine danger. The gay servicewomen of the 1990s want to live more openly, but like the other two groups, not necessarily in the official capacity (none of the women I interviewed formally declared their homosexuality to the military hierarchy). They are, however, confrontational by the simple fact that they are out to more people, co-workers, supervisors and commanding officers than the two other groups of gay servicewomen.

Co-workers, supervisors and commanding officers in the Canadian military have responded in a variety of ways to lesbians' disclosures. In some instances, their reactions have been positive. Daffodil describes how her chief warrant officer, a senior supervisor, changed his language when briefing the troops:

> We were going away on a military exercise to the United States for three weeks and he was briefing the troops on how their wives and partners could contact them while they were away. He used "significant other" instead of "wife" or "spouse," and he looked directly at me when he said it. I know he knows but I have never told him.

Fatima told her supervisor at work that she was gay and gave her partner's identity. His response was, "Okay then, when you come over for dinner Friday night you will bring Natalie."

Not all lesbians in the project reported such positive reactions. Kay was a corporal with over six years military service when she found herself geographically separated from her partner. She decided to explore the possibility of getting posted to the same base as her partner on the basis of compassionate grounds. Service members can apply to the military for a cancellation of, or a request to, move for personal or family reasons. When she approached her commanding officer and explained the nature of her request, he replied, "This is for 'compassionate' postings, not 'passionate' postings." This comment not only suggested that heterosexuals have bona fide compassionate reasons to be with their partners, it displayed prejudicial and stereotypical attitudes towards lesbians and their sexuality.

Beth's experience illustrates the prejudicial attitudes of a co-worker as well as the ever-present fear of discrimination associated with coming out:

> [We were chatting and] he said, "Well, Rock Hudson ... is gay and I never watch his shows. I stopped buying Elton John and Melissa Ethridge because they are gay ... my children will never be exposed to gays ... and I am really, really happy because my son loves playing with trucks and my daughter loves playing with dresses. It was just the happiest moment in my whole life when I noticed that about them." [After that,] I was a bit stand-offish because of where he stood in the pecking order at work and he was really high up there ... I didn't what to piss him off because he had an ear with our boss.

Despite the liberalization of policies and changes in the consciousness of commanding officers, gay women hesitate to come out officially in the Canadian military. None of the nine gay women interviewed had officially declared their homosexuality by signing a declaration for same-sex status nor did they officially request partner benefits. The official declaration process appears to be a great barrier. In addition to explicitly qualifying their relationship using the term "lesbian," the military requires that gay women apply for approval from National Defence Headquarters for some of the same-sex benefits. Some gay women expressed apprehension for the future. Their fear is based on the negative retributions that could result from the imposition of new policies in a system known to have traditional and oppressive values for all women, particularly for lesbians. The present policies and practices of the Canadian Forces do not take into consideration the past context of legitimated discrimination and the still present anti-homosexual culture. Gay women in the Canadian Forces experience conflict and fear between wanting the same rights and benefits as heterosexuals, while dealing with their internalized homophobia, the homophobia of others, heterosexism, gay bashing and institutional barriers. Isabelle, a more senior lesbian of sixteen years military service, is still apprehensive: "They're still in the process of changing all those amendments. So, it still is a little bit scary but I am not feeling as scared as I used to. I am having more of a life but it has been such a long time that I have felt this way that [now], I am just like scared for nothing." Isabelle has lived most of her military career in fear: fear of the discrimination that her lifestyle entailed (interrogations and release) and entails (a homophobic culture). Consequently, she now finds it hard to relax and trust.

Elaine joined the military just ten years ago. She is keenly aware of the homophobic attitudes where she works as a technician repairing aircraft electronic equipment: "The master corporal in the shop right now gives me the impression he is a redneck. He doesn't know and I am not about to tell him [that I am gay]."

The "intersection" between being a woman and a lesbian in a military atmosphere has particular consequences. All women manage and negotiate their femininity and sexuality in the face of a hypermasculine culture, which has no space for femininity or non-traditional female heterosexuality. Moreover, femininity and homosexuality are the antitheses of the military's collectively defined manhood. Gay military women continue to live in an environment that until very recently attempted to eradicate lesbians. Though the military eliminated their overtly discriminatory policies, current policies act as impediments to gay servicewomen living an open and accepted lesbian lifestyle in their military communities.

Organizations like the military reflect the articulation of gender relations, ideological positions, political and cultural practices, power dynamics and different "sexualities" found in the general population. In this context, however, this articulation is overt, formal and often extreme. My analysis demonstrates how the past has shaped this actualization. Heterosexuality, as a norm, is a negotiated social process and cultural ideal that has been, and is still, controlled by a patriarchal system. As more heterosexual women gain greater economic independence, they challenge the material basis of male domination. Lesbians add to this threat by being more emotionally and sexually independent from men. Thus, through their simple existence, lesbians threaten an important means and pillar of male domination: the institution of heterosexuality. In the military, their presence is an even greater threat to the institution of masculinity. Given the all-encompassing role male domination plays in the military, the acknowledgement of lesbianism represents a radical event deserving careful study.

Notes

This chapter would not have come to fruition if not for the support of several organizations and numerous people. As such, I would like to acknowledge and thank McGill University, Fonds pour la formation de chercheurs et l'aide à la recherche, the O'Brien Foundation and the Social Sciences and Humanities Research Council of Canada. I also thank the anonymous reviewers; Baukje Miedema, Janet Stoppard and Vivienne Anderson, the book editors; and Beth McAuley, the publication editor. I am also very grateful to Carmen Poulin for her support and to the participants who shared their stories.

1. The following authors discuss sexuality in its wider, more general or narrower, specific contexts. In Jeff Hearn, Deborah L. Sheppard, Peta Tancred-Sheriff, and Gibson Burrell, eds., *The Sexuality of Organization* (Newbury Park: Sage, 1989), see David L. Collinson and Margaret Collinson, "Sexuality in the Workplace: The Domination of Men's Sexuality," 91–109; Barbara A.Gutek, "Sexuality in the Workplace: Key Issues in Social Research and Organizational Practice," 56–70; Albert Mills, "Gender, Sexuality and Organization Theory," 29–44. See also Jeff Hearn and Wendy Parkin, *Sex at Work: The Power and Paradox of Organization Sexuality* (New York: St. Martin's Press, 1995); Jeffery Nevid, Lois Fichner-Rathus, and Spencer Rathus, *Human Sexuality in a World of Diversity*, 2nd ed. (Toronto: Allyn and Bacon, 1995); Judith Stiehm, "The Military Ban on Homosexuals and the Cyclops Effect," in Wilbur J. Scott and Sandra Carson Stanley, eds., *Gays and Lesbians in the Military: Issues, Concerns, and Contrasts* (New York: Aldine de Gruyter, 1994), 149–162; Sarah Oerton, "Sexualizing the Organization, Lesbianizing the Women: Gender, Sexuality and 'Flat' Organizations," *Gender, Work and Organizations* 3 (1996), 26–37; and Jeffery Weeks, *Sexuality* (London: Tavistock, 1986).

2. Michel Foucault, *Histoire de la sexualité* (Paris: Éditions Gallimard, 1976).

3. Throughout this chapter I use the term "gay woman" interchangeably with the term "lesbian." Commonly, the term gay is used to refer to men and lesbian to women. However, the women interviewed in this study almost uniformly identified

themselves and others as gay women and seldom used the word lesbian. All the quotations referred to in this chapter are drawn from the interviews with these women.

4. The names of the gay women in this chapter have all been changed to protect their identity. I also changed, when necessary, information about these women if it would have compromised their identity. The military is similar to a relatively large but close-knit family. Thus, it is easy to identify individuals with very little information. For reasons of confidentiality, therefore, the place where the interviews occurred and detailed information about individuals, such as their rank or occupation, is not given.

5. See the following reference for a comprehensive discussion of this perspective, Sandra Harding, ed., *Whose Science? Whose Knowledge? Theorizing From Women's Lives* (Ithaca, NY: Cornell University Press, 1991).

6. The following two authors speak to the control and negotiation of sexuality in the workplace: Albert J. Mills, "Gender, Sexuality and Organization Theory," 29–44, and Deborah L. Sheppard,"Organizations, Power and Sexuality: The Image and Self-Image of Women Managers," 139–157, in Hearn et al., eds., *The Sexuality of Organization.*

7. Catharine MacKinnon, "Feminism, Marxism, Method, and the State: Toward Feminist Jurisprudence," *Signs* 8 (1983), 635–658.

8. Adrienne Rich, "Compulsory Heterosexuality and Lesbian Existence," *Signs* 5 (1980), 631–660.

9. For a discussion of sexuality in the context of the military culture, see Brian Adam, "Anatomy of a Panic: State Voyeurism, Gender Politics, and the Cult of Americanism," in Scott and Carson Stanley eds., *Gays and Lesbians in the Military: Issues, Concerns, and Contrasts,* 103–118; Judi Addelston and Michael Stirratt, "The Last Bastion of Masculinity: Gender Politics at the Citadel," in Cliff Cheng ed., *Masculinities in Organizations* (Thousand Oaks, CA: Sage Publications, 1996), 54–76; R. W. Connell, *Masculinities* (Berkeley: University of California Press, 1995); Barton Hacker, "From Military Revolution to Industrial Revolution: Armies, Women and Political Economy in Early Modern Europe," in Eva Isaksson, ed., *Women and the Military System* (New York: St. Martin's Press, 1988), 11–29; Barton Hacker and Sally Hacker, "Military Institutions and the Labour Process: Noneconomic Sources of Technological Change, Women's Subordination, and the Organization of Work," *Technology and Culture* 28 (1987), 743–775; and Deborah Harrison and Lucie Laliberté, "How Combat Ideology Structures Military Wives' Domestic Labour," *Studies in Political Economy* 42 (1993), 45–80.

10. Dana M. Britton and Christine L. Williams, "Don't Ask, Don't Tell, Don't Pursue: Military Policy and the Construction of Heterosexuality," *Journal of Homosexuality* 30 (1995), 1–21.

11. Rhoda Unger, from the Website of the Women's Studies Electronic Discussion List. <http://WMST-L@umdd.umd.edu>. July 23, 1997.

12. Stiehm, "The Military Ban on Homosexuals and the Cyclops Effect," indicates that the United States military disproportionately discharged more women than men for homosexuality.

13. For a discussion on this theme, see Melissa S. Herbert, "Guarding the Nation, Guarding Ourselves: The Management of Hetero/Sexuality Among Women in the Military," *Minerva* 15 (1997), 60–76.

14. For more information on how heterosexuality underpins the military culture, see D. Burrelli, "An Overview of the Debate on Homosexuals in the U.S. Military," 17-32, and G. Harries-Jenkins and Christopher Dandeker, "Sexual Orientation and Military Service: The British Case,"191–204, in Scott and Carson Stanley, eds., *Gays and Lesbians in the Military: Issues, Concerns, and Contrasts.*

15. The following authors, whose work appear in Scott and Carson Stanley, eds., *Gays and Lesbians in the Military: Issues, Concerns, and Contrasts*, discuss the repressive atmosphere and restrictive regulations often imposed: M. Anderson-Boers and J. Van der Meulen, "Homosexuality and the Armed Forces in the Netherlands," 205–218; Rosemary E. Park, "Opening the Canadian Forces to Gays and Lesbians: An Inevitable Decision but Improbable Reconfiguration," 165–179; and Wilbur Scott and Sandra Stanley, "Sexual Orientation and Military Service," xi–xx.

16. The research has been limited to the last thirty years for practical reasons; namely, it coincides with the unification of the army, navy and air force and their respective rules and regulations. Once three distinct and separate forces, they integrated in 1967 and became the Canadian Armed Forces.

17. For a better understanding of the Canadian military's code of laws, see Ronald D. Lunan, "Military Tribunals under the Charter," *The National Journal of Constitutional Law* 2 (1993), 197–216.

18. Park, "Opening the Canadian Forces to Gays and Lesbians."

19. See Karen Davis, "Organizational Environment and Turnover: Understanding Women's Exit from the Canadian Forces" (master's thesis, McGill University, 1994); and Shirley Robinson, "The Right to Serve: Women and the Combat Issue," *Forum* 3 (1988), 22–24.

20. For world statistics, see E. Addis, "Women and the Economic Consequences of Being a Soldier," in E. Addis, V.E. Russo, and L. Sebesta, eds., *Women Soldiers: Images and Realities* (New York: St. Martin's Press, 1993), 3–27, and for statistics specific to Canada, see Brenda Branswell, "It's a Man's World," *Maclean's* (May 1998), 22–23; and Leesa Tanner, *Gender Integration in the Canadian Forces — A Quantitative and Qualitative Analysis*, ORD Report R9901 (Ottawa: Directorate of Military Gender Integration and Employment Equity, 1999).

21. Wendy Chapkis, "Sexuality and Militarism," in Isaksson ed., *Women and the Military System*, 106–113. For statistics specific to the Canadian military, see the Canadian Forces' May 1997 publication called *Defence 2000 News* (101 Colonel By Drive, Ottawa, Canada). The entire edition is dedicated to gender integration.

22. The military is constituted by two groups, officers and non-commissioned members. In general, we think of officers as the leaders and managers and the non-commissioned members as blue-collar workers and supervisors. Each group is demarcated by seven and eight ranks or levels of authority, respectively. In both groups, however, the rank structure is also segregated into junior and senior ranks

differentiating those with more seniority, experience and institutional authority from those with less.

23. Park, "Opening the Canadian Forces to Gays and Lesbians."

24. Ibid.

25. "Armed Forces Given 10 years to End Bias," *Canadian Human Rights Advocate* 5 (February 1989), 1–3.

26. Park, "Opening the Canadian Forces to Gays and Lesbians."

27. News Release/Communiqué AFN: 57/92, *Change to CF Sexual Orientation Policy* (Ottawa: National Defence Headquarters, 1992).

28. This case can be found in the Supreme Court Records under *Egan v. Canada*, (1995), 2 S.C.R. 513.

29. CANFORGEN 094/96, *Same-Sex Partner Benefits* (Ottawa: National Defence Headquarters, 1996).

30. CANFORGEN 055/97, *Relocation, Isolated Post, and Military Foreign Service Regulations — Same-Sex Partner Benefits* (Ottawa: National Defence Headquarters, 1997); CANFORGEN 074/97, *Same-Sex Partner Benefits* (Ottawa: National Defence Headquarters, 1996).

31. Based on field observations, another group also exists. This latter group is constituted of women who joined the military in the early 1970s (that is, before the witch-hunt era). No one from this group, however, was interviewed in the context of this study. Therefore, no reference to this group is included in the present chapter.

32. In the United States, homosexuality is still discriminated against. The "Don't Ask. Don't Tell. Don't Pursue" policy in the United States military has not really changed things, as lesbians can still lose their jobs if they come out.

CHAPTER FIFTEEN

FROM AIRBRUSHING TO LIPOSUCTION

THE TECHNOLOGICAL RECONSTRUCTION OF THE FEMALE BODY

Fabienne Darling-Wolf

℘

I STARTED DIETING at age twelve. From then on, my childhood memories are tinted by the subtle awareness of the many inadequacies of my less-than-ideal female body. I remember kneeling at the toilet, two fingers stuck down my throat, desperately attempting to purge myself from the guilt of a piece of chocolate cake. I remember my sister teaching me how to apply thinning cream — and developing an incredibly itchy rash thereafter. I remember dying my hair in the company of my mother. I remember only allowing myself to eat one apple per day. I remember spending entire afternoons with my best friend, fixing each other's hair. I remember tearing off the pages of women's magazines that offered an incredible variety of beauty tips, which would require entire days to perform adequately. In a word, I remember being socialized into dominant ideals of femininity.

These memories are both painful and precious. Precious because they represent moments of bonding with my female friends and family members. Indeed, I have found that in many situations beauty rituals can be a means of connecting with other women, even across the significant differences of race, class, culture or age. Painful, because for me these memories represent the beginning of a conscious awareness of the fact that my female body was not only a source of pleasure, but also a source of social control, discrimination and, ultimately, oppression.

Numerous feminists suffer from a similar ambiguity. As both victims and critics of dominant representations of femininity, feminist scholars have developed a political understanding of the female body that recognizes it as a crucial site on which culture and ideology are inscribed, as well as a site of struggle against dominant ideology.

In this chapter, feminist interpretations are used to investigate the significance of cultural constructions of the female body and how such constructions can evolve according to the dominant ideology of a specific historical moment. Current conceptions of the female body as controllable through the use of science and technology are far from neutral, and it is important that we, as feminist scholars and activists, continue to develop a critical understanding of the dominant cultural constructions of the female body, including those promoted in popular cultural texts.

FEMINISM AND THE BODY

Feminist analyses of the body have long linked cultural constructions of femininity to women's oppression. In 1792, Mary Wollstonecraft compared the female body to a cage from which women were prevented escape by their socialization into beauty ideals. Some 160 years later, Simone de Beauvoir would recognize cultural constructions of the female body as a central component of women's oppression. She argued that in western societies being a woman is defined as a singularity, an odd condition when compared to the male norm. The biological processes of the female body are constituted as unusual proceedings — often requiring remedy — impeding a woman's intellectual development. De Beauvoir concluded that because the male body is defined as the norm against which all humans are judged, the female body is constituted as not only different, but also deviant, and consequently inferior.[1] Or as Susan Bordo — a current feminist theorist — puts it, "The 'generic' core is usually ... a white or male body passing as the norm for all."[2]

Women's identification with the body has also been recognized as a source of oppression because western societies separate the mind from the flesh and consider the former superior to the latter.[3] Feminist medical anthropologist Emily Martin reminds us that it is by virtue of the dictates of their bodies that men's and women's separate roles have been argued as natural.[4] During the 1700s, women were constructed as captives of their bodily functions — and consequently concerned with inferior "bodily" matters. This made it easier to depict them as inferior to men, who were associated with the mind.[5] This body/mind dualism has also been used to argue the inferiority of people of colour, who have been constructed as closer to "bodily functions" and nature.[6] Having thus been argued to not quite fit human characteristics, female and non-white bodies could conveniently be excluded from the Enlightenment ideal of universalism. Culture, therefore, can make "women both human and nonhuman."[7]

Cultural ideals of femininity and female attractiveness are closely linked to this definition of separate and unequal roles. Diametrically opposed standards of physical beauty have been used as a means to further associate women with the body and justify unequal treatment. Clear gender differentiation is a necessary step in constructing the female body as deviant from the male norm. Marilyn Frye argues that to keep the structure in place and presented as natural, the oppressor and oppressed must be constructed as very different from each other. Thus the forces that make us mark and announce our sex are among forces that constitute women's oppression. Frye writes:

> Persons with authority recommend and supply cosmetics and cosmetic regimens, diets, exercises and all manner of clothing to revise or disguise the too-hairy lip, the too-large breast, the too-slender shoulders, the too-large feet, the too-great or too-slight stature. Individuals whose bodies do not fit the picture of exactly two sharply dimorphic sexes are often enough quite willing to be altered or veiled for the obvious reason that the world punishes them severely for their failure to be the "facts" which would verify the doctrine of two sexes.[8]

The division of humanity into two clearly defined groups supported by diametrically opposed standards of attractiveness is also used to construct sexuality — that is, compulsory heterosexuality — from the male point of view. This heterosexual paradigm works like this: "socially, femaleness means femininity, which means attractiveness to men, which means sexual attractiveness, which means sexual availability in male terms."[9]

Femininity, then, is not a politically neutral construct. The notion that women are vastly different from men has been used to limit women's power. It is no coincidence that feminist challenges to cultural ideals of femininity prompt extreme reactions from conservative forces and that constructions of female attractiveness should be used against feminist activists. For instance, the action of throwing bras into a large trash can at the 1968 protest of the Miss America pageant was particularly disturbing to the public because it rejected one of the clearest symbols of gender differentiation. Even though no bras were ever burned during the protest, this fairly innocuous action was used by the media to construct the myth of American feminist activists as ugly "bra burners" and to dismiss their anger as sexual frustration.[10] Such a reaction clearly indicates that the female body is a primary site of struggle for feminist scholars and a central location of the contest for power.[11]

THE EVOLVING FEMALE BODY

If cultural constructions of the female body are a site where culture and ideology are inscribed, varying standards of attractiveness can tell us a lot about the specific ideology of our time. Historically, the female body has represented identity and place. Up until the early-twentieth-century, the well-fed bourgeois female body was a symbol of material prosperity. Today, the thin body represents the upper class.

Historical and cultural developments can clearly affect constructions of the female body and accompanying ideals of female attractiveness. For instance, cultural theorist Stuart Ewen links changes in cultural representations of the body to the advance of modernity, characterized by the development of speculative capitalism and the increased reliance on science and technology that followed the Industrial Revolution. He argues that as the dominant system of profitability came to be based on financial speculation (or as he puts it "thin air," rather than more materially grounded land-ownership), the female body followed suit. Ewen identifies an increased emphasis on slenderness as an emblem of changing ideology, which parallels similar changes in architecture (symbolized by the slick skyscraper) and the development of increasingly minimalist design. Like buildings and designs, the female body became an icon of the new order.[12]

The development of science and technology also affected dominant metaphors of the body. Feminist theorist Ruth Berman notes that modern scientific method and the development of new capitalist technologies prompted the characterization of the body (and even life) as a machine to be monitored and used effectively.[13] The time-and-motion studies applied to factory work in the United States at the turn of the century are an extreme manifestation of such a characterization. These studies carefully measured and timed workers' every movement to "scientifically" determine work pace for optimum productivity. A similar influence is also evident in the realm of reproduction, where every stage of labour has become standardized and timed, and where the baby has come to be viewed as a product to be successfully manufactured by doctors.

With the advance of science and technology, the body also became increasingly fragmented into parts, each under the supervision of a different expert. Western medicine started offering a different specialist for each body part, a cast of technicians and engineers carefully monitoring the system, helping it perform efficiently and intervening in case of malfunctions. "The then-dominant metaphors for this body — clocks, watches, collections of springs — imagined a system that is set, wound up, whether by nature or by God the watchmaker, ticking away in predictable, orderly manner."[14]

Although the modern body was originally perceived as being beyond human control, it increasingly became seen as malleable, and manageable through technological or scientific intervention. From this ideology of control, a new conception of escape from the biological constraints of the body emerged.

NEW AND IMPROVED BODIES

In a culture in which organ transplants, life-extension machinery, microsurgery and artificial organs are common place, a new ideal of human freedom from bodily determination has evolved. Susan Bordo links this evolution to the development of postmodern conditions, the progress of consumer capitalism, and the proliferation of products and images that are offered to viewers as an array of subjectivities from which each individual is free to choose. Characterized by the rejection of the belief in all-encompassing forces (God the watchmaker) in favour of an understanding of power as increasingly fragmented and dislocated, postmodern ideology constructs the body as under human control. Even nature can be subjected to human will through increasingly sophisticated manipulations. The body itself becomes a crucial site for experimentation either with or against the laws of nature.[15] Supporting Bordo's assertion, Anne Balsamo observes that the female body has become a site for technological intervention, as exemplified by the proliferation of cosmetic surgical techniques.[16] Today the body is conceived as the raw material on which doctors intervene.

Indeed we are increasingly assured that we can escape the natural processes of the body, particularly those of the burdensome female body with its hormone changes, disturbing bulges and unusual organs. Processes such as aging, reproduction, fat accumulation and even death are presented to us in newspapers and magazines as challenges, frontiers to be conquered, rather than natural parts of life. One example of such a construction was the recent excitement in the United States over the fact that a woman managed to give birth at age sixty through artificial insemination and hormonal treatment. While concern was expressed over the disturbing implications of women's newfound ability to conceive past menopause, this birth was mostly framed in the American media as a scientific success. The woman herself was not interviewed but her doctors were praised. She was the raw material; they were the technicians and experts.

In popular culture current representations of the female body certainly follow this dominant ideal. As might be expected, since media sources are foundations where cultural ideals are constructed and perpetuated, media ideals of femininity have undergone an evolution similar to those of society at large. Models have become increasingly thin, and through advertising, we are now offered a variety of solutions to escape the tyranny of our bodies. Advertising has learned to create a wider range of identities, which women are told they can choose from and achieve through consumption (generally of beauty products). The use of such products may even grant women a level of respectability and recognition they may never have otherwise achieved. In a recent phenomenon, the media reconstructed Monica Lewinsky from scandalous whore to "respectable woman" after she appeared in an interview sporting a new line of makeup giving her a "softer, stylish new look." As a *Toronto Star* article noted, "North American women may be divided on their opinions of Monica Lewinsky as a person, but many appear to agree on one point — they love her lipstick."[17]

Such media representations of the ideal female body are facilitated by fairly recent technological developments. The production process of feminine representations have been freed from all biological constraints. While image manipulation, such as airbrushing, has long been possible, the capacity for manipulation afforded by new imaging technology has incredible new proportions. With the stroke of a few keys, digital editing allows magazine editors to correct the too-hairy lip, the too-large breast, the too-slender shoulders, the too-large feet, the too-great or too-slight stature. It allowed film editors to give leading American actor Julia Roberts — deemed too fat — a new body in the movie *Pretty Woman*.[18] Even Kate Moss, Calvin Klein's ultra-thin supermodel, could lose twenty pounds on the computer screen — a clear example of digital imagery moving beyond biological feasibility. Today's supermodels have evolved into cultural icons that bear no relation to real women.

But technology is nevertheless offered as the "real life" solution for women to reach this unrealistic, or unreal, ideal. Advertising offers women a postmodern body on a silver platter. Often using quasi-feminist terminology of women's rights (to a thin, toned body), liberation (from unwanted hair) and freedom of choice (of deodorant), ads for breath fresheners, hair removal devices, liquid diets, cosmetics and plastic surgery services assure women that consumption can free them from the trappings of the body. Technological intervention is often presented as acceptable, or even desirable, in popular cultural texts. For instance, in an analysis of *The New York Times'* coverage of the silicone breast implant controversy, I found that the newspaper readily accepted plastic surgeons' framing of the issue as one of mere personal choice and self-fulfillment.[19] The American media are much quicker to come to the defence of women's right to have silicone implanted into their bodies than to the defence of women's right to a safe abortion, access to affordable healthcare or equal pay for equal work. The term "elective" surgery used by both the media and plastic surgeons to refer to plastic surgery reinforces such an ideology. As Kathryn Morgan points out, "The term ... appears to distinguish cosmetic surgery from apparently involuntary and more pathologically transforming forms of intervention on the bodies of young girls in the form of, for example, footbinding or extensive genital mutilation."[20] As a possible side-effect of this acceptance of increasingly intrusive technological intervention, Myra MacDonald identifies a disturbing shift in media representations of attractiveness from an emphasis on ornamentation to actual reshaping of the female body.[21]

Even the most troublesome markers of ethnicity or race can be remedied with the simplest technological intervention. Where modernity tied the body to the exercising machine, the new ideal comes up with instant solutions. Telling women they can have it all — a high paying job, a family and freedom from embarrassing body odours — advertising constructs multiple identities for women to consume, regardless of the shape, size or colour of the body they happen to be in. Defying the very materiality of the body, this new imagery renders bodies irrelevant, at least on paper.

How Irrelevant Are Bodies?

Often argued by postmodernist scholars to be divested of political significance, advertising imagery is sometimes presented as a playful fantasy for viewers' enjoyment — a fantasy that everyone can use in empowering ways. Advertising, however, may not be as neutral and playful as this argument proposes. A sense of freedom of choice is part of the basic ideology of advertising.[22] By constituting viewers as actors and creators of meaning rather than passive receivers, advertising effectively hides the dominant ideology it promotes, becoming more effective in the process. Freedom, independence, pleasure, are reduced to matters of style and consumption, and the choice of advertising is largely illusory.

Furthermore, considering the history of scientific and technological interventions on the female body, the ideological underpinnings of the discourse of beauty representation and its relationship to technology should be carefully examined. Science is a hegemonic system that has been used to argue the inferiority of women and minorities. A system of domination presenting itself as objective and impartial, and consequently effectively hiding the dominant racist and sexist ideology it promotes. Even the language used to describe biological and technological processes is far from neutral. In an essay on feminist transformations of science and society, Ruth Berman gives the example of physicists referring to successful missiles as "boys" and unsuccessful ones as "girls."[23] Similarly, Emily Martin notes that medical descriptions of biological processes often put a positive spin on processes associated with the male body, and apply negative connotations to those associated with the female body. While the male reproductive system is described as "remarkable" because of its ability for constant production, female gonads are conceptualized as wastefully sitting on the shelf.[24] Menstruation is also framed in negative terms as failed production, even though most of the time women do not want to reproduce.

While the role assigned to technology is often that of transcendence, transformation and control, the technologized object — the raw material — is constructed as inferior or primitive.[25] For instance, Martin argues that doctors conceptualize the female body as a less than satisfactory incubator compared to more technologically mediated reproductive methods. She notes that cesarean sections are often considered superior to vaginal births, which are deemed too stressful for the baby. Moreover, technological intervention on the female body can be justified by the successful production of a healthy child. Women's anger at being forced to undergo a C-section is easily dismissed as irrational if the procedure results in the successful production of a baby in good health.[26] Similarly, female bodies undergoing cosmetic surgery are described by plastic surgeons as the raw material from which doctors create beauty. In *Backlash*, one surgeon told Susan Faludi, "It's very individual. We are sculptors."[27] Again, favouring the skills of the technician or even the artist, the cosmetic surgeon's eye redefines the female body as an object for technological reconstruction.

Such a construction contributes to an ideology — clearly present in the language used by plastic surgeons — of the female body as inherently flawed and pathological. In the United States the American Society of Plastic Surgeons managed to convince the Federal Food and Drug Administration to let silicone breast implants stay on the market by arguing that the condition of having small breasts was actually a disfiguring disease called "micromastia." Cosmetic surgery journals similarly abound with references to "abnormalities" and "deformities" needing to be corrected. Not all bodies, however, are equally affected by such deformities. The deviant female body naturally requires more attention than the more perfect (white) male body. There has not been any controversy over men's right to access potentially dangerous penile enlargement surgery.

THE "PERFECT" FEMALE BODY

This construction of the female body as flawed, promoted by plastic surgeons and perpetuated in the media, becomes even more disturbing when taking into account what kinds of female bodies are constructed as particularly in need of remedy. On top of the list of candidates for technological correction are too-long Jewish noses, too-flat African-American ones, "Oriental" eyelids[28] and, of course, any sign of aging. Technology is offered as a solution to those unfortunate characteristics that pull women away from the young, white middle-class ideal. Plastic surgeons recognize that bone structure is different in all racial identities, but they nevertheless evaluate ideal proportions through the measurement of Caucasian faces, promoting one standard based on a Caucasian ideal. As Morgan puts it, "What is being created ... is not simply beautiful bodies and faces, but white Western, Anglo-Saxon bodies in a racist, anti-Semitic context."[29]

But the discourse of cosmetic surgery is not the only cultural text that constructs ethnicity and race as abnormalities. Numerous feminists have noted that the western cultural construction of female beauty promoted in the media is largely based on a white, middle-class ideal. As Kobena Mercer reminds us, "an *aesthetic* dimension, concerning blackness as the absolute negation or annulment of 'beauty,' has always intertwined with the rationalization of racist sentiment."[30]

Furthermore, in recent years in media representations of attractiveness, the appearance of women of different ethnic and racial backgrounds has done little to challenge this racist ideology. According to bell hooks, "this new representation is a response to contemporary fascination with an ethnic look, with the exotic Other who promises to fulfill racial and sexual stereotypes, to satisfy longings."[31] In her analysis of the *Sports Illustrated Swimsuit Issue*, Laurel Davis found that white models were still the standard and that models of a different ethnicity were either very light-skinned or constructed as exotic Others.[32] Mia Consalvo comes to a similar conclusion in her analysis of the on-line version of *Glamour* magazine.[33] Even today, the symbolic form of what it is to be female is white.

The current ideal of bodily escape has particularly disturbing implications for those whose bodies are most specifically targeted as deviant — those whose bodies are not white enough, not young enough, not middle-class enough, not thin enough, not abled enough. Furthermore, technological intervention on the numerous "deformities" of race, ethnicity, age or excessive flesh, might also become increasingly difficult to reject. Morgan warns against the definition of normal bodily variations as "problem areas" and the increased pressure to seek technological remedies. She notes that, in another interesting co-optation of feminist ideology, women who refuse to use cosmetic technologies are becoming stigmatized as "unliberated" or "refusing to be all they could be."[34] A similar pattern can already be observed in the case of reproductive technologies, where women are pressured to submit themselves to fertility treatments, and those wishing to give birth without technological intervention are judged irresponsible or selfish, and are sometimes legally prevented from doing so. Even more disturbingly, in the case of cosmetic intervention, Morgan suggests that "the naturally 'given,' so to speak, will increasingly come to be seen as the technologically 'primitive'; the 'ordinary' will come to be perceived and evaluated as the 'ugly'."[35] Mastectomy patients who opt against reconstructive surgery sometimes express their surprise at how benign their scar looks when compared to the vocabulary of disfigurement and abnormality used by doctors.[36] But the harshest judgement is reserved for those women who refuse to submit to the fat-free ideal. Fat people — and especially fat women — are the one group in most western cultures that remain a safe target of jokes, expressions of contempt and overt discrimination.

Fat bodies clearly challenge the ideal of bodily escape. They are blatantly sexual, unapologetically physical, primitive, uncultured, out of control. Consequently, fat bodies are under the most pressure to submit to technological reconstruction. Those who remain fat, or even wiggly, in spite of exercising machines, diet pills, weight loss programs and liposuction are deemed lacking in moral character: "The firm, developed body has become a symbol of correct *attitude*; it means that one 'cares' about oneself and how one appears to others, suggesting willpower, energy, control over infantile impulses."[37] The fat female body in particular raises the specter of an insatiable appetite both sexual and otherwise. In her essay on hunger as ideology, Bordo links the control of women's food intake to the control of female sexuality. Indeed, sexual metaphors permeate advertisements for food. But while men are encouraged to un-self-consciously dig in, "their total lack of control ... portrayed as appropriate, even adorable,"[38] women are held to a more contained standard. They can only indulge in low-calorie meals, fat-free desserts or Weight Watchers' dinners. Women who exhibit the most control over their bodies, such as anorectics, receive the most praise from society. In fact, food advertisements targeted at women often exploit the characteristic thought processes of eating disorders, including constant thinking about food, or binging and purging. Women judged to exercise too little control receive only contempt, especially from the media.

Of course, in contrast to the dominant stereotype of fat people as lazy and not wanting to "help themselves," those whose bodies do not fit the cultural norm might actually be spending the most time and effort attempting to control their "unruly" bodies through constant dieting, chemical intake or liposuction — the dangerous procedure through which fat is scraped and sucked out of "problem areas."[39] Recognizing this fact, however, would entail admitting the failure of science and technology to fix the abnormality of excess flesh, or admitting that excess flesh is not abnormal at all. In their unabashed physicality, fat bodies remind us too clearly that the current ideal of bodily escape is but a fantasy.

BODIES THAT REACT

Unfortunately, imagery of the body does not stop at the level of the text. In our critiques of cultural constructions of femininity and physical attractiveness, we must keep in mind that we are talking about actual material female bodies and not just theoretical constructs. "Cosmetic surgery is not simply a discursive site for the 'construction of images of women,' but a material site at which the physical female body is surgically dissected, stretched, carved, and reconstructed according to cultural and eminently ideological standards of physical appearance."[40] The distinction between imagery and actual female flesh cannot always be ignored. In the past, digital imagery was routinely used in plastic surgeons' offices to show women what they would look like with a new nose, larger breasts, tighter skin or western eyelids. But the physical body, no matter how docile, did not always play its part. Unlike pixels on a screen, female bodies react. They swell up and droop and create scar tissue. Surgeons had to stop using the technology for fear of lawsuits, or at least carefully warn their clients against the not-so-playful rebellion of their own bodies against surgical knives.

Even without surgical intervention, cultural constructions of female attractiveness have real-life consequences on women's bodies. Robin Lakoff and Raquel Scherr describe the hierarchy of skin colour within the African-American community which defines lighter-skinned women — those closer to the white ideal — as most attractive. The women they interviewed in their study speak of the pain of being deemed ugly because of the darkness of their skin within the community supposed to provide them with support against the larger racist cultural environment. The authors argue that the statement "black is beautiful" has been such a powerful affirmation of African-American pride precisely because it so clearly works against dominant constructions of beauty.[41] In Patricia Foster's *Minding the Body*, women of various ethnic backgrounds and in various social positions describe their struggles with the many characteristics that make most women's bodies not fit the dominant ideal.[42] Their testimonies remind us that for feminist theory to be useful, gendered bodies cannot be displaced from the socio-cultural environment in which they evolve.

ON RECLAIMING THE BODY

I do not mean to imply in this essay that women who attempt to conform to the cultural ideal of femininity are passive dopes of dominant ideology. Importantly, in the patriarchal environment in which we evolve, the pain and effort required to fit the ideal might be worth a try. A photographer friend of mine told me once that the models he photographed could expect a $75,000 raise after breast enlargement.

There is clearly much more to women's relationship with the body than false consciousness, and feminist theory has come to recognize the complex and varied ways women employ to survive, resist and challenge dominant patriarchal ideology.

For instance, while body piercing or tattooing have sometimes been characterized as forms of self-mutilation by feminist scholars,[43] they can also be interpreted as forms of resistance to dominant ideals of femininity. In the small town where I currently live this fact was illustrated by teenagers' vehement protest of a law that would have required parental consent for body piercing for youth under the age of eighteen. Young protesters argued that body piercing was only meaningful as an act of rebellion against parental supervision. While body piercing as oppositional may be somewhat questionable, these teenagers already understood that their bodies were a significant site of struggle against the dominant ideology of their culture. The law was repelled.

Finally, experiences grounded in the female body, including the particular pressures it is subjected to, are also a possible site for connections. My "beauty memories" described at the beginning of this essay are a painful reminder of how disconnected I felt from my own body growing up in a culture particularly obsessed with appearance. And they are also a source of pleasure at the feelings of closeness I experienced in those moments when I shared beauty secrets with other women. I agree with Elspeth Probyn that it can be liberating to be able to play with fashion without being accused of false consciousness. However, I also agree with her when she notes that "we need to question how far playing with style can go before it becomes yet another way of conforming to the dominant ideology of women as objects."[44]

In order to put our bodies to work against the dominant ideology, we need to find ways of reappropriating dominant constructions of the body so that we can define our bodies in our own terms and create more positive imagery and metaphors. For instance, using late-twentieth-century capitalist ideology, the female body and its monthly cycles could be interpreted as flexibly adjusting to changing conditions in the environment in which it evolves.[45] We must learn to reclaim the female body as a site of political struggle on which feminist claims can be voiced, as a site of "action through transformation, appropriation, parody, and protest."[46] We must also learn to use our bodily instincts and experiences to develop a critical understanding of our own selves and of each other. Female bodies are not simply passive targets of technological reconstruction, or sites for playful experimentation. They are also a potentially powerful source for our developing theories to counteract hegemonic control of women's bodies.

Notes

1. Simone de Beauvoir, *The Second Sex* (1952; reprint, New York: Vintage Books, 1989).

2. Susan Bordo, *Unbearable Weight: Feminism, Western Culture and the Body* (Berkeley: University of California Press, 1993), 34.

3. Ruth Berman, "From Aristotle's Dualism to Materialist Dialectics: Feminist Transformations of Science and Society," in Alison Jaggar and Susan Bordo, eds., *Gender/Body/Knowledge* (New Brunswick, NJ: Rutgers University Press, 1989), 224–255.

4. Emily Martin, *The Woman in the Body* (Boston: Beacon Press, 1992).

5. Donna Wilshire, "The Uses of Myth, Image, and the Female Body in Revisioning Knowledge," in Jaggar and Bordo, eds., *Gender/Body/Knowledge*, 92–114.

6. Ynestra King, "Healing the Wounds: Feminism, Ecology, and Nature/Culture Dualism," in Jaggar and Bordo, eds., *Gender/Body/Knowledge*, 115–141.

7. Muriel Dimen, "Power, Sexuality, and Intimacy," in Jaggar and Bordo, eds., *Gender/Body/Knowledge*, 38.

8. Marilyn Frye, *The Politics of Reality: Essays in Feminist Theory* (Freedom, CA: The Crossing Press, 1983), 25.

9. Catharine MacKinnon, *Toward a Feminist Theory of the State* (Cambridge, MA: Harvard University Press, 1989), 110.

10. Rita Freedman, *Beauty Bound* (Lexington, MA: Lexington Press, 1986), 52.

11. Myra MacDonald, *Representing Women: Myths of Femininity in the Popular Media* (New York: Edward Arnold, 1995).

12. Stuart Ewen, *All Consuming Images* (New York: Basic Books, 1988), 178.

13. Berman, "From Aristotle's Dualism to Materialist Dialectics," 224–255.

14. Bordo, *Unbearable Weight*, 245.

15. Ibid., 245–275.

16. Anne Balsamo, *Technologies of the Gendered Body* (Durham, NC: Duke University Press, 1996).

17. Natalie James, "Women Go Wild for Lewinsky New Lipstick," *The Toronto Star*, 15 March 1999. In 1999, Monica Lewinsky was involved in a sexual liaison with President Bill Clinton while she was an intern at the White House.

18. Jean Kilbourne, *Slim Hopes: Advertising and the Obsession with Thinness* (Northampton, MA: Media Education Foundation, 1995), video.

19. Fabienne Darling-Wolf, "Framing the Breast Implant Controversy: A Feminist Critique," *Journal of Communication Inquiry* 21 (1997), 77–97.

20. Kathryn Morgan, "Women and the Knife: Cosmetic Surgery and the Colonization of Women's Bodies," *Hypatia* 6 (1991), 25–53.

21. MacDonald, *Representing Women*, 125.

22. Judith Williamson, *Decoding Advertisements* (New York: Marion Boyars, 1978).

23. Berman, "From Aristotle's Dualism to Materialist Dialectics," 248.

24. Martin, *The Woman in the Body*, 48.

25. Morgan, *Women and the Knife*, 47.

26. Martin, *The Woman in the Body*.

27. Susan Faludi, *Backlash: The Undeclared War Against American Women* (New York: Corwn, 1991), 216.

28. Balsamo, *Technologies of the Gendered Body*, 62.

29. Morgan, *Women and the Knife*, 36.

30. Kobena Mercer, *Welcome to the Jungle: New Positions in Black Cultural Studies* (New York: Routledge, 1994), 102, emphasis in the original.

31. bell hooks, *Black Looks: Race and Representation* (Boston: South End Press, 1992), 73.

32. Laurel Davis, *The Swimsuit Issue and Sport: Hegemonic Masculinity in Sports Illustrated* (New York: State University of New York Press, 1997).

33. Mia Consalvo, "Cash Cows Hit the Web: Gender and Communications Technology," *Journal of Communication Inquiry* 21 (1997), 98–115.

34. Morgan, *Women and the Knife*, 40.

35. Ibid., 41.

36. Wendy Chapkis, *Beauty Secrets: Women and the Politics of Appearance* (Boston: South End Press, 1986), 26–29.

37. Bordo, *Unbearable Weight*, 195, emphasis in the original.

38. Ibid., 111.

39. In *Backlash*, Susan Faludi notes that a 1988 congressional subcommittee placed the death toll of liposuction at twenty. She adds, however, that the figures are probably actually higher, as patients' families are often reluctant to report liposuction as the cause of death for fear of accusations of vanity and shallowness on the part of the victim (p. 221).

40. Balsamo, *Technologies of the Gendered Body*, 58.

41. Robin Tolmach Lakoff and Raquel Scherr, *Face Value: The Politics of Beauty* (Boston: Little, Brown and Co., 1984), 245–276.

42. Patricia Foster, *Minding the Body: Women Writers on Body and Soul* (New York: Doubleday, 1995).

43. Lakoff and Scherr, *Face Value*, 161.

44. Elspeth Probyn, "Theorizing Through the Body," in Lana Rakow, ed., *Women Making Meaning: New Feminist Directions in Communication* (New York: Routledge, 1992), 86.

45. Martin, *The Woman in the Body*.

46. Morgan, *Women and the Knife*, 44.

CHAPTER SIXTEEN

FROM RAZOR GIRLS TO BIONIC WOMEN

EXTRAORDINARY CYBORG WOMEN IN POPULAR CULTURE

Mia Consalvo

☙

WHEN I PUT IN MY CONTACT lenses, do I become a cyborg? What does being or becoming a cyborg "mean" in contemporary western society? Theorists examining cyborgs in fact and in fiction have started to grapple with questions such as these. I believe the figure of the cyborg could be considered as a convergence of competing or collaborating discourses about bodies, technologies and genders. After all, cyborgs are most often described as hybrids of humans and machines, incorporating both organic and technological components. What happens when these allegedly disparate elements come together? In this chapter, I explore this convergence in three parts: in the first two sections, I look at theories concerning cyborgs, especially how theorists take either celebratory or cautionary approaches. I attempt to delineate two opposing lines of argument, which are drawn somewhat shakily, as some theorists are unsure of the future of the cyborg, and therefore give qualifications to their statements. However, enough theorists have "taken sides" to look at both celebratory and cautionary tales. I draw not only from theoretical discourse but also from popular representations. Additionally, it is helpful to look at different "types" of cyborgs. Sheryl Hamilton suggests that there are three ways theorists use the figure of the cyborg: as a metaphor, of which Donna Haraway's[1] is the best example; as a popular representation — such as Arnold Schwarzenegger's character in the film

The Terminator and the Borg in the television series *Star Trek: The Next Generation* and *Star Trek: Voyager*, and the literal cyborg — people either living in a cybernetic information system, or people with mechanical/electronic devices enclosed in or as part of their bodies.[2]

In the third part, I apply a framework drawn from these theories to a case study of one cyborg figure found in popular culture — Molly Millions in William Gibson's cyberspace trilogy. By applying these theoretical insights to one example, some of the assertions, beliefs, contradictions and confusions surrounding cyborgs may be made clearer.

Cyborgs and Cautionary Tales

Cautionary tales about cyborgs call on the listener to carefully consider the drawbacks and pitfalls as well as the potentials that come with the integration of bodies and technologies. These cautionary tales are not particularly difficult to find. It is important to note, however, that although I am making arguments about cyborgs, I will be referring at times to theorists who were not or are not using the actual figure of the cyborg in their arguments, but are instead making statements about similar domains — bodies and machines, or bodies and technologies. These arguments show how our thinking has developed historically; the various theories explore the problems associated with drawing lines — or understanding the lines drawn — between the body/machine, body/technology fusions.

One cautionary tale concerns gender and the figure of the cyborg. In this tale, the line of argument has historical roots. Going to the writing of Marx, we see how the development and introduction of machines brought greater numbers of women into the paid workforce: brute strength (usually provided by male workers) was often no longer needed to operate the new technology. More specifically, the arrival of the sewing machine further specialized the workforce and women displaced men and children as the operators of these machines. As Marx suggests, this process represents a feminization of the workforce and a beginning of a linkage between female bodies and machines.[3]

This nineteenth-century link is again illustrated in James Beniger's *The Control Revolution*. A historical look at the development of technology and work flows, the analysis shows a photograph of a woman at a typewriter with the caption reading "The Type-Writer." When this machine was first introduced, the operators themselves were called "type-writers." Here, the link between women and machine is made more apparent. Why was this linkage being made? As Mark Seltzer writes, there is no equivalence without the act of making equivalent. So, for an equivalency to "appear" natural, we must use time and effort to give "examples" and "facts" that make the equivalency seem taken for granted. And once two things are made to seem equivalent (such as women and nature, for example), work must be done if we want to break or challenge the equivalence. If women's bodies, which had traditionally been associated with the "natural," were then associated with the "technical," there was a reason — it was a way for men to maintain their control over women and women's use of technology.[4]

One indicator of this reason can be found in the popular culture being produced during the nineteenth century, when increasing mechanization was taking hold. Fritz Lang's film *Metropolis*, for example, tells the story of a mad inventor who steals the "essence" from the woman Maria and puts it into a robot he has constructed and named Maria. The robot Maria is evil and was designed to keep the workers in the city from protesting their conditions. Due to her hypersexualized form, however, she provokes a riot. The workers flood the city and destroy her by burning her.

In this film we see a link between machines and women's bodies, but this time the machine *is* a woman's body. This representation introduces a double discourse: on the surface, the robot Maria represents sexuality out of control.[5] In one scene, she is shown dancing provocatively with little covering her body. She is depicted as a temptress, enticing people to do the wrong thing. This notion of woman as sexually out of control was typically used to control the actions of women, who were seen as slaves to their emotions and passions, unable to control themselves. However, this figure is also a robot, a technological device, which represents technology out of control.[6]

The concern with technology incorporates more traditional fears about women. Thus, a solution is found. Just as women's "out of control-ness" can be held in check, so too can technology's potential threat. The view of the cyborg (or robot) as gendered is negative, in that it represents a way to limit both women's bodies and machines.

This focus on gender has also taken a more contemporary turn with the work of Claudia Springer and Anne Balsamo. Springer echoes Wollen's argument that modernist visions of machines and women tended to map fears of technology onto women's bodies in order to more adequately control both. However, she focuses on recent representations of cyborgs, which have taken a decidedly masculine form. She argues that figures such as Robocop and the Terminator (from the films of the same name) are examples of exaggerated masculinity, musculature gone out of control. The fear of technological advancement, or technology's incursion into the body, is projected outward, with a reassertion of masculine strength and agency. But, she argues, there is a contradiction at work in these representations. These bulging cyborgs represent earlier, mechanical visions of technology. As in Marx's age of production (before the feminization of the workforce), machines were large, loud and powerful; they took up space. This is what the Terminator represents. Springer argues that these figures represent for men a more traditional, powerful form of masculinity. However, most powerful machinery today is represented by the computer and microelectronics. Additionally, computers are sleek and smooth, hiding their "parts" on the inside. Springer proposes that the newer vision of technology presents a problem for traditional masculinity because the new vision of fluid, concealed technology more likely represents feminine bodies. This version of "feminine technology" is represented in the film *Terminator 2: Judgment Day* by the T-1000 cyborg, which has been sent back in time to kill the future leader of the resistance movement, John Connor. The T-1000 is ultimately eliminated by the more masculine cyborg, the T-100, which has also begun to function as a "father figure" for the young John Connor. Thus, traditional masculinity prevails, and the threat of a more feminine, "soft" technology is neutralized.[7]

While the gendering of the technology here has shifted from feminine to masculine, what I think is important to remember is that we are doing the remapping ourselves. Machines can be associated with the masculine as well as the feminine, depending on the purposes to be achieved. If the need is to control the technology or control our fears about it, a figure such as the robot Maria can be constructed. However, if the need is to avert the "crisis in white male subjectivity" as Hamilton claims,[8] men can be associated with cyborgs.

While Springer points to the way cyborgs or machines can be positioned as both masculine and feminine, I believe Anne Balsamo takes an even more cautionary approach. She suggests that even as we compulsively assign genders to cyborgs, the cyborg itself serves as a powerful tool, questioning all dualisms and constructions of otherness. She writes that although technology is giving us new ways to reconfigure the human body, gender remains a heavily guarded border. In her book, *Technologies of the Gendered Body: Reading Cyborg Women,* she explores how different technologies (such as virtual reality (VR), cosmetic/reconstructive surgery, bodybuilding and computerized visualization processes) could potentially change or challenge our gender dualisms, but instead end up drawing the line even more rigidly between male and female configurations. Balsamo believes gender operates as perhaps the last naturalized marker of the human body, which would explain why it would be so tenaciously guarded by some, and fiercely contested by others.[9]

Balsamo goes on to suggest that the figure of the cyborg offers us the possibility of questioning the constructedness of otherness as well as of our own identities, but current cultural and technological practices tend to camouflage this critical function. Virtual reality, for example, promises a "body-free" existence in cyberspace free from sex, race and all other elements that construct identity. However, the discourse surrounding virtual reality omits any questions that would focus on the actual body of the user, and overlooks the political and economic consequences of these different bodies. Ironically, what is currently available as bodies in cyberspace or VR are the traditional raced and gendered bodies we now inhabit, thereby reinforcing differences that exist in reality. Balsamo argues that VR, as it is currently conceived, will not fulfill the promise of existing outside the body nor will it seriously take up the cyborg's challenge of the constructedness of the "other."

These cautionary tales, I believe, point out some of the reasons for being cautious when we encounter cyborgs and demonstrate some ways to understand/analyze the cyborg as we encounter it in popular culture and everyday life. I now turn my attention to some more celebratory theorists who suggest either how to overcome these problems or how to conceptualize cyborgs through a more positive approach.

Cyborgs and Celebratory Tales

One of the first proponents of the cyborg or "man/machine" hybrid was Norbert Wiener, the "father" of cybernetics (the study of information and its flow). In the 1950s, Wiener believed that communication and control were vital to the development of systems consisting of men and machines. He saw the possibility of developing machines that could duplicate some human functions. He believed that feedback — the ability to receive information from the environment, process it and modify output — was the key factor. By integrating feedback, machines could function as humans do. However, Wiener seemed uninterested in debates over whether machines were truly "alive." He wanted to avoid such existential questions and simply look at how machines resemble humans. By doing this, David Tomas argues, Wiener was displacing the question of life. In Wiener's schematic, machines did not have to mimic the outward appearance of humans, they simply resemble humans in their functional ability.[10] Thus, there was no "natural" animosity between humans and machines, no "essential" difference. In Wiener's view, the more humans and machines could interact based on common functioning, the better. While Wiener doesn't comment on the concept of the cyborg as such, his arguments may ascribe a positive value to the cyborg, the ultimate interaction of human and machine.[11]

The positive vision of the cyborg has persisted over the last fifty years. Present-day theorist Allucquére Rosanne Stone feels that as humans enter cyberspace worlds such as virtual reality and Internet chat rooms, we enter cyborg habitats and become cyborgs ourselves. This is because of our reliance on communications technologies and our growing inability to function without them. While she acknowledges that there are many traditional, gendered, power-inscribed interactions taking place in this space, she feels that there are new and exciting practices occurring that need to be investigated. She argues that our assumption that only one self inhabits our body is perhaps a false assumption. Just as gender and race theorists have questioned the "natural" or "essential" identities of gender and race, we need to consider how our notion of one self/one body is also a construction. Stone traces the development of this one self/one body belief throughout human history. She argues that as our bodies are increasingly "anchored" in space with such things as addresses, Social Security numbers, legal names and the like, they are seen as the appropriate holder for only one legitimate self.[12]

While Stone believes that we may have multiple selves residing within our lone bodies, she urges us to remember the existence of this one body while we are in cyberspace. She reminds us that this work of "disappearance" of the body in Cartesian and dualist thought was effected by the invisible labour of those who were unable to escape the constraints and associations of the body — mainly women, children and minorities.

Donna Haraway presents perhaps the most imaginative metaphor and figure of the cyborg yet conceptualized. Haraway looks to the cyborg to operate as a metaphor for radical, progressive political ends. For her, the cyborg is a way to confuse the boundaries of dualisms that we have constructed around humans and animals, humans and machines, and the physical and non-physical. As I hope I have shown, these lines are not set in stone, but shift and change as the need arises. Haraway proposes the figure of the cyborg to throw into relief the constructedness of these dualisms. Since the cyborg is not exclusively human or machine, this boundary has been breached; by calling into question one such dualism, the cyborg can question all dualisms. The cyborg also calls into question the beginning point or origination of all claims. If everything is implicated in everything else, if there is no "pure" nature or "pure" identity to fall back on, how can we make claims about knowledge? Haraway suggests that our claims must be situated: rather than having a (false) position from which to proclaim knowledge, the cyborg forces us to consider how competing claims make knowledge fragmentary, partial and situated. However, Haraway does not feel that we should dispense with all value judgements; instead, we should be more concerned with how we evaluate what counts as knowledge.[13]

Even as Haraway calls for this cyborg vision, she acknowledges that it is only part of the picture. Just as cyborgs can be about challenging systems of knowledge production, they can also be about the imposition of a "grid of control" over the planet. While she suggests that we hold onto both of these views, she obviously prefers the former and gives more time to it in her essay "A Cyborg Manifesto." Herbert Schiller would argue with her on this point. He believes that technologies made in the service of transnational corporations and the military most often stay faithful to the services to which they are put. This is in contrast to Haraway's claim that cyborgs, as illegitimate offspring of the military-industrial state, are unfaithful to their fathers. In Schiller's conceptualization, our future would look more like the worlds presented in the film *Blade Runner* and Gibson's novel *Neuromancer*, with cyborgs (or androids, which are completely artificial lifeforms) serving humanity in slavery, or as part of a totalized system of commodification.[14]

Here I have slid from the celebratory into another cautionary tale, and that seems to be the problem with cyborgs. As Donna Haraway writes, they resist classification and easy demarcation of their bodies and functions.[15] However, even as we wrestle with what we want cyborgs to be or represent for us, I believe they provide an important function, beyond the functions I have already argued here. That is a reminder of the reality of the body. As Stone suggests, even if we spend all our time in VR, we cannot and must not forget the "body" we have (temporarily) left behind.[16] Some postmodern theorists, such as Arthur and Marilouise Kroker and Jean Baudrillard, argue that the physical body has disappeared, replaced by either "panic bodies" or "simulacra" that both seem to be fake or representational rather than "real." These bodies (which these theorists claim we are living in now) are entirely constructed through contemporary discourses of cultural fears and images.[17]

I believe we must argue, as Anne Balsamo does, that this attempt to erase the body is mistaken. Although discourse surrounding the body may be changing, there is still a "real" body that we must live in/through. Disability theorists like Rosemarie Garland Thomson argue forcefully that even as the body is constructed through discourse, there is and always will be a physical component to the body that mediates these constructions. To believe otherwise is to deny the lives and experiences of people with disabilities and illnesses who are forced to daily accept that there is indeed a material component to their bodies.[18] The cyborg figure, as I would reconceptualize it, includes the belief that bodies are "real" just as technologies surrounding them are real.

Thomson's theory aids me here in suggesting a new component to the cyborg metaphor — disability. She argues that people with disabilities are often themselves an "illegitimate fusion" of body and machine, with wheelchairs, hearing aids or canes. They experience their bodies as hybrids and the boundaries between what is real and artificial are often confused. In addition, they challenge the categories of "normal" and "abnormal" as well as gender, since women with disabilities are not seen as truly "feminine." I believe Thomson gives us a new lens with which to focus our view of the cyborg. Haraway herself has argued that people with disabilities may feel they have become hybrids, in conjunction with the communications technologies they may rely upon.[19]

I believe this newly reconceptualized cyborg metaphor could be a valuable addition to feminist theory about the body. As a figure, the cyborg operates to continually remind us of the constructedness of the divisions of gender, body/machine and ability/disability. The "extraordinary" cyborg (to borrow Thomson's term) gives feminists a way to analyze cultural representations, as well as a way to begin investigation of "actual" cyborgs — either all of us enmeshed in the cybernetic information system we call western society, or those of us living with prosthetic devices. I believe in this way the cyborg can be an extremely helpful figure for feminists who are intent on theorizing the body.

POPULAR CULTURE — MOLLY MILLIONS

The conceptual framework I have just discussed is an entry point for the analysis of Molly Millions, a female character from William Gibson's 1980s trilogy — *Neuromancer, Count Zero* and *Mona Lisa Overdrive*. While I have mainly been concerned with how theorists have seen the cyborg as a celebratory or cautionary figure, I would now like to focus more exclusively on Molly Millions as one popular representation of a cyborg. I hope to show how in reality, these approaches are generally combined, giving us a more contradictory, nuanced reading. The character Molly appears in *Neuromancer* and *Mona Lisa Overdrive*, although in the second novel she is using another name and the reader does not know it is Molly until about halfway through the story. In both novels she hires herself out for various jobs — mostly illegal or questionable — such as engaging in data theft or providing "protection" for those who need it.

Molly is a cyborg, as she has several prosthetic devices implanted in her body. Most noticeable are her mirrored shades, which are set into her eye sockets. These give her enhanced vision, as well as allowing her to see in the dark. In addition, she has small, razor-sharp blades that extend and retract from her fingernails, giving her the street-slang nickname "razor girl." Molly also has enhanced neural reactions that give her a quicker response time to danger. Molly works in *Neuromancer* and *Mona Lisa Overdrive* as a "street samurai" — someone who is hired to provide protection and work as a "hired gun" for groups or individuals running scams or illegal operations. While most of Gibson's characters are enhanced to some degree, I find the figure of Molly fascinating in her non-traditional female role of "hired muscle." I believe Molly represents the supreme commodification of the body[20] as well as a traditionally female return to the body (notwithstanding its technological modifications). In addition, Molly demonstrates our deep investment in the myth of control and our beliefs in liberal individualism. I will discuss each of these in turn.

COMMODIFICATION OF THE BODY

As Susan Wendell writes, in western society the body is idealized, and with this idealization comes commodification. The body is treated as a thing that can be worked on or worked over; it can be enhanced, manipulated, conditioned and treated.[21] We can see this process at work in any advertisement for aerobics or health clubs in which the body is treated as raw material that can be improved upon. Likewise, products such as coloured contact lenses, hair dyes, wrinkle creams, makeup, push-up bras and "tummy tuckers" suggest that the body is pliable, that we can reshape or reconfigure our bodies to be more in line with what we would like them to be.

While theorists like Susan Bordo[22] see this process as problematic, I argue that Molly, while fictional, takes this process to its logical extreme. Molly sells her body for her work. While this is nothing new, Molly actively adds technological devices to her body, altering her appearance and physiology to further her ends. She cannot take off these devices at the end of the day — they have become part of her, part of her identity. Further, she not only adds these "tools" to her body, but sees her body primarily *as* a tool. In *Neuromancer*, she explains to her partner Case how she paid for her enhancements. For (at least) a few years, she worked as a "meat puppet" (prostitute) in a brothel. In this future, there are devices known as "cut-out chips" that essentially render the user unconscious and allow a software program to function as the body's "personality." The woman or man using the chip doesn't remember their experiences, thereby making sex-work an "easy way" to make money.

The term "meat puppet" is obviously pejorative, as it suggests a pliancy to the body: different clients can request different software programs for their "puppets." A woman's personal agency is not involved, but since the body's persona is not present, no apparent damage is done. Additionally, the term "meat puppet" suggests a certain contempt for the body, reducing it to mere meat, that others can consume. Meat does not have agency, nor does it have a voice. The person acting as a meat puppet can distance herself from her acts, as she can view them as only a "meat thing," as apart from her "real" or "true" personality. Molly herself suggests that she did just that; but a bad experience, where the images of her acts started intruding on her consciousness, forced her to get out of the business. Once again we can see how women's bodies are objects for consumption by men. The presence of the "cut-out" chip reifies the split between men as active consumers and women as passive objects, unable to remember any actions they were taking or what has been done to them.

Molly's work as a meat puppet and as a street samurai demonstrates how the body in Gibson's world has become the ultimate commodified object. In fact, the view of medicine we see through Molly's eyes is something that is happening today, as pointed out by Susan Wendell. Medicine has become a "high-tech service industry" that will cater to our bodily needs. In *Neuromancer*, medicine is increasingly fused with technology, biotechnology and science to serve as an upscale body-modification service. Medicine is no longer about dealing with illness and death, but about enhancing human bodies beyond their present capabilities.

In Gibson's novels, medicine envisions the "natural" body as normal. Prosthetics and implants are designed to raise humans above "normal" levels, making them above average in looks, performance, intelligence and so on. While there are some holdouts who prefer their natural appearance or performances, most people (Molly included) participate in this practice. In this world, disabilities and long-term illness have disappeared. Medicine has advanced to a level where almost anything can be fixed, for the right price. Those unfortunate enough to be "blown apart" can always be constructed and reconfigured to be better than normal. This vision represents a flattening of perspective about differences in the natural body. While different technological enhancements provide people with different experiences of their bodies, nothing less than perfection is expected from any/body.

Molly represents a logical extension of body-commodification. Her figure, and Gibson's larger universe, show us a potential future, if we continue in our current practices of idealizing the body, of seeing our body as somehow separable from our "real" selves.

CYBORG GENDER

In addition to viewing Molly as an exemplar of the commodification of the body, it is also important to see how Molly represents a specifically gendered cyborg figure. As I have explained, Molly is a street samurai, or "razor girl," who is often a protector in illegal operations. Molly is dangerous, as other characters will readily admit. Many male characters, such as Case and the Finn (another underworld figure who, among other things, sells people "privacy" through the use of rooms employing surveillance-dampening devices) acknowledge Molly's superior strength, street smarts, agility and power. I do not want to dismiss this aspect of Molly, as it is often difficult to find such strong female characters in science fiction. As Claudia Springer suggests, most filmic representations of cyborgs are hypermasculine, such as the *Terminator* and *Robocop*.[23]

However, on another level, and specifically within the context of Gibson's universe, this characterization of Molly is specifically gendered. Molly is the "muscle" in these novels, while Case (in *Neuromancer*) is the mind. Case is the console cowboy who gets to "jack in to cyberspace" (where he can manipulate objects and information by using his mind and a keyboard), which is the focus of the novel. While

Molly must protect and help him, he is the one who must find and steal data in cyberspace, and he is the one who drives the plot forward. Through accessing Case's thoughts, we learn that cowboys (who seem to be mainly boys and men) have a certain "relaxed contempt" for the flesh. When Case is unable to access cyberspace, he feels trapped in the "prison" of his own flesh/body. We see an old dualism at work, one that goes back to Plato: women are associated with the body, while men are allied with the mind.[24]

Although this classification might not be so traditional, given Molly's power, these continual references to the flesh as a contemptible "prison" serve to reinforce the hierarchic nature of the dualism: the mind is privileged over the body. At the end of Neuromancer there is a moment where Case has an out-of-body experience and sees himself holding his computer deck, jacked-in to cyberspace. He notes how gaunt, pale and disheveled he looks. However, he is still the hero of the story. While Molly must keep her own body in prime condition to work effectively, Case can be more relaxed about his own body, as it is not a necessary component of his "disembodied" work.

As Stone reminds us, the privilege of disembodiment is usually given only to a few, with the work of other bodies (usually minorities and women) invisibly supporting this practice.[25] Molly supports and protects Case while he is in cyberspace, guarding him as well as accomplishing some tasks of her own, in the "real" world. Molly cannot seem to escape the prison of her flesh, but Case is allowed to transcend his.

THE MYTH OF CONTROL

The figure of Molly also raises interesting questions about the myth of control. Wendell argues that western society believes passionately in this myth, which suggests that if we do everything right, avoid risks, we'll be well and functioning normally.[26] It is here that some contradictions are found in our beliefs regarding technology and progress. As I argued earlier, medicine in Molly's world is treated as a high-tech service industry. While Molly is on a job she breaks her leg. By applying "derms" to her wrist, she can temporarily kill the pain, but she must soon get the leg fixed. After she goes in for this procedure, she has a "regenerator" that she must attach via electrodes to her leg for a period of time. But since she has another job to do, she can't take the time to use it and abandons the machine. She believes she can control the healing process herself by taking care. However, on another assignment she finds out this isn't true. As she climbs a long steep ladder, her leg begins to bother her again. Ultimately, her role is compromised in the operation because of this physical setback. While Molly believed she could control her body, it betrayed her by not acting in accordance with her desires. Further, the medical service she depended on failed her, as it could not cure her quickly enough for her to continue working. Thus, we see the fallacy of the myth of control, even in this technologically enhanced future, where medicine cannot cure us quickly enough — or perhaps well enough.

LIBERAL INDIVIDUALISM

The figure of Molly, as well as Gibson's universe, calls the notion of liberal individualism into question. In this world, individuals have lost much of the larger control of things, as capitalism has become the global economic system and the zaibatsus (large transnational businesses) are in control. Individual wealth is a thing of the past and corporations control the entire economy. There are still wealthy people, but they are mainly high-powered employees of the various zaibatsus. As Case explains in *Neuromancer*, even if you killed the top ten men (or women) in a particular corporation, another ten would be in line to take their place. The economy is largely out of reach of individual minds and wishes; citizens are left with control over smaller things, such as their appearance and their knowledge. This control is not perfect or non-problematic, but it is allowed under the system. People may "choose" to alter their appearance, but they often do so to resemble differing media representations of beauty (male and female). How free, then, is this choice? Under this system, individual control has become even more strongly a myth, while corporate control is more of a reality. Individuals are tracked or watched, their actions recorded and filed for possible future reference. It is only a limited autonomy that is granted to humans — they are no longer seen as "unitary" selves, with one mind and one body, but as a "collective" to be manipulated by corporate needs.

I believe it is this larger system in the Gibson trilogy that most effectively questions our notions of liberal individualism. As Molly and others have become cyborgs, it has not freed them from the imposition of a "final grid of control" over the planet, as Donna Haraway suggests.[27] This world is Haraway's vision turned nightmare, with the cyborg figure inverted to show us everything that can go wrong with our visions of technological advancement. Autonomy and self-determination have become a mockery, a choice not about governance, but about the consumption of the latest fashionable cosmetic surgery and the latest entertainment to view/participate in.

Molly is only a representative of this larger universe. In *Mona Lisa Overdrive* it is suggested that Molly needs to do some favours in order to get back some damaging information about her past. She is under surveillance, only temporarily able to disappear. Though she changes her name, she cannot escape her past; this proves to limit her autonomy and self-determination. This is typical of all humans in Gibson's world, and increasingly so in our own. Escape from surveillance has become so difficult that death may be the only outlet available. Gibson acknowledges this at the end of *Mona Lisa Overdrive*: we see other characters leaving "our" universe by dying to exclusively inhabit cyberspace. They die a physical death, but their "selves" live on in this technological world. How can this be so? Gibson's futuristic novels constantly call our beliefs into question.

As many theorists have argued, cyborgs mix up categories of human and machine. They defy us to define where humanity begins and ends. Whether they want to save us or assimilate us, cyborgs function to map our current boundaries between power and control, bodies and machines.

This exploration of Molly Millions provides us with another tale about a cyborg, both celebratory and cautionary. Molly is a strong female character, known for her ability to get the job done. Yet, Molly is also a slightly updated example of the mind/body split that is so often used against women in western society. Although Molly is a fearsome fighter, she is limited to using her body to advance her career, both in the past as a meat puppet and in the "present" time as a street samurai. She is hired to protect a man, which may seem transgressive, but her role in Gibson's world is not the central concern. Rather, Case (the console cowboy) is the hero of the story, surfing through cyberspace and living a disembodied life. The society that Gibson describes provides more evidence for the cautionary cyborg tale, as individuals in this world are given a sham of free choice, and are largely powerless to effect world and economic affairs. A grid of control has descended — with appropriate restrictions.

Before this picture becomes too dark, it is useful to observe that although Molly may be watched and her choices constrained, she does have some free agency and does indeed "slip under the radar" of detection for a certain period of time. She also chooses her own line of work; and at the end of *Neuromancer*, she is the one who leaves a romantic relationship she had started with Case, citing as a reason that he distracts her from her work. Molly tries — and succeeds, in a limited way — to wrest some control of her life back, and the struggle is continual. This is a useful lesson for us to take away from this tale of cyborgs and technology. Although grids of control and ideologies about bodies, technologies and genders may prescribe (or proscribe) certain actions or beliefs, we must always make our own way and struggle to resist when we have the chance. We, too, are becoming cyborgs, and it is up to us to determine how free or controlled we will ultimately become.

Notes

The author would like to thank the organizers of the CRIAW 1998 "Our Bodies/Our Lives" conference, as well as the anonymous reviewers and Beth McAuley for their good advice and helpful suggestions in revising this manuscript.

1. Donna Haraway, *Simians, Cyborgs and Women* (New York: Routledge, 1991), 149–182.
2. Sheryl Hamilton, "The Cyborg, Ten Years Later: The Not-So-Surprising Half Life of the Cyborg Manifesto," paper presented at the International Communication Association Conference, Montreal, Quebec, May 1996.
3. Karl Marx, *Capital*, Volume 1 (New York: Penguin Books, 1976).
4. Mark Seltzer, *Bodies and Machines* (New York: Routledge, 1992). It is also interesting to note that the same thing happened with the development of computers.

Jennifer Light reports that during the Second World War, women were employed as "computers" to calculate ballistics charts for the US Army. Some of these women were later chosen to help program the computer that would ultimately replace them, as well as erase them from history. Light, "When Computers Were Women," *Technology and Culture* 40 (1999), 455–483.

5. Peter Wollen, "Cinema/Americanism/The Robot," in James Naremore and Patrick Brantlinger, eds., *Modernity and Mass Culture* (Bloomington: Indiana University Press, 1991).

6. Ibid.

7. Claudia Springer, *Electronic Eros: Bodies and Desire in the Postindustrial Age* (Austin: University of Texas Press, 1996).

8. Hamilton, "The Cyborg, Ten Years Later."

9. Anne Balsamo, *Technologies of the Gendered Body: Reading Cyborg Women* (Durham: Duke University Press, 1996).

10. David Tomas, "Feedback and Cybernetics: Reimaging the Body in the Age of the Cyborg," in Mike Featherstone and Roger Burrows, eds., *Cyberspace/Cyberbodies/Cyberpunk* (Thousand Oaks: Sage, 1995).

11. Norbert Wiener, *The Human Use of Human Beings: Cybernetics and Society* (New York: Da Capo Press, 1950). Wiener later did take up the topic of differences between humans and machines, in *God and Golem, Inc.* (Cambridge, MA: The MIT Press, 1964). In this treatise, he suggests that machines are capable of learning and reproduction and can assist humans. However, he makes clear that "we" must determine how machine inventions can and will be used in a human context — to do otherwise is unethical, and perhaps, even sinful.

12. Allucquére Rosanne Stone, *The War of Desire and Technology at the Close of the Mechanical Age* (Cambridge, MA: The MIT Press, 1996).

13. Haraway, *Simians, Cyborgs and Women.*

14. Herbert Schiller, "Technology and the Future," in Jonathan Crary and Sanford Kwinter, eds., *Incorporations: Zone 6* (New York: Zone, 1992).

15. Haraway, *Simians, Cyborgs and Women.*

16. Stone, *The War of Desire and Technology at the Close of the Mechanical Age.*

17. Jean Baudrillard, *Simulacra and Simulation* (Ann Arbor: The University of Michigan Press, 1984); Arthur Kroker and Marilouise Kroker, *Body Invaders: Panic Sex in America* (Montreal: New World Perspectives, 1987).

18. Rosemarie Garland Thomson, *Extraordinary Bodies* (New York: Columbia University Press, 1997).

19. Haraway, *Simians, Cyborgs and Women.*

20. Susan Wendell, *The Rejected Body* (New York: Routledge, 1996).

21. Ibid.

22. Susan Bordo, *Unbearable Weight: Feminism, Western Culture and the Body* (Berkeley: University of California Press, 1993).

23. Springer, *Electronic Eros: Bodies and Desire in the Postindustrial Age.*

24. Judith Butler, *Bodies that Matter* (New York: Routledge, 1993).

25. Stone, *The War of Desire and Technology at the Close of the Industrial Age.*

26. Wendell, *The Rejected Body.*

27. Haraway, *Simians, Cyborgs and Women.*

GLOSSARY

Beauty ideal: The standard of feminist attractiveness promoted within a culture.

Body wisdom: Communication with our bodies that reflects the experiences and contexts of our lives (lifeworlds). Body wisdom recognizes that our bodies are our means of experiencing the world and are not separate from our thoughts, feelings, perceptions, consciousness and spirit nor are they separate from our environments and everyone in our environments.

Body image: An individual's perception of one's own physical appearance.

Breathing: Etymologically related to soul, spirit, mind, courage, wish, desire, breath of air, life. An infinitely valuable resource for connecting with Self. Both a physical and a symbolic function for living. Breathing connects us to all that is.

Chronic illness: An illness that cannot be cured and results in a permanent disease state. Chronic illness may also have exacerbations between periods of relatively good health or may be slowly progressive with no remissions.

Cohort: The cultural and historical context in which a group of people develop.

Colonialism: Political rule by one society or country over another. It is usually associated with one ethnic group dominating another in the latter's own territory — such as European rule over the indigenous peoples of the Americas or of Africa.

Compulsory heterosexuality: A feminist concept based on the belief that the dominant patriarchal ideology defines heterosexuality as the only acceptable sexual orientation and punishes those who do not fit within its narrow definition.

Concept of health/healthiness: An assessment of well-being that is socially formed and located. Concepts of health/healthiness are dynamic and shaped in relation to experiences of the lived body.

Cultural constructions: Representations and definitions (in this case, of the female body) that generally represent the dominant ideology of a specific culture.

Cultural text: The site on which the ideology of a culture appears, is transmitted and sometimes created. Such sites might include popular media representations — movies, television programs, magazines, popular music — but also literature and the arts.

Cyber punk: A genre of science fiction literature focusing on a dystopian future that is controlled by mega-corporations. Individuals living in this system are heavily reliant on advanced technology, often incorporating it into their bodies. One of the most well-known authors writing cyber punk fiction is William Gibson.

Cyber theory: The field of study examining the intersection of humans and ma-chines, or of bodies and machines. This field is heavily influenced by the work of Donna Haraway, especially her essay "A Manifesto for Cyborgs" (reprinted in her 1991 book *Simians, Cyborgs and Women*).

Dissemination: The sharing of research and research findings. It is an essential component of praxis and is not limited to literary forms of represenation. Dissemination may involve art, for example.

Enlightenment: A western philosophical movement of the eighteenth century characterized by rationalistic methods and a burgeoning belief in the funda-mental equality of all human beings. Despite the assertion of a common humanity, however, women and people of colour were excluded from the de-finition of "universal" equality of this time period.

Equilibrium in society: A state of balance between parts within a social system. It is assumed (by some theorists) to be the norm.

Feminist standpoint: An approach to research grounded in feminist values. These values shape the research questions studied, the research methods used and the goals and purposes of the research. Research carried out from a feminist standpoint often focuses on women's experiences that are treated as an impor-tant source of knowledge for understanding how women's lives are regulated by patriarchal social structures and discourses.

Functionalist concepts: The idea that society is a system made up of interdepen-dent parts, all of which function to maintain one another and the totality. In this scheme, disruption of one part necessarily provokes readjustment among the others. This organic framework ignores the issue of human agency.

Health: Most recently used to refer to an individual's total well-being and not simply the absence of disease. Recognized components of health include social, psychological and spiritual well-being.

Hegemonic system: A system of domination that permeates all aspects of society and is consequently presented as natural. The term hegemony generally im-plies that individuals are unconsciously convinced to participate in their own oppression by supporting the system oppressing them.

Ideology: The ideas and objectives that influence a whole group or national cul-ture, and especially shapes their political and social procedures.

Life history/narrative analysis: An interpretive method in which the narratives of peoples' lives are extensively recorded and presented. Interpretation of the nar-ratives focuses both on the uniqueness of individual accounts and how they reflect the broader social and cultural processes and values which they are related to.

Liposuction: A cosmetic surgical technique that consists of draining fat through a tube inserted in "problem areas."

Macrological research: Large-scale research concerned with social structures.

Material-discursive: A term referring to a theoretical perspective in which both material (the physical body, the physical environment, human artifacts, social institutions and conditions created by human activity) and discursive (systems of meaning involving linguistically mediated communication, fashion, mass media and other symbolic forms) aspects of lived experience are considered simultaneously within the same framework.

Micrological research: Research typically completed on a small scale that deals with everyday life.

Modernity: In the context of this book, the period starting in the late nineteenth century, characterized by the rapid development of capitalism brought about by the industrial revolution and an increased reliance on science and technology. Such reliance was accompanied by an optimistic belief in the ability of science to solve humanity's problems.

Normate: A word coined by Rosemarie Garland Thomson to describe and objectify those without a physical disability, just as the disabled are objectified.

Personal power: The power that comes from being aware. Personal power evolves through the awareness that comes with allowing ourselves to experience and contemplate life deeply, fully. It contrasts, balances and transforms the power of dominance or control over someone or something. Rather, personal power resonates with and expands through understanding, compassion, trust and peace.

Pollution: Usually viewed as a human-generated modification to the physical environment that constitutes stress imposed on the ecosystem. Pollution can also be perceived as stress on the social environment imposed from the outside, or it may refer to substances such as cigarettes and illicit drugs that pollute the human body.

Positivist research: Approaches involving methods that maximize the separation between the researcher and the subject matter of research (that is, the participants) as a way of ensuring "objectivity" of the data collected. A concern with the adequacy (or validity) of measurement procedures and instruments (usually numerical and statistical) is also a feature of positivist approaches.

Postmodern ideology: Refers to a shift from a belief in totality — the characteristic of Enlightenment ideology and modernism — to a belief in fragmentation, particularly wtih regards to the location of power. In the cultural sense of the term, postmodern ideology is used to argue that power is disseminated among individuals rather than concentrated in the hands of institutions. In this sense, individuals are seen as free and able to create their own meaning out of cultural texts and to reinterpret the dominant ideology in empowering and playful ways. Postmodern ideology might be used, for instance, to argue that individuals who submit to plastic surgery are exercising the free choice of playfully defining their own identity through cosmetic intervention.

Praxis: When used within the context of research, praxis denotes action. Many feminists believe knowledge should be used to create positive social change.

Reclaiming: To claim, again, a right that is and has always been there.

Resistance to weight preoccupation: Conscious or unconscious strategies an individual uses to preserve a strong, personally defined identity in opposition to a more dominant externally imposed and negative identity. In this case, resistance is used exclusively to mean a healthy objection to pressures to focus on weight to the detriment of a positive self-identity.

Social constructionist approach: A perspective in which emphasis is placed on language (both spoken and written) and on social interaction as determining people's experiences and knowledge. Language shapes both what is taken to be reality and what is regarded as truth. From this viewpoint, people's lived experiences and understandings are considered specific to the time, place and culture in which they live rather than being timeless and universal.

Subjectivity: As used by those working from a social constructionist perspective, this term refers to the state of personhood or selfhood. It includes identity and sense of self, both as actor and acted upon. Key assumptions of a social constructionist perspective include a critical stance towards taken-for-granted knowledge; a belief in the historical and cultural specificity of knowledge; and the grounding of knowledge in social processes, particularly those mediated by language.

The interminably ill: A phrase coined by Cheri Register to describe those with chronic illnesses. It is a pun on the phrase "terminal illness."

Weight preoccupation: Self-evaluation based on the ability to control body weight, size or shape, accompanied by persistent thoughts or discussion of factors perceived to affect the body's appearance. Weight preoccupation is the norm for females in Canada and the US and is usually expressed as a desire to achieve or maintain weight loss, slenderness or a lean and muscular body. Weight preoccupation sometimes leads to health-damaging behaviours.

CONTRIBUTORS

VIVIENNE ANDERSON has a BA in History from the University of London, England. She began her master's degree at the University of New Brunswick but had to interrupt her studies due to illness. In 1982, she was awarded a Natural Sciences and Engineering Research Council Doctoral Fellowship and began her PhD at Simon Fraser University, which she could not complete due to her chronic illness. Since 1986, Vivienne has been a part-time freelance writer and arts critic for the Fredericton *Daily Gleaner*. In 1990, she won second prize in the Children's Literature Section of the New Brunswick Writer's Federation Literary Competition, and in 1991 won second prize in the Non-Fiction Section. E-mail: vivander@nbnet.nb.ca.

DIANE CEPANEC is a graduate student in the Department of Sociology at the University of Manitoba. Her master's thesis explores women's decisions to have facial cosmetic surgery. Her other research interests include gender issues in later life, women's health issues and theoretical issues in the sociology of the body. E-mail: cepanecd@cc.umanitoba.ca.

MIA CONSALVO, PhD, is an Assistant Professor in the Department of Journalism and Mass Communication at the University of Wisconsin-Milwaukee. Her research interests include new media technologies, gender and popular culture. Her most recent work examines the selling of the Internet to women. E-mail: consalvo@csd.uwm.edu.

BARBARA CULL-WILBY, PhD, is the mother of three children. After fourteen years of service to an academic life, she resigned from her tenured position with the University of New Brunswick, Faculty of Nursing, and began a home-based business under the name of Wholecare that unites science, healing and nursing.

FABIENNE DARLING-WOLF, PhD, is an Assistant Professor of Journalism, Public Relations and Advertising at Temple University. Her research interests focus generally on representations of female attractiveness in the popular media, with a specific interest in the Japanese cultural environment. She has published articles in *The Journal of Communication Inquiry, The Reader's Guide to Women's Studies, Herizons* and *Japanophile*. E-mail: fabienne-darling@uiowa.edu.

CHRIS EGAN, PhD, RN, has spent much of the last thirty years in the Arctic working as a community health nurse, in isolated nursing stations, and as a health researcher. Most recently, she was Director of Research and Education for the Nunavut Department of Health. She was educated at the University of Alberta, University of Western Ontario, McMaster University and the University of Manitoba, and is currently Assistant Professor in the Department of Community Health Sciences at the University of Manitoba. E-mail: cegan@arctic.ca.

DEANNA GAMMELL is a doctoral student in clinical psychology at the University of New Brunswick. Her research interests focus on the use of qualitative methods to investigate women's depression. She is currently engaged in research for her dissertation, which involves an exploration of adolescent girls' understanding of depression. E-mail: q08j@unb.ca.

LYNNE GOULIQUER recently completed sixteen years of military service in the Canadian Armed Forces. She is currently enrolled in the graduate program at McGill University where she is completing her PhD in Sociology. Her main research focus is gender and organization, however, she is also interested in sexuality and identity and the social construction of women's illness. She is an active member of a Muriel McQueen Fergusson Centre for Family Violence research team that is investigating the women's transitions out of abusive relationships. E-mail: lgouli@po-box.mcgill.ca.

MICHELLE N. LAFRANCE completed her master's degree in Social Psychology at York University where she worked under the supervision of Marilyn T. Zivian. She is presently a doctoral candidate in clinical psychology at the University of New Brunswick where she works with Janet M. Stoppard. Her research interests include qualitative investigations of therapists' understandings of empowerment and women's experiences of depression. E-mail: n5a3m@unb.ca.

GAIL MARCHESSAULT, RD, PHEc, MSc, is a doctoral candidate in the Department of Community Health Sciences at the University of Manitoba and Associate Editor of *The Healthy Weight Journal.* Her dissertation focuses on cultural understandings of weight in Caucasian and Aboriginal mothers and daughters. She has worked for ten years as a community nutritionist with First Nations people and will be Assistant Professor in the Department of Foods and Nutrition at the University of Manitoba as of January 2001. E-mail: marches@cc.umanitoba.ca.

BAUKJE (BO) MIEDEMA, PhD, was born in Holland. She trained and worked as a psychiatric and a general nurse in Groningen and Utrecht, the Netherlands. After her arrival in Canada she attended the University of Waterloo and moved to Fredericton in 1984 where she completed post-doctorate work with the Muriel McQueen Ferguson Centre for Family Violence Research. She has written numerous scholarly research papers, and is the author of

Mothering for the State: The Paradox of Fostering (Halifax: Fernwood Books, 1999). Since 1998, she has been a Research Associate with the Dalhousie Family Medicine Teaching Unit at the Chalmers Hospital in Fredericton. E-mail: bmiedema@health.nb.ca.

ANITA M. MYERS, PhD, is a Professor with the Department of Health Studies and Gerontology, University of Waterloo. Her areas of speciality include health program evaluation, gerontology, women's health issues and rehabilitation. E-mail: amyers@interlog.com.

ROXANA NG, PhD, has been active in the feminist and anti-racism movements since the mid-1970s. In addition to her scholarship on immigrant women and anti-racist feminism, she is developing a critique of an alternative to western education from an eastern "embodied" perspective. She teaches in Adult Education at the Ontario Institute for Studies in Education of the University of Toronto. E-mail: rng@oise.utoronto.ca.

BARBARA PAYNE, PhD, is an Associate Professor in the Department of Sociology at the University of Manitoba. She received her BA in Psychology/Sociology from York University and her MSc and PhD in Community Health from the University of Toronto. Her research interests focus on aging and health and, in particular, on women's health. Dr. Payne is a core partner in the National Network on Environments and Women's Health (NNEWH), the national Centre of Excellence for Women's Health, located at York University. E-mail: Barbara_Payne@umanitoba.ca.

KATE ROSSITER completed her Bachelor of Arts at Mount Allison University. Kate's academic interests lie in drama, especially in the area of drama for human development. Kate is involved in social action regarding body image and "body oppression" and hopes to eventually combine her interests in drama and social action, but at the moment is still trying to navigate her way through the new experience of living on her own. E-mail: Kmrsstr@hotmail.com.

YVETTE SCATTOLON works as a clinical psychologist at the Mental Health Clinic at Colchester Regional Hospital in Truro, NS. She also works at the Eating Disorders Clinic at the Queen Elizabeth II Health Sciences Centre in Halifax. Her research and clinical interests include women's issues, depression, eating disorders and health psychology. E-mail: scattolon@nrhb.ns.ca.

JANET M. STOPPARD, PhD, is a Professor of Psychology at the University of New Brunswick. With a background in clinical psychology, her research and teaching interests focus on women's mental health and feminist perspectives in psychology. She is the author of *Understanding Depression: Feminist*

Social Constructionist Approaches (New York: Routledge, 2000) and is co-editing a book on qualitative approaches to research on women's depression. E-mail: stoppard@unb.ca.

ADDENA SUMTER-FREITAG is an award-winning playwright and performance poet. Her one-woman play *Stay Black and Die* won the 1998 Frankie Award for Best Fringe Festival Production and was performed at Montreal's Centaur Theatre. A seventh-generation Canadian, Addena grew up in Winnipeg's North End and now lives and works in Yellowknife, NWT. E-mail: xirvinsu@ssimicro.com.

ROANNE THOMAS-MCLEAN is a doctoral student in the Department of Sociology at the University of New Brunswick. She has completed her master's degree in Sociology and her bachelor's degree in Education. Her areas of interest include women's experiences with breast cancer, sociology of the body and sexuality. She has taught courses in sexuality education and the sociology of health and illness. Roanne is supported in her endeavours by her husband and their daughter. E-mail: rtmaclea@nbnet.nb.ca.

PAMELA WAKEWICH, PhD, is an Assistant Professor of Sociology and Women's Studies at Lakehead University in Thunder Bay. Her chapter in this volume is drawn from her recently completed PhD thesis "Contours of Everyday Life: Reflections on Embodiment and Health Over the Life Course" (University of Warwick, UK, 2000). Her main areas of interest are women's health, the sociology of the body and narrative, and life history. She has been active in local and national women's health initiatives and has published articles on the health concerns of immigrant women in Montreal and representations of women's wartime work in northwestern Ontario. Her current research focuses on notions of time and entitlement in women's narratives of health and health practices. E-mail: pwakewic@sky.lakeheadu.ca.

MARILYN T. ZIVIAN, PhD, is an Associate Professor in the Department of Psychology, Atkinson College, and the Associate Dean (Student Affairs) in the Faculty of Graduate Studies, York University. She is interested in the effects of socio-cultural-historical conditions on developmental changes across the life-span. Recent publications and presentations focus on the influence of the media on the body image of young adult males and females and changes in body size of North Americans over the lifespan. E-mail address: mzivian@yorku.ca.